Natural Resources Law of Papua New Guinea

Edited by

ERIC L KWA

Dean, School of Law, University of Papua New Guinea

with a Foreword by

THE HONOURABLE SIR ARNOLD AMET KB, CBE, LLD

Chief Justice of Papua New Guinea

UPNG PRESS AND BOOKSHOP, 2010

Originally published in Sydney by Lawbook Co.

100 Harris St, Pyrmont NSW 2009

It is produced from final proofs provided by Professor Kwa and these have been checked against a copy of the Lawbook text.

ISBN 9980-939-55-9

Copies available from:

UPNG Press and Bookshop
Box 413
University Post Office
NCD 134
Papua New Guinea

Foreword

This is one of a series prepared under the auspices of the Access to Laws in Papua New Guinea Project funded by the Australian Government through the Australian Agency for International Development (AusAID). The Access to Laws Project comprised three components aimed at improving access to the laws of Papua New Guinea. The Project involved updating and authenticating all the current legislation of Papua New Guinea and the extensive case law developed by the courts. The legislation and judicial decisions have been produced in the modern electronic CD-ROM format. Equally importantly, the Project included the production of a number of legal textbooks to record the distinctive developments in the laws of Papua New Guinea.

The book publishing component of the Access to Laws Project was under the direction of the Publications Committee that I had the pleasure of chairing. The other members of the Publications Committee were: the Commissioning Editor, Professor Don Chalmers, the Chief Magistrate, Mr George Manuhu, the Deputy Chief Magistrate, John Numapo, the Hon the Attorney-General, Mr Francis Damen (previously Mr Sao Gabi, Mr Michael Gene), the Access to Laws Project Manager, Mr Bruce Fulton, the Project Team Leader, Mr Eric Kwa (previously Dr Val Haynes), representatives of AusAID (Mr Stuart Schaefer, Ms Pauline Doonar, Ms Debbie Bowman, Mr John Prescott, Ms Katherine Ruiz-Avila), a representative of the PNG Law Society, Ms Catherine Davani and the Dean of the Law School, Mr Eric Kwa (previously Mr Gerry Linge). The Publications Committee was responsible for choosing authors, settling the contents, assessing the quality and appointing referees for each of the texts. At an early meeting of the Publications Committee it was decided that it was appropriate that Papua New Guinean authors or authors with considerable experience in Papua New Guinea should be chosen.

I am delighted that Eric Kwa has agreed to accept the invitation of the Commissioning Editor on behalf of the Publications Committee to edit this text and I thank all the authors for their contributions: Eric Kwa; Alphonse K Malipu; George Muroa; Billy Manoka and Ursula Kolkolo; Lawrence Kalinoe; John Sagir Kawi and Wilfred W Golman; and George Tapya Yapao. I commend the learned authors for their work and scholarship and I am confident that this text, with the others in this series, will be of great value to judges, magistrates, legal practitioners, academics, students and the citizens of Papua New Guinea. If the underlying law is to be developed according to the precepts and principles embodied in our *Constitution* and *The Underlying Law Act* 2000, it is essential that the Papua New Guinea community has access to texts which can state the law of this country concisely, authoritatively and accurately. On behalf of the Publications Committee, I commend the authors for their contribution to this important endeavour.

The Hon Sir Arnold Amet, KB, CBE, LLD

Chief Justice of Papua New Guinea,

Chair of the Publications Committee,

Access to Laws in Papua New Guinea

Port Moresby 2001

Table of Contents

[References are to page numbers]

Foreword ..... *v*

Table of Contents ..... *vii*

Table of Cases ..... *ix*

Table of Statutes ..... *xiii*

1 Introduction

Eric Kwa 1

2 The Importance of Natural Resources, Particularly Non-renewable Resources, to the Development of the Papua New Guinean Economy

Alphonse K Malipu 6

3 Land Tenure Law in Papua New Guinea

George Muroa 14

4 Forestry Law

Eric Kwa 50

5 Fisheries Resource Development and Management in Papua New Guinea: Law, Biology and Economics

Billy Manoka and Ursula Kolkolo 86

6 Water Law

Lawrence Kalinoe 108

7 Project Financing in Papua New Guinea

John Sagir Kawi and Wilfred W Golman 132

8 Statutory Recognition of Customary Resource Owners' Compensatory Rights and Interests

George Tapya Yapao 167

Index 185

Table of Cases

[References are to page numbers]

Ada v Beau [1996] PNGLR 172 106
Administration of the Territory of Papua and New Guinea v Guba and Doriga (App 79, 1969, FC) 35
Administration of the Territory of Papua and New Guinea v Guba (1973) 130 CLR 353; 47 ALJR 621 .... 34, 35, 37, 38
Agevu v The State [1977] PNGLR 99 .... 35, 46
Akipa v Lowa [1990] PNGLR 502 173
Anthony v Commonwealth [1972-1978] ACR 769 15
Attorney-General (Cth) v RT Co Pty Ltd (1956) 97 CLR 146 15
Australian Provincial Assurance Co Ltd v Coroneo (1938) 38 SR (NSW) 700 .... 27, 28

Bain v Brand [1876] App Cas 762 24
Belgrave Nominees Pty Ltd v Barlin-Scott Airconditioning (Aust) Pty Ltd [1984] VR 947 29
Bernstein of Leigh (Lord) v Skyviews & General Ltd [1978] 1 QB 479 .... 18, 19
Boyd v Shorrock (1867) LR 5 Eq 72 28
Brand v Chris Building Co Pty Ltd [1957] VR 625 .... 24, 25
Burnguist, Petition of 220 Minn 48; 19 NW 2d 394 15

Calder v Attorney-General (British Columbia) (1973) 34 DLR (3d) 145 34
Central Pomio Logging Corporation Pty Ltd v The State [1992] PNGLR 20 69
Commissioner for Crown Lands v Page [1960] 2 QB 274 143
Commissioner for Railways v Valuer-General [1974] AC 328 18
Commissioner of Main Roads (NSW) v North Shore Gas Co (1967) 120 CLR 118 15
Commonwealth v New South Wales (1923) 33 CLR 1 .... 18, 19
Corbett v Hill (1870) 39 LJ Ch 547 18
Cuffy v Koslosky 165 Okl 135; 25 P 2d 290; 1Y 15

Dadzie v Kokofu (1961) GLR 90 16
Director of Expropriated Property v Tedep (1964) 113 CLR 318 41
Donigi v The State [1991] PNGLR 376 173
Doriga v Administration of the Territory of Papua and New Guinea (unreported, FC 18) 45

First Assistant Secretary, Department of the Administration v The Administration (1974, FC 55) 45
Frame v Minister for Lands, Surveys and Environment [1979] PNGLR 626 .... 112, 170
Frame v Minister for Lands, Surveys and Environment [1980] PNGLR 433 172
Francis v Ibitoye (1936) NLR 11 24

Gathomo v Murito [1921] EAPLR 102 ... 34
Geita Sebea v Territory of Papua New Guinea (1941) 67 CLR 544 ... 15, 23, 27, 32
Geita Sebea v Territory of Papua (unreported, Central Court of Papua, 1940, 12) ... 32, 34, 40
Gifford v Dent [1926] WN 336 ... 18
Golpak v Kali [1993] PNGLR 491 ... 53
Graham v KD Morris & Sons Pty Ltd [1974] Qd R 1 ... 17
Guba and Doriga v The Administration of the Territory of Papua and New Guinea (1971, FC 18) ... 37

Holland v Hodgson (1872) LR7 CP 328 ... 27, 28
Holmes v US CCA Okl 53 F 2d 960 ... 14

Jaha Development Corporation v Ilagi [1995] PNGLR 76 ... 81
Jaha Development Corporation Pty Ltd v Ilagi, Secretary for Department of Manus (unreported, Ap No 242 of 1989, 1990) ... 80
John Young & Co v Bankier Distiller Co [1893] AC 691 ... 127
Jones v Magruder DC Md 42 F Supp 193 ... 15

Karynette Pty Ltd, Ex parte (1984) 2 Qd R 211 ... 26
Ketson v Imperial Tobacco Co (of Great Britain and Ireland Ltd) [1957] 2 QB 334 ... 17, 18
Kuwait v Aminoil (1982) 66 ILR 518 ... 157

Land Titles Commission Ordinance, Matter of (1962-1971, No 90, 30 March 1977) ... 45
Lavao v The State (Re Kerema Town and Airstrip Land) [1978] PNGLR 15 ... 43
Lemmon v Webb [1894] 3 Ch 1 ... 18
Liamco v Libya (1977) 62 ILR 140 ... 157
Lowa v Akipa [1992] PNGLR 60 ... 173
Lynch v Cunningham 131 Cal App 164; 21 P 2d 154 ... 15

Mabo v Queensland (1992) 175 CLR 1 ... 34
Mancetter Developments Ltd v Garmanson Ltd [1986] QB 1212 ... 30
Manchester Corp v Rochdale Canal Co (1971) 69 LGR 517 ... 15
Manning v Williams (1909) 9 SR (NSW) 903 ... 15
Manus Provincial Government v Kasou [1990] PNGLR 3 ... 68
Mcdui Development v Genia [1990] PNGLR 50 ... 69, 76
Meats v Callender [1901] 2 Ch 388 ... 30
Milirrpum v Nabalco Pty Ltd (1971) 17 FLR 141 ... 34

Newcomen v Coulson [1877] 5 Ch D 133 ... 15, 18

Okoleji v Okupe (1939) 15 NLR 28 ... 36

Papo v Paul Mambei and Placer (PNG) Ltd (OS No 340, 1996) ... 178, 179
Pawut v Bee [1996] PNGLR 26 ... 106
Pickering v Rudd (1815) 4 Camp 219 ... 18

R v Trent River Authority; Ex parte National Coal Board [1969] 2 WLR 653 ... 18
Rahonamo v Enai (Re Hitau) [1971-1972] PNGLR 58 ... 42
Rainbow Holdings Pty Ltd v Central Province Forest Industries Pty Ltd [1983] PNGLR 34 ... 63, 77
Resena v The State [1990] PNGLR 22 ... 26
Reynard v City of Caldwel 55 Idaho 342 ... 14, 15
Rumints v The State and Western Highlands Provincial Government [1993] PNGLR 94 ... 120

Saunders v Smith (1838) 2 Jur 491 ... 18
Sinclair v Mulligan (1886) 3 Man LR 481 ... 36
Southern Rhodesia, Re [1919] AC 211 ... 34
Sovmots Investments Ltd v Secretary of State for the Environment [1977] 1 QB 411 ... 18
Supreme Court Reference No 3 of 1989; Re Forestry (Private Dealings) Act (Ch 217) [1990] PNGLR 222 ... 69
Supreme Court Reference No 7 of 1992; Re Forestry Act 1991 [1992] PNGLR 514 ... 70, 71, 81

Texaco v Libya (1978) 53 ILR 389 ... 157
The State v Asaoka Kouji of Rabaul [1976] PNGLR 292 ... 76
The State v NTN Pty Ltd and NBN Ltd [1992] PNGLR 1 ... 113
Tijani v The Secretary for Southern Nigeria (1921) 2 AC 399 ... 34
Tolian v The Administration (Re Vulcan) [1965-1966] PNGLR 232 ... 45, 46
Tonolei Development Corporation v Lucas Waka – Minister for Forests (unreported, N404L, 1982) ... 76

Van Achterberg, Ex parte (1984) 1 Qd R 160 ... 26
Van Son v Forestry Commission of New South Wales (unreported, NSW Sup Ct, Equity Div, Cohen J, 3 February 1995) ... 122
Vaniak v Muvamastrum Pty Ltd [1994] PNGLR 425 ... 54
Varzin Case [1964] 113 CLR 318 ... 41

Wandsworth Board of Works v United Telephone Co Ltd (1884) 13 QBD 904 ... 18

Table of Statutes

[References are to page numbers]

PAPUA NEW GUINEA

Central Banking Act (Ch 138): 144, 148

Central Banking (Foreign Exchange and Gold) Regulation: 148, 155

Civil Aviation (Aircraft Operators' Liabilities) Act

Sch 1: 18

Companies Act: 73, 124

Conservation Areas Act: 52, 151

Constitution: 2, 3, 4, 21, 41, 49, 150, 167, 168, 169, 170

s 9: 15, 21

s 11: 169

s 19(3)(eb): 81

s 38: 49, 113

s 39: 113

s 53: 20, 21, 40, 41, 46, 49, 69, 112, 120, 155, 168, 169, 170, 175, 178

s 53(1)(a)(i): 170

s 53(1)(a)(ii): 170

s 53(2): 49, 170, 171

s 53(3): 172

s 53(4): 113

s 53(5)(e): 45, 46

s 54: 169

s 57: 175

s 1871: 80

Sch 2: 15, 127

Sch 2.1: 21

Sch 2.1(1): 21

Sch 2.1(2): 21

Sch 2.2: 21, 175

Sch 2.3: 26

Crown Grants Ordinance 1889: 36

s 2: 36

s 20: 36

Crown Lands Ordinance 1890: 36, 44

s 23: 44, 45

s V: 37

s XVM: 37

s XX: 37

Pt I: 36

Dumping of Waste at Seas Act: 151

Electricity Commission Act

s 25: 18

Environment Act 2000: 5, 151

Environmental Contaminants Act 1978: 5, 151, 170, 182

s 61: 168, 182

s 61(1): 182

Environmental Planning Act (Ch 370): 5, 113, 114, 151, 164, 165

Fauna (Protection and Control) Act: 52

Fisheries Act 1984: 86, 93, 94, 96

Fisheries Act 1986: 103

Fisheries Act 1994: 93, 94, 95, 96, 101, 106

s 25(c): 96

s 39: 95

s 40: 95

s 41(1)(e): 95

s 43: 94

s 55: 106

s 57: 106

Fisheries Management Act 1998: 86, 88, 93, 96, 97, 99, 100, 101, 105, 107

s 25: 97

s 25(c): 107

s 26: 97, 98

s 27: 97, 101

s 28: 97, 98

s 29: 97, 103, 106

s 29(1): 106

s 32: 106

s 33: 99

s 33(2): 99
s 33(2)(a)-(d): 99
s 35: 99
s 37: 99
s 41: 99
s 44: 99
s 46: 106
s 49(2)(a)(i): 105
s 49(2)(a)(ii): 105
s 49(2)(a)(iii): 105
s 49(2)(b): 105
s 49(2)(f): 105
s 49(2)(g): 105
s 50: 105
s 51: 105
s 52: 105
s 53(1)(2)(a)-(e): 105
s 54(1): 105
s 57: 105
ss 58-60: 105
s 58(1)(a): 106
s 58(1)(b): 105
s 58(1)(c): 105, 106
s 58(1)(d): 105, 106
s 58(1)(e): 105
s 58(1)(f): 105
s 58(1)(g): 105
s 58(1)(h): 105, 106
s 58(1)(i): 106
s 58(1)(j): 106
s 58(1)(k): 106
s 58(1)(l): 106
s 58(1)(m): 106
s 58(1)(n): 105
s 58(1)(o): 106
s 58(1)(p): 105
s 58(1)(q): 106
s 58(1)(r): 105
s 58(1)(s): 106
s 58(1)(t): 106
s 58(1)(u): 106
s 58(1)(v): 106
s 58(1)(x): 105
s 58(1)(y): 105
s 58(1)(z): 105
s 58(1)(aa): 106
s 58(1)(bb): 105
s 58(1)(cc): 105
s 58(5): 105
s 58(5)(a): 105
s 58(5)(b): 105
s 58(5)(c): 105
s 58(6): 106
Pt III: 97
Pt IV
Div 1: 99
Div 2: 99
Pt V: 105
Pt VI: 105
Pt VII: 105

Fisheries Management Regulation 2000: 97
s 15(1): 105
s 15(2): 105
Pt V: 105

Fisheries Regulation: 94

Fisheries (Torres Strait Protected Zone) Act: 99

Forest Industries Council Act (Ch 217): 70, 179

Forestry Act 1936-1971: 68

Forestry Act 1974: 69, 76, 83
s 6: 63

Forestry Act 1991: 61, 62, 69, 70, 71, 73, 74, 77, 78, 79, 81, 82, 83, 94, 179, 180, 181, 182
s 3: 63, 70
s 4: 70
s 5: 180
s 5(d): 67
s 9: 180
s 10: 180
s 21: 71, 75
s 30: 77
s 30(1): 77
s 42: 71
s 46: 70, 180

s 47: 71
s 49: 71, 77
ss 54-60: 74
s 55(e): 180
s 56: 71, 74, 181
s 56(1): 74, 181
s 56(3): 70, 181
s 57: 61, 180
s 57(1): 180
s 58: 180
s 58(b): 180
ss 61-65: 79
s 61: 71
s 62(2): 75
s 64: 75
s 66: 75
ss 66-72: 75
s 71: 75
ss 87-90: 63
s 87: 78
s 87(1): 79
s 87(4): 79
s 88: 78
s 91(1): 79
s 95: 79
s 103: 76
s 105: 73
s 120: 181
s 120(6): 76
s 128: 181
s 130: 181
s 136: 70
s 137: 70
Div 4: 74
Pt II, Div 2: 71
Pt III: 70
Pt VI: 72
Pt X: 70
Forestry Act (Ch 217): 179
Forestry (Amendment) Act 1993: 71
s 13: 61
Forestry (Amendment No 2) Act 1996: 79
s 3: 180
Forestry (New Guinea) (Amendment) Ordinance 1971: 66, 67
Forestry Operations Control Act 1992: 71, 81
s 3(1): 81
Forestry Ordinance 1936: 3, 65, 66
s 6: 66
s 7: 66
s 8: 66
s 9: 66
s 10: 63, 65
s 11: 65
s 14: 66
s 15: 66
s 17: 66
s 18: 66
s 19: 66
Forestry Ordinance 1936-1937: 64, 65, 66, 67
s 9: 67
Forestry Ordinance 1937: 65
Forestry (Papua) Ordinance 1950: 64
s 4(1): 64
Forestry (Papua) Ordinance 1951: 64
Forestry (Private Dealings) Act (Ch 217): 68, 69, 70, 78, 83, 179
s 4: 68
s 5: 68
s 6: 68
Forestry (Private Dealings) Ordinance 1971: 67
Forestry (Private Dealings) Regulation: 68
s 2: 68
Forestry Regulation 1974: 63, 64, 65, 77, 78, 83
regs 16-18: 63, 77
reg 17: 63
reg 18: 63

Human Rights Act 1971: 49

Imperial Charter 1885: 38, 44
Imperial Ordinance 1887: 38

Imperial Ordinance 1899: 38, 44
s 1(a): 44
s 2: 44
Imperial Ordinance 1903: 38, 40
s 1: 40, 169
s 1(1): 40
Income Tax Act: 162
Indigenous Timber Ordinance 1892: 2, 3, 54, 55, 62, 63, 64, 77
s 11: 62
s 12: 63
International Centre for Settlement of Investment Disputes Convention
Art 54: 157
International Law of the Sea: 97, 100
Interpretation Act (Ch 2)
s 3: 15
Interpretation (Interim Provisions) Act (Ch 2): 16
Investment Dispute Settlement Act (Ch 346): 157
Investment Promotion Act 1992: 73, 74, 100, 154
s 37: 154, 156
s 38: 155
s 39: 155
s 98: 74
s 104: 74

Land Acquisition Act 1974: 170
s 19: 171
s 19(3): 171
s 22: 171
s 23: 170
Land Act 1911-1940
s 5: 43
Land Act 1911: 43
Land Act 1962: 34
s 7: 34
s 83: 46
Land Act 1996: 31, 35, 36, 37, 137, 169, 170, 172, 182
s 1: 170
s 2: 15, 39, 172
s 3(1): 173
s 4: 17, 35
s 4(2): 35
s 5: 43, 44, 45, 46
ss 6-18: 169
s 10: 36, 38, 39, 41, 44
s 10(1): 39
s 10(2): 39
s 10(3): 42, 43
s 10(4): 42
s 11: 36, 38, 39, 41
s 11(1): 41
s 11(2): 42
s 11(3): 42
s 12: 172
s 13: 172
s 14: 172
s 15: 172
ss 19-47: 168, 169
ss 19-48: 172
ss 19-49: 172
s 48: 26
s 23: 172
s 73: 173
s 120: 31
s 120(3): 31
s 120(5): 31
s 132: 36, 153
Pt II: 169
Pt III: 41
Div 5: 172
Pt IV: 41, 168, 169
Pt X: 32
Divs 1-9: 172
Land Act (Ch 185): 42, 169
Land (Amendment) Act 1984
s 15A: 42
Land Disputes Settlement Act (Ch 45): 16, 30, 54, 174
s 2: 20, 168, 173
Land Groups Incorporation Act (Ch 147): 61, 74, 179, 180

Land Ordinance 1906: 40
s 11: 44, 45
s 23: 40
s 33: 39
s 35: 40, 169
Land Ordinance 1911-1914
s 60: 169
Land Ordinance 1911-1940: 44
s 6: 37
s 8: 37, 44
s 10: 37
s 58: 40
s 60: 40
Land Ordinance 1911
s 58: 39
Land Ordinance 1922-1941
s 11: 44
s 69: 40
s 71: 40, 169
Land Ordinance 1922 (New Guinea)
s 6: 39
s 8: 39
s 10: 39
s 11: 45
Land Ordinance 1962: 39, 40, 44, 137
s 17: 40, 169
s 83: 44
s 83(4): 45
s 83(5): 45
s 85: 171
Land Regulation Ordinance 1888: 35, 36
ss 4-6: 37
Lands Acquisition (Development Purposes) Act (Ch 9)
ss 16-34: 168
Pt III: 168
Lands Acquisition (Development Purposes) Act (Ch 192): 173
ss 7-34: 173
Lands Acquisition Ordinance 1914: 40
s 13: 39, 40, 169
s 26: 40, 169
Lands Acquisition Ordinance 1952: 40
s 14: 39, 40, 169
Lands Acquisition (Town Planning) Ordinance 1949: 40
s 4: 39, 40, 169
s 5: 40, 169
Lands (Kila Kila Aerodrome) Acquisition Ordinance 1939: 32, 39
Lands Regulation Ordinance 1888-1889
s 5: 42

Manus Provincial Forest Management Act 1988-1989: 80
Mineral Resource Stabilization Fund Act 1974: 11
Mining Act 1928-1966: 137
Mining Act (Ch 195): 176
Pt XI: 176
Mining Act 1992: 18, 20, 21, 125, 137, 141, 143, 151, 164, 170, 173, 174, 176, 182
s 3: 174
s 3(1): 174
s 5: 19, 20, 53, 154, 173
s 6: 174
s 16A: 160
s 18: 142
s 28(2): 143
ss 33-37: 174
s 67: 176
s 148: 176
ss 154-160: 168, 174, 175
s 154: 122, 174
s 154(1): 175, 176
s 154(2): 175
s 154(6): 175
s 159: 176
s 168: 176
s 173(5): 176
Pt V, Div 2: 174
Pt VII: 174
Div 8: 174
Sch 2: 175
Mining and Petroleum Act
s 5: 177

Mining (Bougainville Copper Agreement) Act 1967: 136, 137, 145, 175

Mining (Bougainville Copper Agreement) Act (Ch 196): 175

Mining (Ok Tedi Agreement) Act (Ch 363): 139, 175

Mining Ordinance 1907: 174

Mining Regulations

s 1(1): 160

Mining (Royalties) Act 1992: 176

Multilateral Investment Guarantee Agency (MIGA) Convention

Art 15: 155

National Capital District Commission Act: 124

National Investment and Development Act: 73

National Parks Act: 52

National Water Supply and Sewerage Act 1986: 122, 124

s 1: 125

s 3: 123

s 4: 123

s 5: 123

s 6(c): 123

s 6(f): 123

s 26(1): 124

s 26(2): 124

s 26(3): 124

s 26(4): 124, 125

s 27: 123

s 28: 123

s 39(b): 124

National Water Supply and Sewerage Act (Ch 393): 123

Native Land Registration Act 1952: 2

New Guinea Timber Agreement Act (1952): 66

Sch, cl 4(1)(a): 66

Sch, cl 10: 66

Sch, cl 12: 66

Sch, cl 14: 66

Oil and Gas Act 1998: 18, 20, 21, 141, 143, 151, 170, 177, 102

s 3: 53

s 6: 19, 20, 154, 177

s 48: 177

s 50: 177

s 83: 142

s 118: 168, 177

s 118(1): 177

s 159: 177

s 159(1): 177

s 165: 160

s 167(4): 178

s 168: 177

s 183: 142

s 184: 142

Organic Law on Provincial Governments and Local-level Governments: 21, 52, 80, 81,

82, 83, 96, 97, 107, 169

s 24: 80

s 27: 80

s 39: 80

s 41(2): 81

s 42: 5, 81

s 42(1)(l): 96

s 44: 5, 81

s 85: 80

s 98: 5, 81, 82

s 98(6): 82

s 115: 5, 81, 82

s 116: 5, 81, 82

Petroleum Act (Ch 198): 125

s 81: 122

Property Land Act 1974-1989

ss 182-194: 26

s 196: 25

s 197: 25

Public Health Act (Ch 226): 124, 127

s 141: 126

Public Health (Sanitation and General) Regulation: 126, 127
reg 55: 127
reg 58: 127
Public Health (Septic Tanks) Regulation: 126
Public Health (Sewerage) Regulation: 126
Public Health (Underground Water Tanks) Regulation: 126

Real Property Act 1845: 36
Real Property Ordinance 1889: 3
Royal Mines Act
s 1688: 19
s 1693: 19

Sandalwood and Rubber Ordinance of 1907: 63
Statute Law Revision (Amalgamation of Laws) Act 1973: 64
Statute of Frauds and Limitation Act (Ch 330): 36

Telecommunications Act: 18
Timber Ordinance of 1903: 64
Timber Ordinance of 1908: 64
Timber Ordinance 1909-1917: 64
Timber Ordinance 1909-1920: 64, 65, 66
s 6: 63
Timber Ordinance 1920: 64
Timber Ordinance 1922: 65
Timber Ordinance 1922-1926: 65
Timber Ordinance 1922-1936: 65
Timber Ordinance 1936-1937: 66
Timber Ordinance (Consolidated) 1909: 2, 54, 63, 64, 74, 83
s 2: 64
s 9: 64
Timber Regulations 1909: 64
Torres Strait Treaty
Art 22: 99
Torres Strait Treaty Act: 107

Valuation Act (Ch 327): 168
Village Courts Act: 16, 29
s 2: 16

Water Act 1912 (NSW): 122
Water Resources Act 1967: 111
Water Resources Act 1982: 5, 108, 118, 170, 175, 176, 179
s 16(4): 179
s 16(6): 179
s 16(7): 179
Water Resources Act (Ch 205): 108, 111, 112, 115, 116, 117, 118, 121, 124, 125, 127,
128, 151, 178
s 2: 111, 125
s 4(1): 125
s 5: 108
s 5(1): 108, 121
s 5(2): 108, 122, 125
s 5(3): 108
s 8: 110
s 9: 110
s 15: 110
s 15(1): 116
s 16: 119, 120, 121, 178
s 16(1): 120, 178
s 16(2): 120, 178
s 16(2)(a): 122
s 16(3): 120
s 16(4)-(14): 119, 178
s 16(4): 178
s 16(6): 178
s 16(13): 119
s 16(14): 178
s 17: 116
s 17(1)(a): 117
s 17(1)(b): 117
s 17(2): 117
s 18: 117
s 19(b): 117
s 20: 117
s 21: 124
s 21(1): 108, 109
s 21(2): 109

s 22: 121, 122, 124
s 22(1): 109
s 22(1)(a): 124
s 22(2): 109, 122
s 22(3): 109
s 22(4): 109, 125
s 22(5): 109
s 22(6): 109
s 23: 111, 120
s 24: 112, 117
s 24(1): 117
s 25: 112
s 27: 112
s 28: 110
s 28(1): 127
s 29: 113
s 30: 113
s 41: 114
s 41(3): 114
s 42: 113
s 45: 114
s 46: 114
s 49: 115
s 50: 114, 115
s 50(a): 114
s 51: 115
s 52(2): 115
s 53: 115
s 53(3): 115
s 54: 115
s 55(4): 116
s 56: 118
s 56(1): 118
s 56(2): 119
s 57: 178
s 58: 117
s 58(2): 126, 127
s 59: 126
s 60: 118, 126
Pt IV: 111
Pt V: 111, 120, 121
Pt VI: 111, 121
Pt VII: 111, 120, 121
Pt IX: 111, 114, 115
Sch 1, Form 2: 127
Sch 1, Form 3: 115
Sch 2: 112, 114, 115
Sch 3: 114, 115, 127, 129
Sch 4: 124
Water Resources Act (Ch 309)
s 16: 168
s 57: 168
Water Resources (Amendment) Act 1970: 111, 112
Water Resources Ordinance 1962: 112
Water Resources Ordinance 1966: 112
Water Resources Ordinance 1967: 112
Water Resources Regulations (Ch 205)
reg 7(2): 128
reg 7(4): 128
reg 7(5): 128
reg 7(6): 128
reg 7(7): 128
reg 15: 112
reg 56: 124
Sch 4: 128
Water Supply (Papua) Act (Ch 328): 123

COMMONWEALTH

Export Finance and Insurance Corporations Act 1981: 157

UNITED KINGDOM

Civil Aviation Act 1949
s 40(1): 18

Chapter 1

Introduction

Eric Kwa

Papua New Guinea (PNG) is an island nation in the southwestern Pacific Ocean, north of Australia and east of Indonesia. The country consists of the eastern part of the island of New Guinea as its mainland, with the larger island masses of New Britain, Manus and New Ireland in the Bismarck Archipelago, Sudest and Rossell, the larger islands of the Louisiades Archipelago, the D'Entrecasteaux Islands, all in the Solomon Sea, and more than 600 smaller islands. The country is located between latitude 0°E and 10°S and longitude 144°E and 156°E. The mainland has a rugged terrain, with a central dividing range, giving rise to two major wetland areas, the Sepik and Ramu river flood plain to the north, and the Fly and Purari river flood plains to the south. The southern wetland supports a wide range of deltaic systems of pure mangrove forests and large sea-grass meadows in the Torres Straits. The Sepik and Ramu flood plain in the north supports a wide diversity of wetland fauna and flora, and contributes sediment outflow into the Bismarck Sea.

PNG is a country rich in natural resources by global standards. PNG's natural resources comprise renewable and non-renewable natural resources. Renewable natural resources include agricultural crops, forests and fisheries and marine resources. PNG is a rich source of non-renewable natural resources, which comprise gold, copper, silver, natural liquefied gas, oil and nickel. Alphonse Malipu, in Chapter 4, examines the importance of natural resources to the development of PNG.

After Independence in 1975, natural resources were being exploited sparingly for measured and planned economic growth. With the fall in the value of the natural currency (the Kina) in 1995, the pressure increased for accessibility to, and exploitation of, more and more natural resources in PNG. This trend is not a phenomenon peculiar to PNG. According to a 1998 report, it was revealed that:

> "As the economy grows, pressure on the Earth's natural systems and resources intensify. From 1950 to 1997, the use of lumber tripled, that of paper increased sixfold, the fish catch increased nearly fivefold, grain consumption nearly tripled, fossil fuel burning nearly quadrupled, and air and water pollutants multiplied several-fold. The unfortunate reality is that the economy continues to expand, but the ecosystem on which it depends does not, creating an increasingly stressed relationship."[1]

There is no doubt that the natural resources of the world are decreasing at an alarming rate. On the other hand, consumption and population are increasing, and the scale of extraction and depletion of natural resources is accelerating. It is imperative, therefore, that PNG take stock of its own resources. PNG must consider formulating and introducing workable mechanisms that will ensure that the country complies with goal 5 of the National Goals and Directive Principles of the *Constitution*.

---

[1] Brown, "*The Future of Growth*" in Brown, Flavin, French, and Starke, *State of the World (A Worldwatch Institute Report on Progress Toward a Sustainable Society)* (WW Norton & Co, New York, 1998), pp 3-4.

The *Constitution* is unique in including a specific provision in relation to PNG's natural resources. The constitutional directive is that Papua New Guineans, as individuals and as a collective body called the state, must use their natural resources for the benefit of the current generation and replenish them for the benefit of future generations. Goal 5 is the PNG country definition of "sustainable development", which became popularised as the universal concept of "sustainability" in 1987.

Goal 5 of the *Constitution* must be considered in the context of resource ownership in PNG. In PNG, natural resources are largely located on land that is communally owned by Papua New Guineans who are grouped into clans and tribes spread throughout the country. The ownership and usufructuary rights over land are determined by custom, which varies from one region of the country to another. Customary ownership is clearly examined in Chapter 3. That chapter also indicates that land is a very volatile and yet very intricate part of a person's life. To a Papua New Guinean, land means life. If a person does not have possession of, or has no rights over, land, he or she is "dead". Land issues in PNG have always been the cornerstone of PNG's development, during both the colonial and post-Independence eras.

Acknowledging the reality that the people own their land and its natural resources and environment, the *Constitution* implores Papua New Guineans to use their natural resources and environment in their locality wisely, or, to use the universal language, to use their natural resources on a "sustainable basis". The desire to "wisely use the natural resources" must also be considered against PNG's colonial past. PNG emerged as an independent state against the backdrop of a colonial past filled with oppression, paternalism, degradation of self and loss of traditional structures and systems by the Australian colonial administration. As a colonial power, Australia extracted natural resources (mostly gold and timber) and large amounts of rubber, tea, copra and coffee for its industries and markets. Little benefit flowed to the people from this exploitation of their natural resources. Papua New Guineans not only lost out on their natural resources, but also were used by the Australians as indentured labourers to work on the minefields, logging areas and agricultural plantations.

The colonial administration also formulated policies and developed laws targeted at extracting the natural resource of the people. The main area of policy development was in respect of land. Land and other natural resource policies and laws were used as a pretext to obtain arable land. Land policy was also directed towards severing customary ownership of the land from the landowners.[2] This practice was rampant in the forestry sector, where the colonial administration accessed customary land and assumed ownership of the lands under the Timber Rights Purchase (TRP) Agreement process, established first by the *Indigenous Timber Ordinance* 1892, and later, by the *Timber Ordinance (Consolidated)* 1909 and the *Forestry Ordinance* 1936. This policy, a devious mechanism, is discussed is some detail in Chapter 4.

The development of natural resources in PNG begins with its colonial political history in 1884. When the British and the Germans finally decided to establish formal links with this remote outlying island, Papua New Guineans were, for the first time, introduced to money and "began to realise" the economic value of their natural resources. Customary lands were the first resource to be sold to the colonial administration. The colonial administration purchased this resource with tobacco, axes, lap laps and tin goods. Thus, the seeds of manipulation, destruction and oppression were sown.

---

[2] See, for instance, the underlying principles of the *Native Land Registration Act* 1952. Papua New Guineans rejected this law, as they saw this as a direct attempt by the colonial administration to "steal" their land.

The next resources to follow the path of exploitation were the mineral resources. These became the property of the Crown under the *Real Property Ordinance* 1889.[3] Following that, forestry fell under the control of the colonial administration under the auspices of the *Indigenous Timber Ordinance* of 1892. The manner in which customary landowners were treated by the colonial administration continues to exist in the form of multinational and multilateral corporations operating in PNG, as well as the elite Papua New Guineans. Chapter 8 follows this devastation by looking at the minerals and forestry sectors, and concludes that ordinary Papua New Guineans are still missing out on the real value of their natural resources. The compensation they are getting is either insufficient or misappropriated (or, for want of a better word, "stolen") right under their noses by the very people they trust – other Papua New Guineans who call themselves "professional", "experts", "educated" or "experienced". Unfortunately, the existing legal system either protects these exploiters or is inadequate to deal with complex high-tech crimes.

The exploitation of the people by the colonial administration was fresh in the minds of the members of the Constitutional Planning Committee (CPC), the committee tasked to formulate a *Constitution* for the emerging state of PNG. The CPC believed that Papua New Guineans should:

> "... develop a sense of respect for all our natural resources and the environment. We should not be afraid to use those resources to contribute to our development, but should be sure not to over-use them to the extent that they are rapidly exhausted, especially at this stage of our history when it is foreign interests who gain by far the most benefit from the exploitation of our natural resources. Our needs should be weighed against the needs of our children, their children and the generations which follow them."[4]

Exploitation of natural resources plays a significant role in the development of PNG. In 1990, the minerals sector alone contributed 69 percent of total PNG exports.[5] In 1996, the mineral sector accounted for approximately 67 percent of total exports, and forestry contributed 15 percent.[6] The table below shows the contribution of each commodity to the national purse over the past ten years. Generally, the natural resources contribution to the national economy has been on a gradual increase since 1990. The signal is very clear: without the utilisation of these natural resources, the PNG economy cannot be sustained.

---

[3] Kwa, *The Environmental Law Aspects of Forestry Resource Development in Papua New Guinea: A Critique* (LLM Thesis, 1994), p 16.

[4] Constitutional Planning Committee, *Final Report of the Constitutional Planning Committee 1974* (Part 1) (Port Moresby: Government Printer, 1974), p 2/12.

[5] Fallon, *The Papua New Guinean Economy: Prospects for Recovery, Reform and Sustained Growth* (AGPS, 1992), p 32.

[6] Bank of Papua New Guinea, *Quarterly Economic Bulletin* (March 1997 Issue), Vol XXV, No 1, p S33.

EXPORT VALUES BY COMMODITY
K Million
(Current prices)

	1990	1991	1992	1993	1994	1995	1996	1997	1998	1999	2000	2001
Minerals & Oil	757	1,006	1,372	1,768	1,782	2,436	2,245	1,839	2,456	3,419	3,284	3,443
Gold	393	667	746	682	702	840	774	719	1,228	1,458	1,657	1,796
Copper	349	324	314	256	367	755	387	260	396	853	689	721
Silver	15	15	11	12	10	13	10	8	19	22	9	11
Oil			301	818	703	828	1,074	852	813	1,086	929	915
Agriculture	206	206	224	271	375	503	578	777	1,021	881	892	836
Coffee	103	80	68	101	205	215	190	326	476	299	330	301
Cocoa	30	34	34	33	29	48	66	73	82	124	131	114
Copra	9	5	12	14	15	27	49	47	39	65	60	55
Copra Oil	12	13	24	20	20	30	51	51	70	89	97	103
Palm Oil	33	53	64	79	78	142	182	207	272	280	245	230
Rubber	2	2	2	3	3	4	4	7	7	12	13	15
Tea	7	5	7	7	4	5	13	10	19	12	16	18
Other	10	14	13	14	21	32	23	56	56			
Forestry	80	90	148	410	494	450	480	433	173			
Logs	65	81	140	400	483	437	465	409	154	280	340	378
Other	79	91	119	79	10	12	10	10	40	233	179	202
Total	1,187	1,474	2,003	2,928	3,144	3,838	3,778	3,468	3,844	4,813	4,695	4,859

Source: Bank of Hawaii: Economic Report: February 2001

However, the development of PNG's natural resources involves various kinds of risks with which investors and the government are particularly concerned. These risks involve political, social, economic and land tenureship issues. These are critical issues that PNG has to deal with appropriately, because its economy is dependent largely on foreign investments that PNG cannot afford to brush aside. Kawi and Golman express this point in Chapter 7. Their analysis is crystal clear: PNG has to be vigilant in overcoming some of its risks before foreign investors can feel welcome in the country. As long as PNG sits on these issues, it stands to lose millions of kina, because investors will look elsewhere. The competition for PNG is coming from its northern neighbours – West Papua, the province of Indonesia and to the west, East Timor, and, further to the north, countries in South-East Asia. As their political systems begin to stabilise, they are beginning to attract the big multilateral companies to invest in their region.

PNG needs to take stock of its natural resources policies and laws, with the aim of standardising them. Currently, PNG has an array of laws and policies governing specific natural resources. In 1996, the Constitutional Review Commission (CRC) reviewed these incoherent approaches, and recommended that the government should seriously consider formulating an integrated policy and law on natural resources.[7] The Law Reform Commission raised a similar concern in 1990.[8] Participants at the 20th Waigani Seminar again made the same call.[9]

[7] Constitutional Review Commission, *Interim Report on Initiative No 3* (Reports 1994-97) 3 (CRC, Port Moresby, 1996).

[8] Law Reform Commission, *New Directions in Resource Management for Papua New Guinea* (Occasional Paper No 20) (Law Reform Commission, Port Moresby, 1990).

[9] Gladman, Mowbray and Duguman, (ed), *From Rai to Rio: Environment and Development in Papua New Guinea* (UPNG Press, Port Moresby, 1996), Vol 1.

The message is very clear. PNG needs to put in place a natural resources development strategy through policy and law that will work for PNG. This new strategy needs to embody sustainable development principles that have been defined by the *Constitution*. The move towards sustaining the natural resources has been started by the fisheries sector already, and Manoka and Kolkolo discuss this in Chapter 5. The *Organic Law on Provincial Governments and Local-Level Governments* (OLPGLLG) has adopted some of the sustainable development principles under ss 42, 44, 98, 115 and 116. PNG has to be bold in harnessing its natural resources law and policy to comply with the National Goals and Directive Principles.[10]

When developing an integrated natural resources law and policy, PNG must not lose sight of the nexus between the environment and natural resources. The two are interrelated and interdependent. Past and continuing experiences have shown that PNG downplays environmental concerns for the seemingly huge financial gains readily available through the exploitation of the country's natural resources. Kalinoe, in Chapter 6, shows the importance of this relationship as it relates to water resources. The *Environment Act* 2000, which has repealed the *Water Resources Act*, the *Environmental Planning Act* and the *Environmental Contaminants Act*, attempts to collaborate these various pieces of legislation to ensure closer scrutiny of the environment and development. Kawi and Golman, in Chapter 7, examine project financing for resource development projects in PNG.

The government has to make a serious commitment to its people and the environment through the reformation of the natural resources sector to comply with the constitutional directive. Successive governments have paid lip service to the development of a coherent system that will adequately cover the management of the natural resources for the benefit of the present and future generations. The time to act is now and not tomorrow.

[10] Law Reform Commission, *New Directions in Resource Management for Papua New Guinea* (Occasional Paper No 20) (Law Reform Commission, Port Moresby, 1990).

CHAPTER 2

THE IMPORTANCE OF NATURAL RESOURCES, PARTICULARLY NON-RENEWABLE RESOURCES, TO THE DEVELOPMENT OF THE PAPUA NEW GUINEAN ECONOMY

*Alphonse K Malipu**

2.1 INTRODUCTION

It is probable that there are few small developing countries around the world that have such an abundance of natural resources as Papua New Guinea (PNG). PNG is a privileged country with a small population, yet it has a commendable export and tax revenue potential from the development of its vast renewable and non-renewable resources.[11] This chapter will focus on the various contributions the non-renewable resource sector, comprising the mining and petroleum (including natural gas) industries, have made to the PNG economy.

2.2 THE NON-RENEWABLE RESOURCE SECTOR

PNG's non-renewable resource sector is a high-risk sector in so far as realising its anticipated receipts, whether they are returns on investment by stockholders of exploration and resource developing companies, or claims on government tax revenues and export receipts. The high-risk factor is associated with its:

(a) initial exploration costs, and subsequent development costs for successful finds, due to their relative and absolute inaccessibility from major towns and existing public infrastructure such as ports, roads, electricity and telecommunication supply lines; and

(b) the fact that the world mineral and petroleum prices are very volatile.

Apart from these two factors, other issues exacerbate the total risks associated with mining and petroleum developments, including ongoing landowner disputes and administrative and political mishandlings at the three tiers of government (national, provincial and local levels). In addition, access to mineral and petroleum reserves requires the use of very costly transport (airfreight and charter helicopters), resulting in capital-intensive development. Operational techniques require the use of the latest technology in mines and petroleum development.

Critics have defended resource extraction methods in developing PNG's mineral and petroleum reserves because of the flow-on level of employment creation and linkage effects. To comply with their mining agreements, some mining and petroleum establishments have taken initiatives to institute training programs or cadetship programs to train and localise skilled expatriate positions requiring some level of specific skill in those sectors. These include Ok Tedi and Placer Pacific's graduate trainee schemes.

---

*Deputy Executive Dean – School of Law and Business Studies, University of Papua New Guinea.

[11] For the purpose of our analysis, we define "renewable resources" as those that can be regenerated within a generation, and "non-renewable resources" as those resources that cannot be regenerated within a generation or even longer. Examples of the former would include commercial aquatic species and forestry, while examples of the latter would include naturally occurring minerals and combustible organic substances such as natural gas and other oil.

2.3 THE DEVELOPMENT OF THE SECTOR

Mining in PNG began in the early 1920s when the Morobe Gold Fields were proclaimed in February 1923, following the rediscovery by William "Sharkeye" Park of Arthur Darling's original 1901 discovery of gold in the Bulolo River.[12] The subsequent operations of this goldfield closed down during World War II, and recommenced in 1965. It is estimated that by June 1977 total mineral extractions amounted to 116 tonnes of gold and 71 tonnes of silver from within the same area.[13] By the mid-1960s, there was an increase in the search for minerals, which subsequently led to the discovery of the Bougainville copper deposit in 1972, and the Ok Tedi copper deposit in 1955. Ever since the discovery and the subsequent development of the Bougainville copper deposit, there has been a substantial impact on PNG's economy. Unfortunately, due to a landowner uprising, this strategic mine was forced to shut down in 1989.

Currently, there are several mining and petroleum projects being developed, and some are operational. These include the Ok Tedi copper mine (which came into operation in mid-1984), Porgera mine (which came into operation in 1990), Misima, Mt Tolokuma and Lihir gold mines, the Kutubu, Gobe and Moran oil fields, the Hides gas field and the proposed Ramu cobolt and nickel mine. There are smaller alluvial mines in operation, such as the Mt Kate, Wau and Mt Victor sites. Due to the recent economic decline, further exploration activities were cut back drastically, as logistical and other associated costs have increased significantly.

2.4 CONTRIBUTIONS OF THE NON-RENEWABLE RESOURCE SECTOR

2.4.1 Government revenue

The government has maintained a consistent set of fiscal strategies that have consisted of both debt and internal revenue financing. Due to worsening economic conditions, exacerbated by low levels of economic activity in the non-mining/petroleum sectors, the government's debt position has increased in recent years, but is not yet a cause for alarm. Indeed, the main source of government revenue constitutes internal revenue, grant aids and borrowings. The former constitutes a significant portion of overall government revenue generation, primarily from income taxes and equity holdings in selected firms. This, in turn, implies that the tax base is narrow. Income tax is collected from a small portion of the labour force that is primarily associated with the formal sector, and from corporate entities.

The internal revenue generated from the non-renewable sector is dependent on a lot of factors, and none is more important than the economic conditions to which corresponding firms are subject. Such conditions include:

(a) the high cost structure they are faced with due to the relative inaccessibility to the respective project sites; and

(b) the dynamic global economic conditions, which are dependent on:

  (i) the relative cost of capital;

  (ii) the world market price of non-renewable resources; and

---

[12] Coopers and Lybrand, *Mining and Petroleum Taxation: A Guide for Operators and Contractors* (Coopers and Lybrand, Port Moresby, 1987).

[13] Garnaut and Ross, *Taxation of Mineral Rents* (Clarendon Press, Oxford, 1983). See also Triton, Millet and Ward, *Mineral and Mining Policy in Papua New Guinea: INA Discussion Paper No 24* (Institute of National Affairs, Port Moresby, 1986), p 4

(iii) the exchange rate.

The performance profitability of the firms in these sectors is determined by these factors. Consequently, the revenue generated by the government is consistent with the upswings and downswings associated with the performance of economic variables.

The government, consistent with existing policies, has decided to participate directly in the development of resources by taking equity. On the one hand, the government has taken up a share of the total risk borne by the resource developers. However, in essence, the government has maximised its potential revenue receipts from this sector. Indeed, the government has enjoyed its share of receipts from some projects in recent years. This has been perceived as a good vehicle to expand the revenue base. There are, however, problems associated with this equity approach. There are issues in relation to the proper role and the primary objective of the state in the development of its non-renewable (and even renewable) resources. This issue is specifically related to environmental issues, which the state could downplay if it perceives that significant financial gains are going to be thwarted.

2.4.2 Export revenue

PNG's total export earnings from the non-renewable sector account for more than 50 percent of PNG's total export earnings. This figure is subject to variations in both the volume of output and the world market prices of the respective minerals and petroleum. Since 1975/1976, there has been an increase in export earnings. This is attributable to the establishment of the Ok Tedi, Misima, Porgera and Lihir mines, the Kutubu, Gobe and Moran oil fields and the Hides gas. A relative price increase for gold and copper, from 1986 to 1988, also contributed to the increase. Export earnings from this sector increased from 50 percent in 1976/1977, to 80 percent in 1988.

2.4.3 Employment and manpower development

Employment creation is insignificant in relation to mining and petroleum operations. This contrasts with other sectors/industries, such as primary industry (agriculture, livestock, fisheries and forestry), manufacturing, construction and the public service. For instance, in 1976 the number of persons employed in the mining and quarrying industry totalled 4,527. By 1983 this figure had increased to 8,018 (primarily due to Ok Tedi's commencement of operations), but it was still insignificant when compared with other activity areas' employment levels.[14] The overall increase was 11 percent from 1978 to 1983, and yearly increases were around 3.7 percent to 4.2 percent.

Interestingly, many firms in this sector assert that they are committed to a more concerted effort in employment creation, such as the training of nationals to allow for the transfer of technology. This has been seen as one area of concern in mining agreements between the firms involved and local landowner groups, the provincial government and, to some degree, the national government. It is argued that there are some jobs that could be taken over by local people. The problem with this has been that local people do not have the necessary expertise.

Firms are committed to allow the transfer of skills to local people to take up jobs currently held by expatriates. There are problems with these initiatives. First, the training is specific, and if

---

[14] Triton, Millet and Ward, Ibid, p 4. See also_Goodman, Lepani and Morawetz, *The Economy of Papua New Guinea: An Independent Review* (Development Studies Centre, Australian National University, Canberra, 1987), p 251, table A34.

people are laid off they may not easily be absorbed in other sectors. Secondly, the transfer of technology could be achieved by local entrepreneurs establishing themselves in the industry. This is difficult because the current operations are on a very large scale. It would be tremendously difficult to develop a nationally owned, operated and managed mining or petroleum project at this stage.

2.4.4 Infrastructure and social services

Public infrastructure and social services are state functions. It therefore follows that receipts from the development of the non-renewable sector should be used to finance the construction of new, and the maintenance of existing, public infrastructures, such as roads, bridges, wharves, jetties and telecommunication services. The government is also expected to fund the establishment of new social services and the continued maintenance of those services, such as health, education, agricultural extension services and business development services. Sadly, due to shifts in macroeconomic policy, the government has not been able to fund all its priority areas under its successive budgets. Many factors have contributed to this dangerous scenario, but the results have been unimpressive.

Given these trends, some provincial governments and local landowners consider that, while they have some claim over the resources on their land, they continue to be left out of essential government services. Therefore, they have negotiated to ensure that resource developers and the state take note of their needs and return part of the profits in the development of their area. This has culminated in special provisions in the respective mining and petroleum agreements, which allow for certain public infrastructure to be established for the people and to allow for accessibility to essential social services.

An interesting aspect of these negotiations and subsequent provisions in the respective mining and petroleum agreements has been the introduction of the tax credit scheme, first initiated in the Porgera Mine Agreement. The tax credit scheme allows the resource developers to fund the provision of some services and/or set up public infrastructures that are seen to benefit local resource owners and other people from the province concerned. Capital funds that are used for such purposes are exempted from corporate income tax. This is, in essence, a form of tax shield for firms directly involved in resource development projects. Under this scheme, several resource developers in PNG have constructed roads, bridges, aid posts, health centres, schools and other social services. These include Placer Pacific (operator of Porgera mine), BHP (operator of Ok Tedi mine), Rio Tinto (operator of Lihir mine), Chevron (operator of Kutubu, Gobe and Moran oil fields), and Highlands Pacific (operator of Hides gas field).

Community and government agencies' attitudes to such services are mixed. Many local people appreciate the services brought to their locality, but others believe that the firms should do more. In some cases, expectations are unwarranted and, consequently, cause anxiety and unreasonable demands. One such situation occurred in Porgera, where certain public infrastructure was set up by force, while landowners received some compensation for alleged environmental pollution in the last two years. In other incidents, the Misima people petitioned the public, seeking exclusive rights to spin-off contracts (in some cases where they would be seen to lack the managerial, logistic and financial basis) to provide the necessary services to the Misima mine.

2.5 PAST AND EXISTING GOVERNMENT POLICIES

2.5.1 General

The government sees its role in the development of its resources as a vehicle to enhance its population's welfare. In some ways, the government's approach to resource development is the same as making "charters" that guide the operations of statutory corporations. These "charters" place profit-making as one objective, and the provision of social service as another objective.

The PNG government has always recognised the importance of the two resource sectors in its economy's growth. In its wider and sector-specific policy pursuits, it has stressed the need for the acceptance of the peculiarities of the two industries and, hence, adopted policies that would best suit the attainment of objectives of all participants concerned. These include the government's export revenues, tax revenues, increased economic benefits to be enjoyed by as many nationals as possible, and the provincial government's royalty benefits, landowners' royalties and spin-off benefits, such as improved accessibility to social services and, more importantly, the investors' desired rate of returns.

Interestingly, the national government did not have any mining policy before independence, or even until the late 1980s. Instead, the government negotiated and signed mining agreements on an ad hoc basis. Of the various mining agreements that were negotiated and concluded in this manner, the main ones were the Bougainville Mine Agreement of 1967 (and the same re-negotiated in 1974), the Ok Tedi Mining Agreement of 1979 and the Porgera Mine Agreement of 1987. It is, in essence, the former two agreements that have served as the basis for further agreements and fostered the understanding of the mining and petroleum sectors to develop further projects.

2.5.2 Principles for development

Potential resource developers should recognise the main principle of development, which can be summarised as "to seek more efficient utilisation of Papua New Guinea's mineral (and petroleum) resources so as to maximise the benefits to the economy".[15]

This general principle can be divided into three. The first principle is that all mineral (and petroleum) resources belong to the people, and the people and the government should receive a "fair share" in the resources' exploitation, or, to use O'Faircheallaigh's words, "to ensure that the benefits are maximised by the majority"[16]. The second principle is that the mining (and petroleum) sectors are very high-risk sectors, and since PNG has to rely heavily on foreign capital to exploit the reserves within these sectors, a conducive fiscal and political environment should be provided. This would enable investors to obtain a reasonable rate of return on their investments without affecting the normal profits in the operations of these projects. The third principle adheres to the former two. That is, for the benefit of the people, the government has the right to regulate the activities of mining companies to maximise potential benefits, where possible, and to minimise potentially harmful social and economic costs.

---

[15] *Papua New Guinea, Medium Term Development Strategy Inception Reports* (Port Moresby: National Planning Office, 1984) 26

[16] O'Faircheallaigh, *Review of Papua New Guinea's Mineral Policy 1974-1983 - Some Preliminary Findings* (Paper presented to a seminar on Economic Policy Issues and Options in Papua New Guinea, University of Papua New Guinea, Port Moresby, 5-7 September 1983).

[16] *Papua New Guinea, Medium Term Development Strategy Inception Reports* (National Planning Office, Waigani, 1984).

The principles correspond to the "resource rent tax" (RRT) or the "additional profits tax" (APT), a concept that was first proposed, in the case of PNG, by Garnaut and Ross in 1975. The APT ensures that the windfall gains arising from either extraction of high ore contents, or due to increases in world market prices, are taxed. The tax rate is applicable on top of the normal 35 percent income tax for mining companies. The corresponding rate for petroleum projects is 50 percent on top of the normal 50 percent corporate income tax. It is applicable after the end of the investment recovery period, and is imposed on the excess of the accumulated receipts over the accumulated value of total expenditure.[17]

2.5.3 The Mineral Resources Development Corporation

The second most important policy instrument in this sector is the *Mineral Resource Stabilization Fund Act* 1974. The Mineral Resource Stabilisation Fund has recently been corporatised and is now known as the Mineral Resource Development Corporation (MRDC). The reasons for the change will be clarified below, but first the Mineral Resource Stabilisation Fund will be explained. It was initially established to allow for a consistent flow of revenue from the minerals sector to the consolidated fund of the national government. Indeed, it was part of the macroeconomic stabilisation policy that was pursued prior to PNG attaining political autonomy up to the early 1980s. The Mineral Resource Stabilisation Fund acted as a stabilising mechanism, ironing out any fluctuations in revenue receipts from the non-renewable sector to the annual budgets. At the time the stabilisation-oriented polices were pursued, the actual flows to the Consolidated Revenue Fund were determined by a board, based on trend analysis and revenue projections, which were not allowed to exceed 20 percent of the previous amount dispensed to the Consolidated Revenue Fund.

2.5.4 The environment

Other policy instruments relate to the fiscal regime, accounting for tax holidays, depreciation allowances, etc. Apart from the fiscal regime, one area that has become increasingly important, even up to the present, is that of environmental management and control. Many adverse environmental incidents have impacted on projects and have caused serious concern. Mining and petroleum agreements are signed, and petroleum development licences and special mining leases are granted, on the condition that the sponsors of major projects satisfy any restrictive conditions, one of which is the environmental plan. However, the responsible department has been downgraded to the Office of Environment and Conservation. It is ill-equipped, underfunded, understaffed and unable to critically appraise a project's environmental plans. It is necessary that the government reviews the status of the Office of Environment and Conservation and takes appropriate action.

The government adopts a balancing approach to resource developments. In more recent times, the scope and ability of the government in reconciling mutually exclusive interests associated with the many opposing parties has been tested in the negotiating process. The government demonstrates maturity in attempting to ensure that resource development proceeds without significant confusion, ambiguities, and conditions for future conflicts. Specific mining agreements between resource developers, state, provincial governments and landowners, initiated for various projects, demonstrate this.

---

[17] Coopers and Lybrand, op cit n 2, p19

2.6 CONCLUSIONS

Small open and developing economies all over the world strive for various avenues to attain structural transformations with respect to their domestic economies. However, if there were no constraints, such objectives would have long been achieved. The fact that there are many constraints hinders the achievement of economic growth with development. In PNG's case, the national government has the same objective but, above all, it needs to ensure that the welfare status of the economy is significantly improved. Only the willing participants in all sectors can bring such an objective to fruition by increased participation. Available data shows that the non-renewable sectors hold promise in bringing some degree of development and growth into the PNG economy.

However, too much dependency on the non-renewable sector is by no means desirable for small open developing economies, including PNG. Therefore, there should be a concerted effort in reducing this dependency by creating an adequate absorptive capacity in the agricultural sector, or the non-renewable sector as a whole. As long as there are sufficient tax revenue earnings from the non-renewable sector, many of these projects in the other sectors can be funded (thus avoiding the option to finance them by debt).

There have been encouraging trends in the development of non-renewable sectors, especially in allowing the relevant, but previously marginalised, parties to participate fully. Since the then Prime Minister and the then Premier for Enga took the initiative in signing the Porgera Mine Agreement between the national government, the provincial government and the land owners, most projects to date have, in varying degrees, replicated these agreements. The problem was that in some of the projects the bargaining power of the parties was not consistently the same and, hence, there have been reported cases where some parties have expressed their disappointment at the rest of the parties/participants. An obvious example occurred when the national government and Placer Pacific did not seal the Enga Highway from Wapenamanda to Porgera. A further example occurred when it was alleged that a mine discharged large quantities of tailings into the Ok Tedi and Fly Rivers, and no considerable effort was made to clean it up. A binding agreement allows every member to adhere to their obligations, while recognising others' rights and, consequently, all parties have a sense of ownership of the project.

REFERENCES

Coopers and Lybrand, *Mining and Petroleum Taxation: A Guide for Operators and Contractors* (Coopers and Lybrand, Port Moresby, 1987).

Garnaut and Ross, *Taxation of Mineral Rents* (Clarendon Press, Oxford, 1983).

Goodman, Lepani and Morawetz, *The Economy of Papua New Guinea: An Independent Review* (Development Studies Centre, Australian National University, Canberra, 1987).

O'Faircheallaigh, *Review of Papua New Guinea's Mineral Policy 1974-1983 – Some Preliminary Findings* (Paper presented to a seminar on Economic Policy Issues and Options in Papua New Guinea, University of Papua New Guinea, Port Moresby, 5-7 September 1983).

Papua New Guinea, Medium Term Development Strategy Inception Reports (National Planning Office, Waigani, 1984).

Triton, Millet and Ward, *Mineral and Mining Policy in Papua New Guinea: INA Discussion Paper No 24* (Institute of National Affairs, Port Moresby, 1986).

Chapter 3

LAND TENURE LAW IN PAPUA NEW GUINEA

*George Muroa**

3.1 INTRODUCTION

In Papua New Guinea (PNG), the significance of land cannot be overstated. About 90 percent of the population lives entirely off the land, engaging in gardening, gathering, fishing and hunting for daily sustenance.[18] Land is perhaps the most important resource in the world, because it sustains life itself. Indeed, this is the only planet that supports living things known to man. That is why people all over the world have to fight to keep possession of their land. In the early days of European colonisation, Europeans travelled all over the world in search of new lands or territories. Discoveries of the continents of North and South America, Australia, Asia and Africa were the result of such European colonial expansion.

In western society, land is deemed to be a commodity that can be bought and sold. By distinction, land in PNG is not an alienable commodity; it is a sacred resource that links the past, present and future generations. The present owners or holders of customary land are deemed to hold land in trust for future generations.

PNG has a dual system of laws governing land tenure. On the one hand is the common law, supported by statutory law, governing non-customary land, and on the other hand is customary law governing customary land.[19]

3.2 DEFINITION AND NATURE OF LAND TENURE

In the perception of most people, land is the solid portion of the earth's surface. However, in law, land means more than that, and this is illustrated by the following definitions.

3.2.1 Common law definition

Under common law, land is an immovable property and means a definite portion of the earth's surface. In more general terms, land comprehends any ground, soil or earth whatsoever, including fields, meadows, pastures, woods, moors, water, marches and rock.[20] In its more limited sense, it denotes the quantity and character of the interest or estate that a person may own in land.[21] Thus, under common law, land may include any estate or interest in land, either legal or equitable, as well as easements and incorporeal hereditaments.[22] The ownership of land also extends to the airspace above the surface of the land. At common law, trees, crops and permanent fixtures, such as fences and buildings, are deemed to be part of the land.[23] Thus, under the common law

---

* Lecturer in Law, Papua New Guinea.

[18] See Kalinoe, *Water Law and Customary Water Rights in Papua New Guinea* (UBS Publishers' Distributors Ltd, New Delhi, 1999), Ch 1.

[19] The details of customary and non-customary land etc are discussed later in the chapter.

[20] *Reynard v City of Caldwel* 55 Idaho 342; 42 P 2d 292 at 296; *Holmes v US* CCA Okl 53 F 2d 960 at 963.

[21] *Holmes v US* CCA Okl 53 F 2d 960.

[22] *Reynard v City of Caldwel* 55 Idaho 342; 42 P 2d 292 at 297; *Jones v Magruder DC* Md 42 F Supp 193 at 198; *Lynch v Cunningham* 131 Cal. App 164; 21 P 2d 154; *Cuffy v Koslosky* 165 Okl 135; 25 P 2d 290; 1Y; *Petition of Burnguist* 220 Minn 48; 19 NW 2d 394 at 401.

[23] *Geita Sebea v Territory of Papua New Guinea* (1941) 67 CLR 544; *Newcomen v Coulson* (1877) 5 Ch D 133. Cf *Attorney-General (Cth) v RT Co Pty*

definition, land includes the soil and everything below and above it that is annexed in such a manner that it becomes part of the soil. If land is acquired, there is a presumption that the transferee takes the land above and below the surface.[24] The common law concept of land is summed up in the Latin maxim *cujus est solum ejus est usque ad coelum et ad inferos*, which, translated literally, means that the person to whom the soil belongs also owns the space above it and everything below it down to the centre of the earth. Legally, land is indestructible, in the sense that, although the surface may be destroyed, the space that remains is land.

The definition of land as noted is significant for a number of reasons. The most important of these is that it determines the nature and extent of the rights of the landowner vis-a-vis his or her neighbours and the rest of the community. Such rights and their limitations are examined below.

3.2.2 Customary law definition

It is not easy to define land under PNG customary law[25] because of the fact that custom varies from place to place. One needs to study closely the relevant customary law of a particular area to decide exactly what land means. However, generally land under customary law refers to the physical soil, that is, the land itself. It does not include trees, crops and permanent fixtures. Customary law, therefore, recognises that a lineage or other group may own the physical soil, whereas growing crops and other improvements thereon may be claimed by individual members of communities, including those who might be strangers to the communities but who have been invited to occupy land.

3.2.3 Statutory definition

The *Interpretation Act*[26] defines land to include messuages, tenements and hereditaments, corporal and incorporeal, of any tenure or description, whatever the estate or interest therein may be.[27] Under s 2 of the *Land Act* 1996, land is defined to include an interest in land, whether arising out of, and regulated by, custom or otherwise.

Although the distinction between land and other rights in land is generally clear under the customary system, there are statutory modifications for specific purposes. The Village Courts, which are established under the *Village Courts Act* to resolve disputes by applying the relevant customs, are expressly denied jurisdiction over disputes involving the ownership of land under the general law. They do, however, have jurisdiction to hear disputes concerning the ownership of land by custom, and rights by custom to its use, and make interim orders pending the determination of the substantive issue by the Land Court. For this purpose, s 2 of the *Village Courts Act* defines land to include "a reef or bank and a house or other structure built on or over water, *but does not include things growing on land*". The *Land Disputes Settlement Act*[28] extends

---

Ltd (1956) 97 CLR 146; *Commissioner of Main Roads (NSW) v North Shore Gas Co* (1967) 120 CLR 118; *Anthony v Commonwealth* [1972-1978] ACR 769, for information on certain fixtures that are not deemed to form *partes soli*.

24 *Manchester Corp v Rochdale Canal Co* (1971) 69 LGR 517. Thus, in *Manning v Williams* (1909) 9 SR (NSW) 903 it was held that the power to resume land did not entitle the Crown to resume a stratum to the depth of 50 feet, but the whole must be assumed *ad inferos*.

25 "Customary law" means the customary law of the indigenous people of PNG as adopted under Sch 2 as part of the underlying law and declared under s 9 of the *Constitution* as part of the sources of law in PNG. The term "traditional law" is used interchangeably with the term "customary law" in this chapter. For a detailed discussion of the meaning of "customary law", see Amankwah, "Post-Mabo: The Prospect of the Recognition of Customary Law in Australia" (1994) 18 UQLJ 15-37.

26 *Interpretation Act*, Ch 2, s 3.

27 Corporeal refers to the physical soil and structures thereon. Incorporeal rights are the legal rights over the land, eg, easements, rent charges, etc, which are less substantive.

28 *Land Disputes Settlement Act*, Ch 45.

the definition in the *Village Courts Act* further. Section 2 of the Act defines land to mean customary land, and includes "a reef or bank; a house or other structure built on land or over water; things growing on land or in water over land; earths and minerals on or under land; and an interest in land".

Thus, whereas the definition of land in the *Land Disputes Settlement Act* includes things growing on land or in water over land, and earths and minerals on or under land, the *Village Courts Act* does not include things growing on land. It is not clear whether or not land refers to improvements, which, under custom, generally belong to those who effected them. Such improvements, provided they are effected by a person other than the owner or owners of the land, can be owned and removed by the improver.[29] As such, it could be argued that the phrase "things growing on land" in this instance refers to improvements, rather than those things naturally growing on land that form part of the land and are therefore owned by the owner of the land.

3.3 CLASSIFICATION OF LAND

Land in PNG is divided into two basic categories; customary land, which is also referred to as unalienated land, and non-customary land, which is also referred to as alienated land. The former category comprises a little over 97 percent, or 46,310,419 hectares, and the latter comprises a little less than 3 percent, or 1,305,281 hectares, of the total landmass in the country.[30] Unalienated land is land that is owned and controlled by indigenous peoples according to their customs. The expression "customary land" is normally used in legislation to refer to this category of land. Customary land has been defined to mean land that is owned or possessed by an automatic citizen, or community of automatic citizens, by virtue of rights of a proprietary or possessory kind that belong to that citizen or community and arise from, and are regulated by, custom.[31]

Alienated land, on the other hand, is largely land alienated from the traditional sector, either voluntarily or by compulsory process. Alienated land also includes land acquired by declaration as waste and vacant or ownerless. It comprises two basic subdivisions, namely state land and private freeholds. It should be noted that, although alienated land represents less than 3 percent of the total land area of PNG, it accounts for prime urban and agricultural land in the country. For instance, alienated land accounts for over 40 percent of the arable land in the Gazelle area of East New Britain Province, which is a very fertile area of the country.[32] The distinction between state land and private freehold is that the private owner controls his or her land for his or her own benefit, whereas state land is held on behalf of the people as a whole for development purposes.[33] Some areas are made available as settlement areas for various agricultural projects and schemes, others for schools, hospitals, roads, etc. Other areas are granted to individuals or companies as state leases for residential, commercial or industrial purposes.

The broad division between alienated and unalienated land carries the implication of the contrast between written and unwritten laws, that is, the former is governed or regulated by the rules and principles of common law and equity, and the latter by customary law. It also expresses diverse theoretical basic principles of the PNG land tenure system, that is, the radical title to alienated

---

[29] In the Ghanaian case of *Dadzie v Kokofu* (1961) GLR 90 at 93, the Supreme Court of Ghana held that the ownership of farms is distinguishable from the land on which the farms are made.

[30] James, *Land Law and Policy in Papua New Guinea* (Law Reform Commission Monograph No 5, Port Moresby, 1985), p 33.

[31] See *Interpretation (Interim Provisions) Act*, Ch 2. It should be noted that the terms "unalienated land", "customary land" and "traditional land" are used interchangeably in this chapter.

[32] See James, op cit n 13, p 33.

[33] The title to all land owned by the government is vested in the state.

land is in the state, while the ultimate ownership of unalienated land vests in the traditional groups. This principle is contained in s 4 of the *Land Act* 1996, which provides that "all land in the country other than customary land is the property of the State". The radical title of the state, however, is subject to any estates, rights, titles or interests in force under any law. All estates, rights, titles and interests, other than customary rights, in land are, therefore, deemed to be held under the state.[34]

3.4 INCIDENTS OF LAND OWNERSHIP

Ownership of land can usually give rise to a number of incidents. The most salient are discussed below.

3.4.1 Rights above the surface of the land

Common law

As noted in the common law definition of land, the airspace above the surface of the land belongs to the owner of the land. Any intrusion of this space without lawful excuse would constitute trespass to land. The fact that the intrusion is insignificant, or that it causes no damage to the surface of the land, is not a defence. Thus, in *Ketson v Imperial Tobacco Co (of Great Britain and Ireland Ltd)*,[35] it was held that an advertising sign fixed on the defendant's building, and which projected about eight inches over the plaintiff's shops, constituted trespass to the plaintiff's land. The defendant was therefore ordered to remove the offending object.

The relevant question one needs to ask is, how far above the surface does the landowner's entitlement extend? It used to be the view in common law, supported by older cases, that the ownership of land generally included all the space above the land vertically upwards for an indefinite distance, and all the earth beneath its surface down to the centre of the earth.[36] However, the accepted view today is that ownership of land above the surface is subject to limitations upon the use of airspace imposed, and rights in the use of airspace granted, by law. This view is supported by more recent cases that have adopted a common sense approach to the issue and imposed a limit on the airspace above one's land. For instance, in *Lord Bernstein of Leigh v Skyviews & General Ltd*,[37] the court had to encounter the difficulties in this area of the law. The plaintiff in this case was the owner of, and resident at, premises comprising a country house and surrounding land in Kent in the United Kingdom. The defendants, whose business was to take aerial photographs of properties and then offer them for sale to the owners, took a single aerial photograph of the plaintiff's premises from a height of several hundred feet. The plaintiff

---

34 The doctrine of radical title is based on two fundamental principles in English common law: that all lands are held for an estate, and that all lands are held of the Crown in one or other of the various tenures. For details, see Mugambwa and Amankwah, *Cases and Materials on Papua New Guinea Land Law and Policy* (Pacific Law Press, Hobart, 1996), pp 120-133. There are several consequences flowing from the classification of land in PNG, and these are discussed in James, op cit n 13, pp 33-34. See extracts in Mugambwa and Amankwah, op cit n 17, pp 119-20.

35 *Ketson v Imperial Tobacco Co (of Great Britain and Ireland Ltd)* [1957] 2 QB 334. See also *Graham v KD Morris & Sons Pty Ltd* [1974] Qd R 1.

36 See *Corbett v Hill* (1870) 39 LJ Ch 547; *Newcomen v Coulson* (1877) 5 Ch D 133; *Lord Bernstein of Leigh v Skyviews & General Ltd* [1978] 1 QB 479; *Wandsworth Board of Works v United Telephone Co Ltd* (1884) 13 QBD 904; *Kelsen v Imperial Tobacco Co (of Great Britain and Ireland) Ltd* [1957] 2 QB 334; *Pickering v Rudd* (1815) 4 Camp 219; *Lemmon v Webb* [1894] 3 Ch 1; *Gifford v Dent* [1926] WN 336; *Saunders v Smith* (1838) 2 Jur 491; cf *Commissioner for Railways v Valuer-General* [1974] AC 328 at 351; *Sovmots Investments Ltd v Secretary of State for the Environment* [1977] 1 QB 411. See also Riddal, *Introduction to Land Law* (Butterworths, London, 1974), pp 44-46; James, *Land Tenure in Papua New Guinea* (UPNG, Port Moresby, 1978), Ch 2; Brown, *Land and Registration* (Cambridge University Press, London, 1976), pp 5-8.

37 *Lord Bernstein of Leigh v Skyviews & General Ltd* [1978] 1 QB 479.

objected to the photograph being taken without his permission, and demanded that the defendants hand over or destroy all negatives and prints of the photograph. The defendants refused to do so. The plaintiff brought an action against the defendants, alleging that they had wrongfully entered the airspace above the plaintiff's premises to take the photograph and were guilty of trespass and actionable invasion of the plaintiff's right to privacy. The plaintiff claimed damages for trespass, and sought injunctions to restrain the defendants from entering the airspace and from invading the plaintiff's right to privacy. The plaintiff further contended that the defendants were not entitled to rely on the statutory defence under s 40(1) of the *Civil Aviation Act* 1949 (UK), since that section was limited to a bare right of passage over land, and did not permit the use of airspace for the purpose of photography. After analysing the authorities, the court concluded:

> "The problem is to balance the rights of an owner to enjoy the use of his land against the rights of the general public to take advantage of all that science now offers in the use of airspace. This balance is in my judgment best struck in our present society by restricting the rights of an owner in the airspace above his land to such height as is necessary for the ordinary use and enjoyment of his land and the structures on it, and declaring that above that height he has no greater rights in the airspace than any other member of the public ... On the facts of this case, even if contrary view, the defendants' aircraft committed a trespass at common law in flying over the plaintiff's land, the plaintiff is prevented from bringing any action in respect of that trespass by the terms of section 40(1) of the *Civil Aviation Act* 1949."[38]

For these reasons, the plaintiff's action failed and judgment was rendered in favour of the defendants. The judgment in this case illustrates the fact that modern legislation renders the flight of aircraft through an owner's vertical airspace as not being a trespass, as long as it is a reasonable height above the ground.[39]

Customary law

One question that arises from the customary law definition of land, is whether land includes ownership of the airspace above the land. On the face of it, it is doubtful whether customary law recognises ownership of airspace over one's land. Usually, it is taken for granted that customary law does not recognise the ownership of airspace. However, it is accepted that a person cannot do anything such as build a house on somebody else's land without permission. The fact that no one can go onto another person's land without permission to do anything on it, means that customary law does recognise ownership of airspace above one's land. Today, because of modern technological advances that make it possible for frequent use of airspace, it is imperative for customary law to redefine the ownership of airspace. The issue would appear to be moot in a culture and age that predated the advent of space technology.

---

[38] Ibid at 907 (Griffiths J).

[39] *R v Trent River Authority; Ex parte National Coal Board* [1969] 2 WLR 653. In the case of PNG, s 25 of the *Electricity Commission Act*, the *Telecommunications Act*, and Sch 1 of the *Civil Aviation (Aircraft Operators' Liabilities) Act*, are examples of limitation imposed by statute or legislation on an owner's right to the superjacent airspace. At common law, gold, silver and other minerals and oils found in the soil belong to the Crown by royal prerogative and were not deemed to form *partes soli*: *Commonwealth v New South Wales* (1923) 33 CLR 1. In PNG, the *Mining Act* 1992 states that all minerals found in or upon land are the property of the state. Similarly, the *Oil and Gas Act* 1998 provides that oil is the property of the state.

3.4.2 Rights below the surface of the earth

Common law

As noted from the definition of land, the owner of the surface of the land is entitled to everything below the surface. Again, the relevant question is, how deep below the surface does the owner's entitlement extend? Is it down to the centre of the earth as expressed in the common law maxim *cujus est solum ejus est usque ad coelum et ad inferos?* There is no direct authority on this point. However, on the analogy of *Bernstein v Skyviews*, the owner's rights to the surface of the land are probably limited to such depth as is necessary for his or her ordinary use and enjoyment of the land and the structures thereon.

At common law, ownership of the surface land does not include gold and silver in mines. At common law, these minerals (so called royal metals or minerals) belong to the Crown.[40] The basis of this proposition is that, at common law, the Crown is the ultimate owner of the land, and that individuals can only own estates or various interests of varying degrees in land, rather than ownership of the land itself, notwithstanding the nature of the interests held. If a person dies intestate, and no living descendants, or collaterals in the absence of lineals, can be established with reasonable inquiries, the land reverts to the Crown as the ultimate owner of the land, and, as such, the Crown is deemed to have the reversionary interest in the subject land. In PNG, ownership of all minerals and petroleum on, in or below the surface of any land in the country is vested in the state.[41]

As noted, at common law, although an individual can own land as a freehold, or an interest in land as leasehold, royal minerals found on, in or under the land belong to the Crown. They do not belong to the individual landowner. The landowner, therefore, owns everything on, above, in or below the surface of the land, except the royal minerals, which are reserved to the Crown. This common law principle evolves from the feudal doctrine that recognised the Crown as the absolute owner of all land in England and that individuals can only own an interest in land, not the land itself, irrespective of the nature or duration of the interest. As such, the royal minerals were rightfully reserved to the Crown as ultimate owner of the land. Hence, where land was granted to an individual, there was an inevitable presumption that the grant was made subject to the reservation of the royal minerals.

Customary law

It appears that, under customary law, ownership of land includes ownership of surface soil and everything below the surface of the land down to the centre of the earth. In theory, therefore, minerals and petroleum, as well as things growing on land or in water over land, form part of the land. This seems to be the extent of the definition in s 2 of the *Land Dispute Settlement Act* discussed earlier in this chapter. This proposition is important, because under customary law no

---

40 See *Commonwealth v New South Wales* (1923) 33 CLR 1; *Royal Mines Act*, ss 1688 and 1693.

41 Section 5 of the *Mining Act* 1992 (No 20 of 1992) vests all minerals existing on, in or below the surface of any land or in any water in PNG, in the state. Similarly, s 6 of the *Oil and Gas Act* 1998 (No 49 of 1998) vests in the state all petroleum and helium at or below the surface of any land in PNG.

stranger can tread on a group's land and claim that the group or any individual right-holder thereof only owns the surface of the land but the stranger owns what is in or under the land. Nor, for that matter, can the stranger dig or extract any minerals or petroleum from the group's land.

In PNG, the reservation does not depend on the limited nature of the common law doctrine of royal minerals, but on mining and petroleum legislation. For instance, the *Mining Act* 1992 vests the ownership of all minerals in the country in the state.[42] Similarly, the *Gas and Oil Act* 1998 reserves the ownership of oils and gas to the state.[43] Such reservation is not to be construed as an unjust deprivation of property contrary to s 53 of the *Constitution*, which prohibits unjust deprivation of property of citizens. The effect of these reservations is that the state is the legal owner of such resources. This is in direct conflict with the customary law, which regards minerals, oils and gas to be part of the land and, hence, owned by the owner of the land. It could be argued that such statutes are unconstitutional, as they contravene s 53 of the *Constitution.*[44]

Consequently, if minerals and petroleum were discovered on, in or under the land, the state would assert ownership over them. The state would then invite the landowners to come forward and negotiate with the government, with a view to making their land available so that the minerals or petroleum could be developed in the interest of the country at large. If the customary landowners refuse or fail to negotiate with the government, the land can be acquired by compulsory process, which is permitted by the *Mining Act* 1992 and the *Oil and Gas Act* 1998 as being for a public purpose under s 53 of the *Constitution*. Section 53 prohibits acquisition of private property, except, inter alia, acquisition for a public purpose. Once the acquisition of the subject land is effected using this procedure, the landowners can only be compensated for the loss of the land and any improvements thereon, not the minerals or petroleum therein. Once the land is acquired, the government can invite developers to develop the minerals or petroleum on the land.

The reservation of minerals and petroleum affects both alienated and unalienated land in PNG. However, no discovery has yet been made on alienated land, and all the discoveries so far have been made on customary land.

The reservation of the ownership of all minerals and petroleum in the country to the state under the *Mining Act* 1992 and the *Oil and Gas Act* 1998 is in direct conflict with the customary law. In most, if not all, parts of PNG, customary law recognises minerals and petroleum as part of the land, and it is, therefore, owned by the owner of the land.[45] To resolve this apparent conflict of laws, it is necessary to invoke s 9 of the *Constitution*, which spells out not only the sources, but also defines the hierarchy of laws in PNG. Section 9 provides that the laws of PNG consist of:

(a) the *Constitution*;

(b) Organic Laws;

(c) Acts of Parliament;

---

42 See s 5 of the *Mining Act*.

43 See s 6 of the *Oil and Gas Act* provides: "Subject to this Act, but notwithstanding anything contained in any other law or in any grant, instrument of title or other document, all petroleum and helium at or below the surface of any land is, and shall be deemed at all times to have been, the property of the State."

44 However, the constitutionality of the provisions of the *Mining Act* and the *Oil and Gas Act* has not yet been challenged before the Supreme Court. It is unclear how the judiciary would approach the issue once its jurisdiction is invoked.

45 This certainly seems to be the case in the Simbu and Eastern Highlands Provinces, where customary landowners assert that what is under their land is theirs and that they would fight tooth and nail to keep it. They would not allow the government or any other authority or individual or group to assert ownership over their minerals and petroleum.

(d) emergency Regulations;

(e) laws made under, or adopted by or under, the *Constitution* or any of those laws, including subordinate legislative enactments made under the *Constitution* or any of those laws; and

(f) the underlying law.

As noted, the above sources of laws appear in order of their importance. The *Mining Act* and *Oil and Gas Act* are Acts of Parliament, listed third in the above hierarchy of sources of laws. On the other hand, customary law is part of the underlying law,[46] and is listed last in the hierarchy. Where there is a conflict between two or more sources of laws, what one generally needs to do to resolve the conflict is to look at the hierarchy of laws under s 9 and decide which law or laws prevail over the other or others, as the case may be. Usually, the law that appears higher in the hierarchy of laws under s 9 will prevail over that which appears lower in the hierarchy. Applying this general principle to the present conflict between customary law and the *Mining Act* and the *Oil and Gas Act*, it is apparent that the Acts of Parliament are superior to custom. Consequently, the *Mining Act* and *Oil and Gas Act* must prevail over custom in this case.

The above argument is reinforced by the fact that, by Sch 2.1 of the *Constitution*, "custom is adopted, and shall be applied and enforced, as part of the underlying law"[47] unless it is, inter alia, inconsistent with a statute.[48] The inevitable conclusion, therefore, is that, in the event of inconsistency between customary laws and Acts of Parliament, the latter must prevail over the former. That being the case, unless the present law on the reservation of minerals, oils and gas is amended, the state is the legal owner of such resources.[49]

Customary land and project development

The denial of recognition accorded to customary landowners' rights to ownership of minerals and petroleum is a very sensitive issue, and is of singular importance as it affects every aspect of major mining and petroleum developments in the country. For instance, landowners who are unhappy about such denial of their rights to ownership often cause major disruptions to natural resource development projects, resulting in the country losing millions of kina in foreign exchange earnings. Despite the sensitive nature of this issue, not much academic research has been done in this area of the law to provide information which policy and law makers can draw on to formulate appropriate policies and laws that are mutually beneficial to the landowners, the government and the developers, and to avoid the frequent disruptions to major natural resource developments in the country.

The notion that one person can own land but another person can own the minerals and petroleum found on, in or in connection with the land, is an alien concept under PNG's customary law and land tenure system. As such, most Papua New Guineans, especially customary landowners, on whose land nearly all the mining and petroleum development activities take place, refuse to accept the concept that the state owns the minerals and petroleum on, in or under their land. Consequently, there have been numerous constant disruptions to new, as well as existing, major natural resource developments in the mining and petroleum industry. In the case of new

46 The other part of the underlying law is the rules and principles of common law and equity of England as adopted under Sch 2.2 of the *Constitution*.

47 *Constitution*, Sch 2.1(1).

48 *Constitution*, Sch 2.1(2).

49 It could be argued that such statutes are unconstitutional, as they contravene s 53 of the *Constitution*. However, it should be noted that the constitutionality of the provisions of the *Mining Act* and the *Oil and Gas Act* has not yet been challenged before the Supreme Court.

development, these disruptions have caused lengthy delays in securing landowner consent or agreement to proceed with the development of the major natural resource in the country. In the case of existing projects, the disruptions result in the mining or petroleum project constantly being shut down. In either case, the disruptions do not only affect the ability of the country to earn foreign exchange earnings, but also affect the ability of the developers to earn foreign exchange to meet their ongoing commitments to their creditors, the government by way of taxes, shareholders and their operating costs. Furthermore, the problems have an adverse impact on the ability of the country to attract foreign investments, as potential investors generally have negative perceptions about PNG as a good investment destination. Moreover, this situation affects economic activities of local companies, groups or individuals who are dependent on major natural resource development for their survival. In addition, it affects those who anticipate expending to provide services to the new natural resource development site, which in turn affects the country's economy generally.

A classical example of disruption caused by dissatisfied customary landowners to a major natural resource development project is afforded by the trouble on the island of Bougainville. The trouble in this instance started because successive governments and developers had systematically suppressed the landowners' rights to the ownership of minerals.[50] The legal suits filed by the landowners of the multi-billion dollar Ok Tedi gold and copper project in the Western Province of PNG in 1994, in the Supreme Court of Victoria and the National Court of PNG, also provide further illustration of disruptions caused by disgruntled landowners. Additional examples are afforded by the constant disruptions caused by disgruntled landowners to the multi-million dollar gold project at Porgera in the Enga Province, and Iagifu and Gobe oil projects in the Southern Highlands Province, in recent months. There appears to be no easy solution to these problems, and the situation is likely to continue for a long time to come unless some solution is found soon which would be mutually beneficial to all parties concerned in the industry.

It appears that the constant disruptions caused to major natural resource developments in the mining and petroleum industry occur because of the denial of the landowners' rights to ownership of minerals and petroleum under the present policy and legal regime, which have many adverse impacts on the country's economy. Perhaps one way in which the current situation can be redressed is to review the existing policy and legal regimes operating in PNG. The review is imperative to introduce amendments to the current policy and legal regimes, to reflect the prevailing perceptions and attitudes amongst customary landowners (who hold over 97 percent of the land in the country) as to the issue of natural resource ownership in PNG. For example, the current law relating to ownership of minerals and petroleum could be amended with a view to:

(a) divesting the state of ownership, and vesting it in the customary landowners; and

(b) increasing the landowners' equity participation from the current 5 percent to around 33 percent in any natural resource development.

In the event that landowners are required to raise capital to pay for their share of the equity, then the state should provide a guarantee for any loan that may be obtained, as, in most instances, the landowners would not have the necessary collateral required by lending institutions. The remaining equity should be divided between the state and the developers. Alternatively, the state should not hold any equity in the development project at all; it should only play a regulatory role rather than taking up any equity. In this case, the state should only collect its revenues from the

50 For detailed analysis on the situation on Bougainville, see Muroa, *Legal Aspects of Compulsory Acquisition of Land in PNG* (LLM Thesis, University of Tasmania, 1987).

imposition of various forms of taxes on the project, including levying withholding tax on interests earned by landowners or landowner companies, tax on incomes accrued to the landowners or landowner companies from the project, company tax, payroll tax, personal income tax, etc. The revenues from these should be used for developments in other parts of the country.

3.4.3 Ownership of fixtures on land

3.4.3.1 Common law

The common law definition of land, in its pristine and unsullied form, would make a landowner the owner of everything found on the land or which attaches to it. This view is summed up in the maxim *quic quid plantatur solo, solo cedit*, which literally translated means that which attaches to the land goes with it. Thus, any person who affixes a thing (chattel) in such a way that in law it becomes a fixture, loses it to the owner of the freehold who is not under an obligation to compensate him or her for the expenses. The rule also applies to leases of land. Thus, fixtures erected by a tenant become part of the land, and, subject to certain exceptions (for example, trade fixtures, which may be removed), cannot be removed by the tenant who affixed them. In land transactions, fixtures pass with the conveyance unless expressly reserved or excluded. Where land is mortgaged, all fixtures, whether attached before or after the mortgage, are part of the mortgagee's security and cannot therefore be removed without the mortgagee's consent.

The maxim *quic quid plantatur solo, solo cedit* is clearly part of PNG law, as the case *Geita Sebea v The Territory of Papua*[51] illustrates. In that case, certain natives in the then Territory of Papua, otherwise known as British New Guinea, who possessed a communal usufructuary right to occupy certain unimproved land with perpetual right of succession in heir community, leased the land to the Crown for a term of 10 years at a yearly rental in 1937. Thereafter, the Crown transformed the land into an aerodrome, levelling, draining and making runways, and the Crown and private firms erected buildings on the land. In December 1937, an Ordinance was enacted, providing for the compulsory acquisition of the said land by the Crown subject to the payment of compensation to the indigenous owners. One of the issues in the litigation was whether structural improvements to the land by the Crown and private firms should be taken into account in assessing compensation payable to the native owners of the land. It was held by Starke J that:

> "The meaning of the word (fixtures) is anything annexed to the freehold, that is, fastened to or connected with, not in mere juxtaposition with the soil. Whatever is so annexed becomes part of the realty, and the person who was the owner of it when it was a chattel loses his property in it, which immediately vests in the owner of the soil ... But an exception has long been established in favour of a tenant erecting fixtures for the purposes of trade, allowing him the privilege of removing them during the continuance of the term *(Bain v Brand* [1876] App Cas 762 at 772). And in determining whether or not a chattel becomes a fixture, the intention of the person affixing it to the soil is material only so far as it can be presumed from the degree and object of the annexation."[52]

In the Nigerian case of *Francis v Ibitoye*,[53] the plaintiff and the defendant were negotiating the sale of land by the defendant to the plaintiff. Before the negotiations were concluded, the

---

[51] *Geita Sebea v The Territory of Papua* (1941) 67 CLR 544.
[52] Ibid at 553.
[53] *Francis v Ibitoye* (1936) NLR 11.

plaintiff, without knowledge or leave of the defendant, proceeded to construct a house on the land at a cost of £120. However, the negotiations for the sale of the land fell through. The plaintiff, therefore, sued the defendant for compensation for the erection of the building. The defendant denied liability to pay compensation, arguing that the defendant's improvement in the nature of the building, being a permanent fixture, formed part of the land. Paul J said:

> "In these circumstances I am asked to hold that the plaintiff can recover from the landowner the cost of the building. I know of no authority for such a claim. ... It is trite law that a building erected in the circumstances I have indicated becomes the property of the landowner without any obligation to re-compensate the builder. The maxim *quicquid plantatur solo, solo cedit* applies without qualification."

In the Australian case of *Brand v Chris Building Co Pty Ltd*,[54] the Supreme Court of Victoria applied the principle that permanent fixtures become part of the land and therefore become the property of the owner of the land. In that case, the defendant, Chris Building Company Pty Ltd, entered into a contract to build a residential house for Mr and Mrs Pulis on the Pulis' land. Mr Pulis pointed out to the defendant's representative the land on which the house was to be built, but in error, he indicated the adjoining block, which in fact belonged to Brand, the plaintiff. The defendant offered to remove the structure and return the plaintiff's land to its previous state or, alternatively, the defendant offered to accept £2,145 from the plaintiff, being the cost, without profit, of the labour and materials. The plaintiff declined both offers and brought these proceedings to restrain the defendant from entering his land and demolishing the house. The main defence was acquiescence and unjust enrichment. It was held:

> "The position therefore is this, that the plaintiff as the owner is entitled to possession; the defendant under an honest mistake which was not contributed to by the plaintiff entered upon the land without any authority or licence of the plaintiff, became a trespasser and proceeded to build a house on it; and when the plaintiff found out, he took immediate steps to prevent the continuance of the trespass.
>
> What does the law say about such a position? I think the correct statement of the position is as set out in *Halsbury's Laws of England* (3rd ed) Vol 14, para 1179, p 639:
>
> > 'When A stands by while his right is being infringed by B, the following circumstances must as a general rule be present in order that the estoppel may be raised against A:
> >
> > (1) B must be mistaken as to his own legal rights; if he is aware that he is infringing the rights of another, he takes the risk of those rights being asserted;
> >
> > (2) B must expend money, or do some act, on the faith of his mistaken belief; otherwise, he does not suffer by A's subsequent assertion of his rights;
> >
> > (3) acquiescence is founded on contract with a knowledge of one's legal rights, and hence A must know of his own rights;
> >
> > (4) A must know of B's mistaken belief; with that knowledge it is inequitable for him to keep silence and allow B to proceed on his mistake;
> >
> > (5) A must encourage B in his expenditure of money or other act, either directly or by abstaining from asserting his legal right.'

---

[54] *Brand v Chris Building Co Pty Ltd* [1957] VR 625.

...

On the face of it, the result of the case seems very hard on the defendant and he may well feel that the decision is unjust; but he must realise that the Court must be guided in its decision by principles of law. It has been said that the plaintiff is hard in insisting on his strict legal right, but it does appear that there were certain negotiations made in an effort to settle the matter. What the offers were that were made I am not concerned to inquire, nor can I say whether either side is reasonable or unreasonable."[55]

Modification of the maxim *quic quid plantatur solo, solo cedit*

Due to the inherent injustice under the maxim at common law, some Australian States have enacted legislation to protect persons in positions similar to the defendant in *Brand v Chris Building Co Pty Ltd*, who mistakenly construct buildings or carry out permanent improvements on other people's lands, or whose buildings encroach upon their neighbour's land. For instance, in Queensland, s 196 of the *Property Land Act* 1974-1989 provides:

> "Where a person makes a lasting improvement on land owned by another in the genuine but mistaken belief that:
>
> (a) such land is his property; or
>
> (b) such land is the property of person on whose land the improvement is made or intended to be made,
>
> application may be made in the Court for relief under this Division."

Section 197 of the Queensland Act gives the court wide powers to grant such relief as it deems to be just and equitable. These include the power to order the landowner to pay compensation to the developer, to order the landowner to give the land or part of it on which the improvement is made to the developer, or to order the developer to remove the structure.[56] With reference to encroaching buildings over the neighbour's land, ss 182-194 of the Act give the court the power to grant such relief as it considers just and equitable, either to the owner of the encroaching building or the owner of the land.[57] Unlike Australia, there is no corresponding statutory provision in PNG, so the common law maxim applies without modification. However, under s 48 of the *Land Act* 1996, the Minister for Lands is required, in certain circumstances, to pay compensation to an outgoing tenant for improvements made on the land by him or her. Otherwise, the outgoing tenant is required to remove those fixtures that are removable, causing as little damage as possible to the land.

It should be noted that customary law also appears to favour the payment of compensation for improvements. Thus, in *Madaha Resena v The State*,[58] Bredmeyer J said:

> "In awarding this compensation, I have endeavoured to apply the customary law, but as no customary law was cited to me or discovered by me which was directly relevant, I have endeavoured to fashion a rule which is applicable and appropriate to the circumstances of the

---

55 Ibid at 628 (Hudson J).

56 See *Ex parte Karynette Pty Ltd* (1984) 2 Qd R 211 for a discussion of these provisions.

57 See, eg, *Ex parte Van Achterberg* (1984) 1 Qd R 160.

58 *Madaha Resena v The State* [1990] PNGLR 22 on appeal at [1991] PNGLR 174.

country in accordance with the matters set out in Sch 2.3 of the *Constitution* ... I can think of two analogies from custom which may be relevant. The first is that I believe under Motuan custom, and under many other customs in PNG, when a wrong has been committed against a group, it can be put right by compensation and it is usual for the payment of that compensation to be marked by a feast at which speeches are made and food and drink is consumed. The compensation is handed over in a ceremony and the feast helps reconcile the hitherto opposed parties. I would like to award a sum to the plaintiffs for this purpose but, as I have heard no argument on it, will not.

The second analogy I draw from custom is this. Mr Shepherd vigorously argued that the buildings on the land erected by the Department of Civil Aviation became the property of the plaintiffs following the Chief Commissioner's decision in April 1985 and hence should not have been removed by the Department of Civil Aviation in February 1989.

I consider that under relevant Motuan custom, these buildings did not pass to the plaintiffs and that Mr Tom Jones' evidence to the contrary was not convincing and is not to be believed. I remind myself that the airstrip and these ancillary buildings were not a blatant act of trespass by the Government. When the airstrip and these buildings were constructed, the Government honestly believed that it was the owner of the land. According to its records, it had taken possession of the land in 1889 and had treated it as its land ever since. Hence the establishment of the State plantation and of the quarantine station and the 1907 Gazette notice reserving it from sale or lease. Of course, the Chief Commissioner found in 1985, after 21 years of litigation, that the Government did not own the land, but, up until that time I consider that the Government did own the land. I consider that the Government believed in good faith that it owned the land."[59]

Tests to determine whether an object is a fixture

Because of the operation of the maxim *quic quid plantatur solo, solo cedit,* it is important to determine whether an object is a fixture and therefore forms *parte soli.* The issue as to whether or not an object is a fixture is, therefore, crucial. Where there is dispute as to whether an object is a fixture or not, the courts generally employ two broad tests to determine the issue: (i) the degree of annexation; and (ii) the purpose or object of annexation as demonstrated below:

(i) **Degree of annexation:** The degree of annexation is determined by the means by which the object or chattel is attached to the land, for instance, whether the object is attached to the land by nails, bolts, mortar or its own weight. As a general rule, an object that is attached to the land by some means other than by its own weight is deemed to be a fixture. In such a situation, the burden of proof is upon the person who alleges otherwise. Conversely, if the object is resting on the ground by its own weight, prima facie it is not a fixture, and the onus of proof is on the person who alleges that it is a fixture. It should be noted that in such a situation the burden of proof is discharged by employing the second test.

(ii) **Object of annexation:** This test raises the question: What was the intention of the person who affixed the object to the land? This question is particularly significant, because if the person's intention was for permanent and substantial improvement of the land or building, it becomes a fixture and is affected by the maxim *quic quid plantatur solo, solo cedit.* If, on

---

59 *Madaha Resena v The State* [1990] PNGLR 22 at 38-39.

> the other hand, the aim was for a temporary purpose for more complete enjoyment of the premises or the object as a chattel, it is not a fixture and remains a chattel.[60]

The two tests are discussed in *Holland v Hodgson.*[61] In that case, George Mason was the owner in fee simple of a worsted mill, at which he carried on the business of a worsted spinner and stuff manufacturer. He mortgaged the mill and all fixtures to the plaintiffs. Subsequently, Mason in bankruptcy assigned all this property to the defendants in trust for the benefit of Mason's creditors. The defendants seized 436 looms in the mill and sold them. The plaintiffs sued in conversion, claiming that the looms were fixtures and therefore part of their mortgage. These looms were attached to the store floors of the rooms of the mill by means of nails driven through holes in the feet of the looms, in some cases into beams which had been built into the stone, and in other cases into plugs of wood driven into holes drilled in the stone for the purpose. It was impossible to remove the looms without drawing out the nails, but this could be done without causing any serious damage to the floor. The defendants contended that the looms were attached to the floor to make them steadier and more capable of convenient use as chattels. The trial judge held that the looms were fixtures. On appeal, the issue turned on whether the looms were fixtures or remained chattels. The appellate court said:

> "There is no doubt that the general maxim of the law is that what is annexed to the land becomes part of the land; but it is very difficult, if not impossible, to say with precision what constitutes an annexation sufficient for this purpose. It is a question which must depend on the circumstances of each case, and mainly on two circumstances, as indicating the intention; viz, the degree of annexation and the object of the annexation. When the article in question is no further attached to the land then [sic] by its own weight it is generally considered to be mere chattel ... But even in such a case, if the intention is apparent to make the articles part of the land, they do become part of the land ... Thus blocks of stone placed one on top of another without any mortar or cement for the purpose of forming a dry stone wall would become part of the land, though the same stones, if deposited in a builder's yard for convenience sake stacked on the top of each other in the form of a wall, would remain chattels. On the other hand, an article may be very firmly fixed to the land, and yet the circumstances may be such as to show that it was never intended to be part of the land, and then it does not become part of the land. The anchor of a large ship must be very firmly fixed in the ground in order to bear the strain of the cable, yet no one could suppose that it became part of the land, even though it should chance that the shipowner was also the owner of the fee of the spot where the anchor was dropped. An anchor similarly fixed in the soil for the purpose of bearing the strain of the chain of a suspension bridge would be part of the land. Perhaps the true rule is that articles not otherwise attached to the land than by their own weight are not to be considered as part of the land, unless the circumstances are such as to show that they were intended to be part of the land, the onus of showing that they were so intended lying on those who assert that they have ceased to be chattels, and that, on the contrary, an article which is affixed to the land even slightly is to be considered as part of the land, unless the circumstances are such as to show that it was intended all along to continue as a chattel, the onus lying on those who contend that it is a chattel ... This, however, only removes the difficulty, one step, for it still remains a question in each case whether the circumstances are sufficient to satisfy the onus. In some cases, such as the anchor of the ship or the ordinary

---

[60] See *Geita Sebea v The Territory of Papua* (1941) 67 CLR 544. See also *Australian Provincial Assurance Co Ltd v Coroneo* (1938) 38 SR (NSW) 700.

[61] *Holland v Hodgson* (1872) LR7 CP 328.

> instance given of a carpet nailed to the floor of a room, the nature of the thing sufficiently shows it is only fastened as a chattel temporarily and not affixed permanently as part of the land. But ordinary trade or tenant fixtures which are put up with the intention that they should be removed by the tenant (and so are put up for a purpose in one sense only temporary, and certainly not for the purpose of improving the reversionary interest of the landlord) have always been considered as part of the land, though severable by the tenant. In most, if not all, of such cases the reason why the articles are considered fixtures is probably that indicated by Wood VC, in *Boyd v Shorrock* [(1867) LR 5 Eq 72 at 78], that the tenant indicates by the mode in which he puts them up that he regards them as attached to the property during his interest in the property. What we have now to decide is as to the application of these rules to looms put up by the owner of the fee in the manner described in the case.
>
> It is established that where an article is affixed by the owner of the fee, though only affixed by bolts and screws, it is to be considered as part of the land, at all events where the object of setting up the articles is to enhance the value of the premises to which it is annexed for the purpose to which those premises are applied ... We think therefore that the judgment below should affirmed."

As illustrated by *Holland v Hodgson,* the object of the annexation test is easier stated than applied to actual situations. The courts use various guidelines to assist them to determine whether or not the object was attached to the land with a view to permanent improvement of the land. For instance, the courts will look at how firmly the object is held to the land. If it is so firmly held that its removal would entail its destruction or cause substantial damage to the land, it is strong evidence that a permanent fixture was intended. However, even if an object is only slightly attached to the land, if the intention was to enhance the value of the land, it may support the inference that it was intended to be permanent. Secondly, the courts may look at the use to which the object is put in relation to the principal use of the land. If the object was a great connection with the main purpose of the land, the chances are that it will be held to be a fixture.[62] Thirdly, the capacity in which the fixer brought the object onto the land is another relevant consideration. Hence, where a proprietor of the land attaches a chattel to the land, he or she is more likely to intend it as a permanent improvement of the land than if a mere lessor or other temporary occupant did so.[63] It should be emphasised, however, that these are guidelines only, and none of them is conclusive. Furthermore, the fact that an object is held to be a fixture or a chattel in one case does not necessarily follow that it is a fixture or chattel, as the case may be, in all situations. Each case, therefore, must be considered on its own facts.

3.4.3.2 Customary law

Things growing or cultivated on land

As noted earlier, customary law recognises the dichotomy between the soil and things on or forming a part of the soil. Thus, the ownership of crops on land can be distinguished from ownership of the soil itself. Hence, if a landowner revokes his or her tenant's permission to the occupation and use of land granted to him or her, the general view is that the tenant is entitled to payment of compensation for improvements that he or she has made to the land. However, as customary law varies from society to society or area to area, the right of the improver to be

---

[62] For example, looms in a mill, as in *Holland v Hodgson*, or chairs fastened together in rows and fixed on the floor of a cinema hall, as in *Australian Provincial Assurance v Coroneo* (1938) 38 SR (NSW) 700.

[63] See *Belgrave Nominees Pty Ltd v Barlin-Scott Airconditioning (Aust) Pty Ltd* [1984] VR 947 at 951.

compensated for improvements, or to remove them, may depend on the customary law of each society or area. For instance, in some societies, custom may permit an outsider to come in and use a group's land for gardening. Generally, in such cases, the person is not allowed to grow cash crops, such as coffee trees. Once the garden is harvested, the person is required to leave without removing any improvements that he or she might have effected on the land, such as trees. The person is not entitled to compensation and is not expected to seek it.[64]

In other situations, an outsider who has some ties with a landowning group, such as a son-in-law, may be invited to move in with his wife's relatives and occupy the land. This situation often arises where the wife's parents do not have any other children, especially male children, to inherit their interests in the group's land. In such a case, the son-in-law would occupy the land for an indefinite period. He can raise his children there and effect whatever improvements he considers necessary, including the cultivation of cash crops such as coffee trees. He can also carry out other economic activities such as operating a trade store. It is rare for such a person and his descendants to be allowed to live on the in-laws' land indefinitely without any interruption. In most instances, as soon as any conflict arises between any of the local people and their in-law and/or any of his descendants, no matter how trite it may be, the former would normally evict the latter from their land. Such a situation can occur no matter how long the in-law may have been occupying the land.[65] Hence, the common law maxim *cujus est solum ejus est usque ad coelum et ad inferos* appears to have no application under the customary law of PNG.

Buildings and other structures

As noted earlier, in customary jurisprudence, land does not include structures or permanent fixtures. However, for the purposes of the *Village Courts Act*, a house or other structure built on land, and not being over water, is deemed to be land. Disputes over such matters or improvements are justiciable by Village Courts under their general jurisdiction. In contrast, a house or other structure built on land, and things growing on land, are within the definition of land for the purposes of the jurisdiction of the Land Courts under the *Land Disputes Settlement Act*. Although buildings, houses and other structures may form part of the improvements to the land, no compensation is payable unless the buildings or other structures are built of permanent or semi-permanent materials. However, even if they are built of permanent or semi-permanent materials, the improver is usually required to pull them down and remove the materials rather than seek compensation for them.[66]

It could be argued that the modern day practice of planting cash crops that tie up the land for a number of years, and the practice of building permanent structures on land, might lead to the modification of the concept of land in the customary land tenure system. Customary law is itself flexible and evolving, and could change to accommodate changing circumstances.[67] However, this argument should not be taken for granted, because, although members of a group are allowed to plant cash crops and build permanent structures on the land, the practice does not affect improvements effected by an outsider invited to the land.

---

64 Such a situation prevails generally in the Highlands of PNG, particularly in the Elimbari, Chuave and Siane areas of Chuave District, Simbu Province.

65 Such a situation exists in the customary law of the Elimbari and Siane areas of Chuave District, Simbu Province.

66 Such is the customary law of the Elimbari and Nambayufa areas of Chuave District, Simbu Province.

67 See Amankwah, op cit n 8 at 21.

Things growing on or in water over land

The phrase "things growing on or in water over land" appears to refer to things naturally growing on land or in water over land, as opposed to improvements such as food and cash crops on the land. This distinction is important, because generally, as noted earlier, it is permissible under customary law for those responsible for effecting improvements to remove such improvements; that is, improvements such as food and cash crops can be separated from the ownership of land itself. Hence, crops, trees and other improvements on the land can be claimed or owned by individual members of the land-owning group. These rights in land owned by individuals are often referred to as usufructs; not land as such. Thus, the usufructuary has no proprietary rights in the land.[68] The basis of this distinction is that labour creates rights and, therefore, the person who is responsible for improvements on the land retains rights to them. Such a person has power to remove the improvements on the land without trespassing.[69] Indeed, it is generally recognised under traditional law that a person is entitled to claim compensation for value added to the land. Thus, again, the common law maxim *cujus est solum ejus est usque ad coelurn et ad inferos* appears to have no application in PNG's land tenure system.

3.4.4 The right to remove fixtures

At common law, an exception is made to the maxim *quic quid plantatur solo, solo cedit*, which entitles an outgoing lessee to remove any fixtures that he or she installed and which he or she uses for his or her trade, domestic or ornamental purposes. These are known as tenant's fixtures, in contrast to landlord's fixtures. Fixtures used for agricultural purposes are not tenant's fixtures.[70] The right to remove fixtures arose under the common law independently of contract, though the right may be limited or excluded by agreement of the parties or by statute.[71] A tenant who wishes to exercise the right to remove fixtures must do so during the currency of the lease. This is important, because if the tenant leaves the premises after the lease expires without removing the fixtures, he or she is deemed to have abandoned them and cannot thereafter remove them. Secondly, a tenant, or any person acting under the tenant's authority, who removes fixtures must make good any damage caused in the process of removing the fixtures and leave the premises in a reasonable and tenantable condition.[72] At common law, there appears to be no provision for payment of compensation to an outgoing tenant for leaving fixtures that cannot be severed.

In PNG, the *Land Act* 1996 has made provision for payment of compensation to an outgoing state lessee for improvements made on the land.[73] However, compensation only applies where, at the expiration of the lease, the outgoing tenant applies for a further lease of the whole or part of the land but his or her application is refused. In such a case, the Minister is required to pay compensation to the outgoing lessee for the value of his or her improvements on the land.[74] An outgoing lessee who does not apply for a further lease upon its expiry, is not, therefore, entitled to compensation for improvements on the land. In this case, the tenant

---

68 See Lynch, "Customizing the Law" in Sack (ed), *Problems of Choice: Land in Papua New Guinea's Future* (ANU Press, Canberra, 1973), pp 87-96; James, op cit n 13, Ch 2.

69 This is true in the case of improvements made by members of the land-owning group itself, but in the case of an outsider, once he or she has left the group after harvesting his or her garden, he or she must seek permission to re-enter the land to remove improvements.

70 Note that in *Meats v Callender* [1901] 2 Ch 388, fixtures used for market gardening were regarded as trade fixtures, and were therefore removable by the tenant.

71 See *Mancetter Developments Ltd v Garmanson Ltd* [1986] QB 1212 (CA).

72 Ibid.

73 See *Land Act* 1996, s 120.

74 *Land Act* 1996, s 120(3).

may remove such of the improvements as are severable on or before the expiration of the lease, doing as little damage as may reasonably be done to the land.[75]

3.4.5 Compensation for improvements

Compensation for improvements is not an automatic right. Whether or not a person should be compensated for his or her improvements will depend on the circumstances of each case. Generally, an outsider who has had a long occupation of the land cannot be compensated, because he or she would have benefited more than enough from the long occupation of the land. Similarly, an outsider invited to merely garden on the land has no right to compensation for improvements once the garden is harvested. This situation must be distinguished from the situation where a person has been invited to settle on the land and led to believe that he or she would be there permanently, and on the basis of that belief he or she has carried out improvements, but soon after the improvements are added onto the land, the improver is evicted or forced to leave without gaining any benefit from his or her improvements. In such situations, the improver's in-laws and, in particular, those who stand to benefit from the improvements, are required to compensate the outgoing improver, usually before he or she leaves the land to return to his or her own group.[76] It should be noted, however, that the obligation to pay compensation is of a moral rather than legal nature and, as such, in most instances payment of compensation depends on the goodwill of the landowners.

3.5 NATURE OF OWNERSHIP OF LAND

3.5.1 Common law

As noted earlier, under common law individuals can obtain grants from the Crown that may be registered and owned individually subject to the royal minerals and the Crown having a reversionary interest therein. In PNG, alienated land is either owned by the government or by private individuals as freeholders or leaseholders. Generally, freeholders own the land outright and can do whatever they want with the land. On the other hand, leaseholders hold their land subject to the terms and conditions by which the grants have been made.[77]

3.5.2 Customary law

Under PNG's customary law, customary land is owned by a lineage or other groups such as a clan or tribe, not by an individual or individuals. In other words, land is owned communally. This doctrine of communal ownership of land in PNG was given judicial recognition by the court in *Geita Sebea v The Territory of Papua*,[78] and is authority for the proposition that the colonial administration in PNG, unlike the situation in Australia, recognised communal native title. In that case, certain lands were leased in 1937 by the villagers of Kila Kila in Port Moresby to the administration for a period of 10 years. After improvements were effected on the lands, the administration enacted the *Lands (Kila Kila Aerodrome) Acquisition Ordinance* 1939, under which the lands that were the subject of the lease, with the improvements thereon, together with

---

75 *Land Act* 1996, s 120(5). For detailed treatment of the subject, see Muroa, Amankwah and Mugambwa, *Land Law in Papua New Guinea* (LBC Information Services Ltd, Sydney, 2001), Ch 5.

76 See note 11 for the area where this custom applies.

77 For terms and conditions of state lease, see Pt X of the *Land Act* 1996.

78 *Geita Sebea v The Territory of Papua* (1941) 67 CLR 544.

an additional 38 acres of lands, were acquired by compulsory process. The customary owners claimed compensation for the land including improvements. However, the administration claimed that the customary claimants were only entitled to the unimproved value of the land, because, firstly, the claimants did not own the land, and secondly, the improvements would not be of any use to the claimants if they were found to have owned the land and therefore improvements under the common law doctrine of *quic quid plantatur solo solo cedit.* Gore J, in the court of first instance, found that the Kila Kila land belonged to Kila Kila village, that is, to the community, and what they had was the possessory title to the usufruct.[79] On appeal to the High Court of Australia, the court made a similar finding that the subject lands were communally owned by the Kila Kila group, and that they should be compensated for the permanent improvements as well as the lands comprised in the acquisition, and it was immaterial whether the improvements were of any use to the villagers. This case is significant because it affirms that customary ownership entails rights in rem, not merely rights of user or usufructuary rights.

Individual members of the landowning groups only possess what is known as usufructuary rights, or rights of user, to use land for various purposes consistent with the group's socio-political and economic interests, as opposed to proprietary rights in land. The individual's usufructuary rights are capable of being inherited by members of his or her family in perpetuity, unless the right-holder's lineal or collateral descendants are extinct. Where lineal or collateral descendants are extinct, the land reverts to the landowning group, which would then reallocate it to another person or other persons from the group itself. In some societies, such as in the Highlands of PNG, if a person dies leaving no lineal or collateral relatives, a distant relative who is not related by blood, but is a descendant of a common ancestor, can assume the usufructuary rights of the deceased.[80] In other societies, someone who has done good deeds for the deceased, such as slaughtering a pig for him or her or looking after him or her during an illness, may be allowed to assume such rights of the deceased. In any event, the land must remain within the group and must not be allowed to be alienated out of the group.[81]

In PNG, land is not an alienable commodity. It is the most sacred resource in the lives of the people. The importance that Papua New Guineans accord their land transcends its market or economic value. Land is not simply an asset that can be used for economic production or traded for cash; it is the basis of the people's existence and an essential part of their social, political and economic life.[82] This is because land provides security for the people and the future descendants.[83] Thus, Dr Sack notes: "to say that in PNG land owns the people, instead of the people owning the land, is almost true".[84]

---

79 See *Geita Sebea v The Territory of Papua* (unreported, Central Court of Papua, 1940, 12), cited in Mugambwa, Amankwah and Muroa, *Land Law in Papua New Guinea* (LBC Information Services Ltd, 2001), para 1.10.

80 This is true under the customary law of the Elimbari and Siane local-level government areas of Chuave District, Simbu Province.

81 Such a custom exists in parts of Simbu and Eastern Highlands Provinces.

82 For further reading on the importance of land in PNG, see Dove, Miriung, and Togolo, "Mining Bitterness" in Sack (ed), *Problems of Choice: Land in Papua New Guinea's Future* (ANU Press, Canberra, 1973), pp 181-183. The same subject has been discussed in Sack (ed), ibid, pp 32-39, 40-48, 97-106, and 151-158. See also Zorn, "Fighting Over Land" (1976) 4 MLJ 7 at 9; Antoninus, "The Tolai Land Case" in *Appendices to Land Tenure in PNG* (UPNG, 1976), pp 106-109; *The PNG Commission of Inquiry into Land Matters Report* (CILM *Report*), Ch 3; Haynes, "Succession to Land in PNG: Choice of Law" (1981) 9 MLJ 74 at 74; Trebilcock and Knetsch, "Land Policy and Economic Development in PNG" (1981) 9 MLJ 101 at 114.

83 Lynch, "Customizing the Law" in Sack (ed), op cit n 65, p 90; Dove, Miriung and Togolo, in Sack (ed), ibid, p 183; Olewale "The Price of Progress" in Sack (ed), ibid, p 43.

84 Sack, "The Triumph of Colonialism" in Sack (ed), ibid, pp 200-209.

3.6 MANNER OF ACQUISITION BY THE GOVERNMENT AND RESTRICTIONS ON ACQUISITION

When the British colonisers first arrived in PNG, they realised that (Papuans) Papua New Guineans had customary land tenure systems governed by their customary law. Since the declaration of the protectorate in 1884, successive administrations adopted specific policies to recognise and protect the existing indigenous land rights.[85] In Papua, after the declaration of the protectorate, one of the main concerns of the British Imperial Government was to respect and protect the land rights of the natives against European settlers. Thus, Commodore Erskine solemnly assured the native people at the time of declaring protectorate over Papua: "your lands will be secured to you [and that] no acquisition of land, whensoever or howsoever acquired, within the limits of the Protectorate hereby established, will be recognised by Her Majesty".[86] This assurance was further strengthened by the instructions issued to Special Commissioner General Scratchley to explain to the natives that he was sent to "secure to them the safety of their persons, the enjoyment of their property and particularly to protect them from being deprived of their lands by force or fraud".[87]

In New Guinea, the situation was similar to that in Papua. Germany also proclaimed New Guinea a colonial protectorate in 1884. The German Government assumed formal control in 1885 when the first representatives of the New Guinea Company arrived. The *Imperial Charter* of 17 May 1885 gave the company the right to administer New Guinea until 1 April 1899, when the German Imperial Government took over the administration of the Territory. Although no express assurances were made to the native New Guineans to protect their land rights or interests therein, as in the case of early British colonials to the Papuans, specific instructions were issued to the New Guinea Company to recognise and respect native land rights and interests in New Guinea.[88] The German administration, as their British counterparts in Papua, thus recognised and respected existing native rights and interests in land.[89]

The effect of annexation on customary land rights or title therein has been considered in a number of cases from some Commonwealth countries. For instance, in Australia,[90] Canada,[91] Nigeria,[92] Zimbabwe[93] and Kenya,[94] the courts have conclusively determined that, by virtue of annexation, the radical title to all the land in the country is vested in the Crown subject to such usufructuary rights as the natives might have in the land. According to Mugambwa and Amankwah,[95] the courts in PNG have not conclusively determined the effect of annexation of Papua on customary

85 For further readings on the policies of the early colonial administration with respect to native land rights, see James, op cit n 19, Ch 3; Montgomery, *A Handbook of Information for Senior Land Settlement Officers* (Department of Lands, Surveys and Environment, Port Moresby, 1979), p 7; Oram, "Land and Race in Port Moresby" in *Appendices to Land Tenure in PNG* (UPNG, 1976), p 36; Leyser, "Title to Land in the Trust Territory of New Guinea" in *Appendices to Land Tenure in PNG* (Part 1) (UPNG, 1976), p 77; Sack, "The Triumph of Colonialism" in Sack (ed), op cit n 65, pp 200-208; Haynes, *Land Law and Land Policy in PNG: Text, Cases and Materials* (Part1) (UPNG Press, 1983); Specer, "The Expropriation and Sale of German Plantations in the Mandated Territory" in *Appendices to Land Tenure in PNG* (Part 1) (UPNG, 1976), pp 86-89.

86 Sack (ed), op cit n 65, p 204. For detailed discussion on colonial land policies, see Ch 1.

87 Oram, op cit n 68, p 36; Haynes, op cit n 68, p 4.

88 Leyser, op cit n 68, pp 77-85; Sack, "The Triumph of Colonialism" in Sack (ed), op cit n 65, p 204; Sack and Sack, *The Land Law of German New Guinea* (ANU Press, Canberra, 1975), pp 1-3.

89 Leyser, op cit n 68, p 79; Sack in Sack (ed), op cit n 65.

90 See *Milirrpum v Nabalco Pty Ltd* (1971) 17 FLR 141 (overruled in *Mabo v Queensland* (1992) 175 CLR 1).

91 See *Calder v Attorney-General (British Columbia)* (1973) 34 DLR (3d) 145.

92 See *Amodu Tijani v The Secretary for Southern Nigeria* (1921) 2 AC 399.

93 See *In re Southern Rhodesia* [1919] AC 211.

94 See *Gathomo v Murito* [1921] EAPLR 102.

95 Mugambwa and Amankwah, *Cases and Materials on Papua New Guinea Land Law and Policy* (Pacific Law Press, Hobart, 1996), pp 7-8.

title and land in general. However, in a number of cases[96] the courts have expressed the view generally that upon annexation the radical title to all land was vested in the Crown subject to such usufructuary or proprietary rights as the natives might have in land. Further, annexation at international law is an act of state, and the Crown could decide whether or not to recognise native customary rights. In *Geita Sebea v The Territory of Papua,*[97] Gore J, when considering the issue of the effect of annexation over land in Papua, said:

> "In the Territory of Papua, which was acquired by settlement, there was not importation of the common law of real property with respect to native lands, nor have native lands been brought under the Torrens system. It has been suggested that the lands held by natives are allodial but I do not think that there is such a thing as an allodium existing in modern times. The conception of the term here is that the title to native lands is higher than a fee simple and has no derivative fountain. In my judgment, it is not so but on constitutional grounds the radical title is in the King and whatever estate the natives have is the recognition of the security promised by Commodore Erskine's proclamation."[98]

A major legislative change to the common law position with respect to the effect of annexation occurred in 1962, with the enactment of the *Land Act* 1962. By s 7 of that Act:

> "All land in Papua New Guinea other than customary land is the property of the State subject to any estates, rights, titles or interests from time to time in force under any law in force in Papua New Guinea or part of Papua New Guinea."

---

96 See *Geita Sebea v The Territory of Papua* (unreported, Central Court of Papua, 1940, 12); *The Administration of the Territory of Papua and New Guinea v Daera Guba* (1973) 130 CLR 353. In the latter case, Barwick CJ assumed, without deciding, that the declaration of the protectorate or the annexation of British New Guinea did not vest in the Crown the ultimate title to all the land in the Territory.

97 *Geita Sebea v The Territory of Papua* (unreported, Central Court of Papua, 1940, 12).

98 Quoted in Mugambwa, Amankwah and Muroa, op cit n 58.

This provision has been retained in successive land legislations of the country, including the current *Land Act* 1996.[99] The effect of this provision is that the state has radical title to all non-customary land, subject to any estates, rights, titles or interests in land in force under any law. Land in this context includes private freeholds and leaseholds. All estates, rights, titles and interests, other than customary rights, held by a person at any time in such land are deemed to be held under the state.[100]

The policy of recognising and protecting native land rights and interests in both British Papua and German New Guinea implied respect for existing native land ownership and the land tenure systems. Consequently, whereas at the time of the first settlement of the Australian colonies all lands were deemed waste and the property of the Crown, in Papua and New Guinea the assumption was that all land except that which was *truly waste and vacant* belonged to the people under traditional tenure.[101]

3.7 CONVERSION OF LAND TO FREEHOLD OR LEASEHOLD

3.7.1 Acquisition by private individuals

Acquisition of land from customary owners by private individuals or companies, such as settlers and missions, both in Papua and New Guinea, preceded the declaration of the protectorate and subsequent annexation. In 1888, the administration enacted the *Land Regulation Ordinance* 1888. The Ordinance imposed restriction against private individuals from acquisition of customary land, and made it an offence for anyone breaching the restriction. A similar restriction was also enacted in the Ordinance prohibiting customary landowners from dealing directly or indirectly with private individuals or companies for the purposes of disposing of customary land. The object of the Ordinance was to regulate dealings in relation to customary land, so that customary landowners did not lose their land to private interest at the expense of their future land requirements, and so as to allow acquisition for development purposes.

In *The Administration of the Territory of Papua and New Guinea v Guba and Doriga,*[102] there was a dispute as to the law governing land acquisition during the pre-annexation period, that is, whether custom or common law governed the acquisition. Frost J thought that the answer turned on the status of the Territory at the time of the purchase, and the social organisation of the people. He concluded that as British New Guinea, at the date of the purchase in question, was a protectorate and populated by "uncivilised tribes" having no system of law, the only solution was that English law was applicable to a purchase by the Crown, as in the case of an uninhabited colony acquired by cession or settlement. Yet, he was not prepared to apply the strict standards

99 See *Land Act* 1996, s 4.
100 *Land Act* 1996, s 4(2).
101 See *The Administration of the Territory of Papua and New Guinea v Guba Doriga* (1973) ALJR 621 at 637-638; *Arthur Agevu v The State* [1977] PNGLR 99.
102 *The Administration of the Territory of Papua and New Guinea v Guba and Doriga* (App 79, 1969, FC).

for land dealings required by English law that were contained in the *Statute of Frauds* and the *Real Property Act* 1845, which required the agreement to be evidenced in writing and the transfer to be by deed.[103] His Honour thought that neither of these statutes could be considered applicable because of the illiteracy of the population at the relevant time. Ironically, in arriving at this conclusion, His Honour preferred to follow the Canadian case of *Sinclair v Mulligan*[104] on this point, rather than the Nigerian case of *Okoleji v Okupe*,[105] where the *Statute of Frauds* was held applicable to protect illiterate people.

Although pre-annexation acquisitions were prima facie inconsistent with the assurance given by Commodore Erskine at the time of the proclamation of protectorate, it could be argued that land purchased *before* the protectorate was not caught by the terms of Erskine's proclamation. Nevertheless, the British Imperial Government decided to regularise such transactions. Consequently, the administration, immediately upon annexation, enacted the *Crown Grants Ordinance* 1889, which provided for the issue of Crown grants to any person who acquired land from native owners prior to 1888.[106] The provisions of this Ordinance were directed at regularising land acquisitions, not only by private interests, but also by the administration.[107] It could be argued that the *Crown Grants Ordinance* is a recognition of the dubious nature of land purchases during the pre-annexation period.[108] Additionally, the administration enacted the *Crown Lands Ordinance* 1890, which provided machinery for dealing with and giving effect to private land acquisitions in the Territory. Under Pt I of the Ordinance, private purchasers from indigenous Papuans were given the opportunity to apply for the recognition of their grants within six months of the publication of the notice in the *Gazette* inviting claims in that regard.

Provisions similar to those found in the *Land Regulation Ordinance* above have been retained in successive land legislations of the country. The current *Land Act* 1996 made no provision expressly prohibiting private land acquisition from customary owners. However, s 132 of the Act imposes general restrictions on customary landowners from disposing of their land to persons or bodies other than to citizens in accordance with custom. The provisions are, nevertheless, broad enough to affect private persons acquiring land from customary landowners. Section 132 reads:

> "Subject to Sections 10 and 11,[109] a customary landowner has no power to sell, lease or otherwise dispose of customary land or customary rights otherwise than to citizens in accordance with custom, and a contract or agreement made by him to do so is void."

3.7.2 Acquisition by the administration

Acquisition in Papua

Since the indigenous people owned most the land in PNG, the administration had to acquire land needed for development from them. The power of the administration in Papua to acquire land was

---

103 These requirements are now contained in the *Statute of Frauds and Limitation Act*, Ch 330.
104 *Sinclair v Mulligan* (1886) 3 Man LR 481.
105 *Okoleji v Okupe* (1939) 15 NLR 28.
106 See *Crown Grants Ordinance* 1889, s 2.
107 By s 20 of the *Crown Grants Ordinance* 1889, there was a requirement that the administrator must execute an instrument evidencing acquisition of land by the Crown from native owners. It is said that the High Court questioned the capacity of the administration to bind the Crown as to its title to land that it had already acquired. That Ordinance would, therefore, be limited to facilitating a record of title rather than the confirmation of the Crown's title and, presumably, to regulating future land purchases. See James, op cit n 13, p 64.
108 Ibid, pp 63-64.
109 Sections 10 and 11of the *Land Act* 1996 permit the government to generally acquire customary land, and customary land owners have the capacity to dispose of their land to the government provided the latter meet certain prerequisites which are discussed in detail below.

purportedly based on the terms of the Special Commissioner John Douglas' Special Commission, which provided that he was appointed for the protectorate:

> "in all respects to represent our Crown and authority in matters accruing therein, and further to take all such measures, and to do all such things in the said Protectorate as in the interests of our service you may think expedient, subject to such instructions as you may from time to time receive from us or through one of our Principal Secretaries of State".[110]

In *Daera Guba v The Administration of the Territory of Papua and New Guinea*,[111] one of the issues contested before the Full Court (Mann CJ, Frost SPJ and Prentice J) was whether the Special Commissioner had power to acquire land. It was argued by the native claimants that the instructions to John Douglas, as Special Commissioner, to protect the natives in the free enjoyment of their lands and possessions, indicated that there was no power of purchasing land at all, and that this was confirmed by Erskine in 1884 saying that no acquisition of land in the protectorate would be recognised by Her Majesty. It was held, however, that having regard to Douglas' task to act on behalf of the Crown in an "uncivilised country", this general power should be given full effect and was wide enough to include the power to purchase land. It was also held that the right to sell land was incidental to free enjoyment of it, and the particular words contained in the terms of Douglas' Special Commission were not inconsistent with the power to purchase land. The court held further that the assurance to recognise and protect native land rights seemed to refer to the activities of undesirable persons purchasing lands from the natives, and was not intended to bind the Crown.[112]

On appeal to the High Court of Australia,[113] the court observed that the policy of the British Government at the time of the declaration of the protectorate was that the natives should not be disturbed in the use or enjoyment of their land, except insofar as the government might acquire land by compulsory process for public purposes, or supervise any permitted purchase by private individuals. In essence, the policy of preserving the use of the land by the natives was to be implemented by preventing persons other than the Crown from purchasing land, or interest in land, from the natives.[114] The administration's power to acquire land was subsequently accorded legislative recognition, so that the officers of the administration had power to purchase land, and the natives had the power to sell land to them.[115] The power is retained in the present *Land Act* 1996, which permits the Minister for Lands to acquire customary land outright on such terms and conditions as are agreed on between the Minister and the landowners.[116] Also, the Minster is permitted to lease customary land for purposes of granting special agricultural or business leases over the land.[117]

One of the issues that featured prominently on appeal in the High Court in *The Administration of the Territory of Papua and New Guinea v Guba Doriga*,[118] was whether the natives had the

---

110 James, op cit n 93, p 4.

111 *Daera Guba v The Administration of the Territory of Papua and New Guinea* (1971) FC 18 (Full Court). See also the High Court decision on appeal in the same case in the *Newtown* case, *The Administration of the Territory of Papua and New Guinea v Guba Doriga* (1973) 130 CLR 353; 47 ALJR 621 at 627.

112 (1971) FC 18 (Full Court).

113 See *The Administration of the Territory of Papua and New Guinea v Guba* (1973) 47 ALJR 621.

114 Ibid at 629 (Barwick CJ).

115 See *Land Regulation Ordinance* 1888, ss 4-6; *Crown Lands Ordinance* 1890, ss V, XVM and XX; *Land Ordinance* 1911-1940, ss 6, 8 and 10.

116 See s 10 of the *Land Act* 1996.

117 See s 11 of the *Land Act* 1996.

118 *The Administration of the Territory of Papua and New Guinea v Guba* (1973) 47 ALJR 621, most commonly referred to as the *Newtown* case. James,

capacity to dispose of land to strangers, including the administration, in accordance with custom. In that case, the administration claimed that its officers validly purchased the subject land in 1886 from the native owners who had the capacity to sell. The native claimants (respondents) argued that their forbears, who owned the land at the time of the declaration of the protectorate, had no capacity to dispose of land absolutely to any strangers under the customary law of the time. The High Court held that the natives at the time of the purported sale had the capacity to dispose of their land outright to any strangers, including the administration.

Acquisition in New Guinea

In New Guinea, the power of the administration to acquire land was based on the terms of the *Imperial Charter* of 17 May 1885. Unlike the ambiguous terms of Douglas' Special Commission in Papua, the *Imperial Charter* expressly granted the New Guinea Company the exclusive right to acquire land in New Guinea. The Charter also granted the company the right to occupy and dispose of ownerless or waste and vacant land, and to enter into direct negotiations with the natives and acquire from them native land or rights over land.[119] At the same time, the *Imperial Charter* made specific provisions for the New Guinea Company to recognise and respect native land rights.[120] On 10 August 1887, the Board of Directors of the New Guinea Company, in accordance with the provisions of the *Imperial Ordinance* of 20 July 1887, issued directions to the company to institute thorough investigations prior to acquisition of land, with a view to ascertaining whether or not the land was cultivated or otherwise used by the natives.[121]

The power of the New Guinea Company to acquire land in New Guinea was accorded legal recognition in the *Imperial Charter* 1885. The *Imperial Ordinance* 1899, regarding the assumption of local sovereignty over the protectorate of New Guinea, provided that as from 1 April 1899 the power of acquisition of land in the protectorate would pass to the German administration.[122] The 1899 Ordinance, therefore, recognised the power of the German administration to acquire land in New Guinea. This was later reinforced by the *Imperial Ordinance* 1903. The Ordinance authorised the administration to resume or restrict the use of land in the public interest.[123]

Acquisition during joint administration

In 1902 Australia took over the administration of Papua from Britain, after the formation of the Commonwealth of Australia in 1901. After World War I, Germany gave up the colony of New Guinea, and Australia took over the administration of New Guinea in 1921 under the Mandate System of the League of Nations. Australia administered Papua and New Guinea separately until after 1945, when they were jointly administered as one colonial unit, by virtue of the provision of Art 5 of the United Nations Trusteeship Agreement, as the Territory of Papua and New Guinea. Successive Australian administrations in Papua and New Guinea stated a commitment to the

---

commenting on the decision of the court, said: "The High Court decision falls within the genus of colonial precedents which asserts that a 'primitive' people, recognise a conception of 'ownership' of land and have a legal system enabling the outright transfer of their land by sale to Colonial Administrators, missions and settlers." See James, "The Role of the Court in Attempts to Recover Alienated Land" (1994) 2 MLJ 270 at 271.

119 See Sack and Clark (ed), *German New Guinea: The Annual Report* (ANU Press, Canberra, 1979), p 13; Sack and Sack, op cit n 71, pp 1-3; Montgomery, *A Handbook of Information for Senior Land Settlement Officers* (Department of Lands, Surveys and Environment, Port Moresby, 1979), p 2.

120 Leyser, op cit n 68, pp 77-85; Sack, "The Triumph of Colonialism" in Sack (ed), op cit n 65, p 204; Sack and Sack, op cit n 71.

121 Sections 1-4 of the *Directions Regarding the Procedures of the Acquisition of Land by the New Guinea Kompagnie* of 10 August 1887, in Sack and Sack, op cit n 71, pp 19-22; Sack and Clark (ed), op cit n 102, p 14.

122 This Ordinance is reproduced in Sack and Sack, op cit n 71, pp 11-12.

123 Ibid, pp 85-95.

principles to recognise and protect the land rights of the natives.[124] The succeeding Australian administrations abolished private land dealings with natives, but nonetheless retained the power of compulsory acquisition.[125]

3.7.3 Modes of acquisition by government

It is possible for the government and customary landowners to enter into an agreement for the acquisition of customary land. The agreement in this case must be voluntary.[126] However, once the land has been purchased or leased, the subject land becomes government land absolutely for all purposes, or, in the case of leased land, for the duration of the lease.[127]

Where land is leased, the land reverts to its customary status after the expiration of the lease. Furthermore, where land is leased, during the currency of the lease, the customary owners retain reversionary rights, which they may protect through legal action.[128]

Acquisition by agreement

This mode of acquisition is the most common means by which the government acquires customary land. By s 10 of the *Land Act* 1996, subject to s 11 of the Act, customary land must be acquired in accordance with this section, and must be authenticated by such instrument and in such manner as is approved by the Minister for Lands.[129] The Minister can acquire land on behalf of the state on such terms and conditions as are agreed between the Minister and the customary landowners.[130] If acquisition of land by agreement fails, the government can invoke the compulsory acquisition power to effect the acquisition.

Acquisition by compulsory process

Under this mode of acquisition, the government acquires land from customary owners to carry out its essential development programs in the public interest. Acquisition for public purpose is a prerequisite to the exercise of the compulsory acquisition power, and compensation is payable for such acquisition.[131] However, because land is an important resource in the lives of Papua New Guineans, acquisition of land from customary landowning groups is not always easy, as people do all in their power to keep their land. Quite often, landowners either reject government negotiations to acquire their land, or demand exorbitant compensation. Where a minority group (landowners) has refused "unreasonably" to give up their land, or interests therein, for development programs beneficial to the public at large, the government can invoke the power of compulsory acquisition, and take the land in the interest of the public and compensate the landowners. The compulsory acquisition power, therefore, becomes an extremely necessary

---

124 James, op cit n 19, p 29; Leyser, op cit n 68, pp 78-79.

125 See *Land Ordinance* 1906, s 33; *Land Ordinance* 1911 (Papua), s 58; *Land Ordinance* 1922 (New Guinea), ss 6, 8 and 10; *Lands Acquisition Ordinance* 1914 (Papua), s 13; *Lands Acquisition (Town Planning) Ordinance* 1949, s 4; *Lands Acquisition Ordinance* 1952, s 14. There was also a specific enactment, the *Lands (Kila Kila Aerodrome) Acquisition Ordinance* 1939, which was enacted specifically to resume the lands on which the Kila Kila aerodrome was constructed. The land laws of Papua and New Guinea differed, and it was not until the enactment of the *Land Ordinance* 1962 that the land laws of the two territories were amalgamated.

126 Although the government has power to compulsorily acquire customary land, there is no statutory basis for the government to compulsorily lease such land.

127 See definition of "Government land" in s 2 of the *Land Act* 1996.

128 See discussion on leases in Mugambwa, Amankwah and Muroa, op cit n 58, Ch 5.

129 *Land Act* 1996, s 10(1).

130 Ibid, s 10(2).

131 See *Constitution*, s 53. Also, see Muroa, "Constitutional Constraints on Power of Eminent Domain" (1995) 23 MLJ at 95-118.

measure for taking land needed for development programs in the event that landowners fail to voluntarily surrender their land to the government for such purposes.

The power of compulsory acquisition was first exercised in 1886, when the administration in Papua required land at Hanuabada, in Port Moresby, for a cemetery site. Rev WG Lawes, a missionary of some ten years experience in the Port Moresby area, raised an objection that compulsory acquisition would be in breach of the promise made to natives when the protectorate was declared, that is, that their land would be preserved for them. However, despite this objection, the land was compulsorily acquired and has remained a cemetery.[132]

In Papua, however, no provision for compulsory acquisition of land was included in land legislation until the *Land Ordinance* 1906 was enacted. This Ordinance,[133] together with the *Land Ordinance* 1911-1940,[134] made provisions for the government to compulsorily acquire land, both alienated and unalienated, from any owner. One important compulsory acquisition that was made by the administration in 1940, was the lands involved in the case of *Geita Sebea v The Territory of Papua*.

As indicated earlier, in New Guinea, provision for compulsory acquisition was first made in the *Imperial Ordinance* 1903, which expressly allowed the administration to resume or restrict any land or interests therein "in the public interest in return for compensation".[135] When Australia took over the administration of German New Guinea, it made provision in the *Land Ordinance* 1922-1941[136] for the administrator to acquire land compulsorily for certain public purposes. The acquisition of land under this process must be for public purpose, and compensation must be payable for the land so acquired. These are basic principles of the exercise of the compulsory acquisition powers, and were continued in force in the successive land legislation of the country.[137] The above principles are protected in the *Constitution* of the independent state of PNG,[138] and form the basis of the current law which is set out in the *Land Act* 1996.[139]

The compulsory acquisition power was sometimes abused during the colonial administration. Some early land acquisitions were made through excessive pressure being put on the landowners. For instance, when the lease of the site of Iduabada Technical College, held by the administration from the customary landowners, expired in 1953, the landowners refused to renew the lease or sell the land. However, considerable pressure was exerted on them, and, after seven years, they relented and agreed to let the administration take their land for £25 per acre.[140] In another case, the administration needed a piece of land, which was owned by the natives of Kila Kila and Pari villages, for the Taurama Army Barracks in Port Moresby. The administration compulsorily leased the land from the native owners, and paid very little rent on the grounds that the land was

---

132 See Oram, op cit n 68, p 39; Haynes, op cit n 68.

133 *Land Ordinance* 1906, s 23.

134 *Land Ordinance* 1911-1940, s 58.

135 *Imperial Ordinance* 1903, s 1(1). This Ordinance is reproduced in Sack and Sack, op cit n 71, pp 85-95.

136 *Land Ordinance* 1922-1941, s 69.

137 See *Land Ordinance* 1906, s 35; *Land Ordinance* 1911-1940, s 60; *Land Ordinance* 1922-1941, s 71; *Imperial Ordinance* 1903, s I; *Lands Acquisition Ordinance* 1914, ss 13 and 26; *Lands Acquisition (Town Planning) Ordinance* 1949, ss 4 and 5; *Lands Acquisition Ordinance* 1952, s 14; *Land Ordinance* 1962, s 17. The application of the 1914 Ordinance was expressly excluded from native lands, while the 1952 Ordinance applied to such lands if required for a purpose connected with the defence or public safety of the country. The *Lands Acquisition (Town Planning) Ordinance* permitted the administration to acquire or resume land by compulsory process for the purposes of town planning, and compensation was payable for lands so acquired. The 1962 Ordinance amalgamated all the land laws of the country and included some new provisions, including, among other things, a new method of acquisition by compulsory process and improved provisions regarding compensation payments. See Montgomery, *Land settlement Branch Manual* (Department of Lands, Surveys and Environment, Port Moresby, 1978), pp 113-120. The 1949, 1952 and 1962 Ordinances applied to both Papua and New Guinea.

138 See *Constitution*, s 53.

139 Sea *Land Act* 1996, Pts III and IV.

140 See Oram, op cit n 68, pp 36-53.

needed for national defence. The administration subsequently acquired the land by compulsory process and offered to pay £2 an acre, but the people rejected that offer. An independent arbitrator subsequently awarded them £20 per acre.[141]

Numerous instances have been documented where land was also confiscated as punishment of individuals or groups for various offences perpetrated, or alleged to have been perpetrated, without compensation being paid.[142] One very well-known instance of this situation was the land in issue in the case of the *Director of Expropriated Property v Tedep,*[143] commonly known as the *Varzin* case. Although the dispute in that case was based on the title to the land in issue, and not on confiscation per se, the manner in which the land was taken initially best illustrates this point.[144] In another case, certain lands were fought over by various clans that made overlapping claims to them, although none of them was able to keep permanent settlements on the lands. However, the administration was reported to have acquired them without compensating customary right-holders for the loss of their rights there.[145]

Acquisition by lease

By s 11 of the current *Land Act* 1996, the Minister is authorised to lease customary land for the purpose of granting a special agricultural and business lease of the land.[146] Where the Minister leases customary land, an instrument of lease in the approved form, executed by or on behalf of the customary landowners, is conclusive evidence that the state has a good title to the lease and that all customary rights in the land, except those which are specifically reserved in the lease, are suspended for the period of the lease to the state.[147] It must be noted that no rent or other compensation is payable by the state for a lease of customary land.[148]

The provisions of the preceding legislation, that is, s 15A of the *Land (Amendment) Act* 1984,[149] were enacted to give effect to an indigenous scheme developed in the 1970s, known as the lease-leaseback scheme. The scheme was designed to afford customary owners access to credit facilities from financial institutions. The section authorised the Minister for Lands to lease customary land for a period of 25 years, in most cases for the purpose of creating special agricultural or business leases. Upon conclusion of the lease agreement, the land became government land, and the state would, in turn, grant a state lease for agricultural or business purposes to the customary owners, who were required to establish business groups to acquire the land. The title acquired by the customary business groups under the scheme could be used to obtain mortgage loans from the commercial banks to develop the land acquired.[150] The security

141 For further information on similar instances of abuse of the compulsory acquisition power, see Oram, "Urban Expansion and Customary Land" in Sack (ed), op cit n 65, pp 171-172. See Dove, Miriung, and Togolo, "Mining Bitterness", ibid, pp 181-189, for the analysis of the circumstances surrounding the acquisition of the land for the immense Bougainville copper project in the North Solomons Province, where the police force, armed with batons, shields, teargas and other modern police paraphernalia, were said to have been deployed against peaceful demonstrations by simple, defenceless people whose livelihoods were at stake.

142 See James, op cit n 19, pp 107-109; *CILM Report*, Ch 4; Chatterton, op cit n 124, pp 8-15; Sack and Clark (ed), op cit n 102, pp 236 and 354; Leyser, op cit n 68, p 32; Sack, "Early Land Acquisition in New Guinea: The Native Version" in *Appendices to Land Tenure in PNG* (UPNG, 1976), pp 110-121.

143 *Director of Expropriated Property v Tedep* [1964] 113 CLR 318.

144 See Leyser, op cit n 68, p 82, for details of the circumstances surrounding the acquisition of the land.

145 *CILM Report*, p 46.

146 *Land Act* 1996, s 11(1).

147 Ibid, s 11(2).

148 Ibid, s 11(3).

149 *Land (Amendment) Act* 1984 (No 23 of 1984). This Act amended the *Land Act* (Ch 185).

150 See Hulme, "Credit, Land Registration and Development: Implications of the Lease-Leaseback Scheme" (1983) 11 MLJ 91. The land acquired for grant as state leases for agricultural or business purposes under the scheme did not require an inquiry to be made to ascertain the needs of the owners

of title to such land is further enhanced by s 11(2), which provides that a copy of the lease document is conclusive evidence of the state's title to the land. There is, therefore, little room for disputes over the use of the land during the currency of the lease. Mortgagees will, therefore, more readily enhance credit based on the security of the land.

3.8 CONDITION PRECEDENT TO ACQUISITION OF LAND

One major condition must be satisfied before customary land can be acquired either by agreement or compulsory process. The condition is stipulated in s 10 of the *Land Act* 1996, which requires that the Minister must not acquire customary land unless satisfied, after reasonable inquiry, that the land is not required, or likely to be required, by the customary landowners or by persons on whom the land will or may devolve by custom.[151] Where the Minister is satisfied, after reasonable inquiry, that any customary land is not required or likely to be required for a certain period, but that the land may be required after that period, he or she can only lease the land from the customary landowners for the whole or part of that period.[152] Breach of this condition precedent may affect the validity of an acquisition.

In *Rahonamo v Enai (Re Hitau)*,[153] the administration effected acquisition of customary land under s 5 of the *Lands Regulation Ordinance* 1888-1889, which made it unlawful for the administrator to purchase customary land until, by sufficient inquiry, he or she had become satisfied that such land, the use or usufruct thereof, was not required, nor likely to be required, by the native owners. The customary landowners argued that the subject land was not validly acquired, because the administration failed to comply with the condition precedent to the acquisition of customary land, in that it failed to conduct reasonable inquiry to satisfy itself whether or not the customary owners required the land, or were likely to require the land, prior to its acquisition. The issue that the Supreme Court had to consider was whether or not customary owners could impugn a purchase of customary land by the administration on the ground of "the state of satisfaction in the mind of the administrator". There was nothing in the material before the court to show how the administrator made any inquiry, and whether he became satisfied that the land, or the use or usufruct thereof, was not required, nor likely to be required, by the native owners. However, the court held that, in all the circumstances, a presumption arose that the appropriate inquiry had been made by the administrator, as a result of which he became satisfied that the land was not required, nor likely to be required, by the native owners.

Clarkson J realised that there may well be cases where the factual situation would not justify the presumption that the prerequisites specified in s 5 of the Act were duly complied with. In such cases, the burden of showing the due performance of the prerequisites to the lawfulness of the acquisition would be on the administration. His Honour also appeared to be of the view that once the administrator had carried out the appropriate inquiry, it was irrelevant whether he or she was satisfied rightly or wrongly that the land was not required, nor likely to be required, by the customary owners.

Another case in which the court considered the effect of the predecessor provisions of s 10(3) of the *Land Act* 1996, was *Safe Lavao v The State (Re Kerema Town and Airstrip Land)*.[154] In that case, the administration in 1963 purported to acquire a large portion of land in Kerema, known as

---

of the customary land, as would be the case in normal acquisitions.

151 *Land Act* 1996, s 10(3).

152 Ibid, s 10(4).

153 *Rahonamo v Enai (Re Hitau)* [1971-1972] PNGLR 58.

154 *Safe Lavao v State (Re Kerema Town and Airstrip Land)* [1978] PNGLR 15.

the Kerema Town and Airstrip land. An instrument in relation to the acquisition was registered under the *Land Act* 1911. In 1967, the appellant and others claimed to be the owners of the lands comprised in the purported acquisition, and that they had never sold the land to the administration.

Pritchard J expressed the view that when a law in PNG affects traditional or customary rights, especially in relation to land, that law will be strictly construed where it purports to deprive the people of their right to assert ownership or interest of any sort in the land. It was established in evidence that the land to which the state claimed ownership was never sold by the appellants. They had manifested an unwillingness to sell. In the circumstances, His Honour held that this apparent unwillingness to sell land placed the appellants clearly within the situation envisaged in s 5 of the *Land Act* 1911-1940, which provided that it must not be lawful for the Lieutenant-Governor to purchase or lease land from the native owners until, by sufficient inquiry, he had become satisfied that the land was not required, or likely to be required, by the owners. After holding that the second limb of s 5 was a mandatory and not directory provision, His Honour went on to hold that the instrument of transfer contained no suggestion that anyone had even bothered to ask if the vendors had considered whether or not they would possibly have a need for the land in the future. His Honour concluded that the question appeared to have been ignored.

3.9 WASTE AND VACANT OR OWNERLESS DECLARATION

"Waste and vacant" (in Papua) or "ownerless" lands (in New Guinea) denote lands which were deemed by the administration to be owned by *nobody*. They were not alienated lands,[155] nor were they customary lands, and they had no apparent owners.[156] Where land appeared to be without apparent owners, or where land was deemed to be unoccupied land, the administration would acquire it as administration land by declaring it as waste and vacant or ownerless using this procedure. Although the power of declaring land waste and vacant or ownerless was a form of compulsory acquisition, the acquisition need not satisfy the criteria of public purpose. The condition for investigation and satisfaction required in s 10 of the *Land Act* 1996 does not apply. However, customary owners were required to object to the declaration within three months.[157] Moreover, no compensation was payable upon acquisition as in the case of compulsory acquisition.[158]

155 This category of land (alienated land) is largely land alienated from the traditional sector, either voluntarily or by compulsory process, and comprises state land and private freeholds. See James, op cit n 19, p 21.

156 However, it could be argued that in PNG there has never been such a thing as "ownerless" or "no man's" land, because all land in PNG society has always been owned by the people, irrespective of whether or not it has been cultivated. Even in this case, there is a requirement for prior investigation and satisfaction by the government before declaration is made. See discussions in Chapter 1 of this book.

157 See *Land Act* 1996, s 5.

158 James, op cit n 19, Ch 4; Chatterton, op cit n 124, pp 8-15.

In Papua, the policy was first incorporated into the *Crown Lands Ordinance* 1890. This Ordinance,[159] together with the *Land Ordinance* 1906,[160] enabled the administration to acquire land as waste and vacant or ownerless, provided that it "was not used or required or reasonably likely to be required by [the natives] for building, agricultural or other industrial purposes". An example of such acquisition was the declaration in 1901 of the areas in respect of Paga and Tuaguba Hills in Port Moresby as Crown lands, on the grounds that the natives had not used the lands for 15 years and did not require them for agriculture.[161] The *Land Ordinance* 1911-1940, on the other hand, enabled the administration to acquire lands which had never been alienated, and of which there appeared to be no apparent owners, as waste and vacant or ownerless.[162]

In New Guinea, the policy was first recognised in the *Imperial Ordinance* 1899. Section 2 of the Ordinance provided that special property rights and other privileges enjoyed by the New Guinea Company, by virtue of the *Imperial Charter* 1885, should pass to the German Imperial Administration. These rights and privileges included the rights to acquire land as waste and vacant or ownerless.[163] When Australia took over the administration of New Guinea, the policy was also incorporated into the *Land Ordinance* 1922-1941.[164] The Ordinance contained somewhat similar provisions to the *Land Ordinance* 1911-1940 (Papua), in that it enabled the administration to acquire lands that had never been alienated and of which there appeared to be no apparent owners.

The *Land Ordinance* 1962 slightly modified the power of waste and vacant or ownerless declarations. Under the Ordinance, expropriation was by way of a notice published in the Gazette, declaring that the land was not customary land.[165] The subject land was then deemed conclusively not to be customary land. If the customary owners contested the declaration, the land was deemed to be customary land until the claim of ownership on the part of the customary owners had been resolved by the Land Titles Commission or by the Land Courts.[166]

---

159 See *Crown Lands Ordinance* 1890, s 23.

160 See *Land Ordinance* 1906, s 11.

161 See Oram, op cit n 68, p 38; Haynes, op cit n 68, p 7.

162 See *Land Ordinance* 1911-1940, s 8.

163 See *Implementation Order for the Imperial Ordinance* 1899, s l(a), dated 1 April 1899. The *Implementation Order* can be found in Sack and Sack, op cit n 71, pp 13-14.

164 See *Land Ordinance* 1922-1941, s 11.

165 See *Land Ordinance* 1962, s 83. The declaration under the 1962 Ordinance was usually referred to as a "Section 83 Declaration".

166 *Land Ordinance* 1962, s 83(4) and (5). However, a different view was taken in the *Matter of the Land Titles Commission Ordinance* (1962-1971, No 90, 30 March 1977). In that case, O'Neally AJ purported to state a general principle that the legislative provisions on the power of waste and vacant or ownerless declaration were merely regulatory, and did not create or extinguish any authority or right of the Crown to waste and vacant or ownerless lands effectively vested in the Crown. If this general principle is correct, then, in the event of any dispute by the customary owners thereof as to the validity of a declaration, the land would be deemed to be administration land until it was established otherwise. There are very few waste and vacant or ownerless declarations made now, although s 5 of the current *Land Act* has provision for doing so if the need arises. However, the validity of a declaration under s 5 of the Act is now doubtful by virtue of s 53(5)(e) of the *Constitution*, which permits legislation to provide for the acquisition of ownerless or abandoned property "other than customary land". It could be argued, however, that in the light of the view taken by the court in *The Matter of the Land Titles Commission Ordinance* above, such lands are not customary lands, but state lands, and therefore do not fall within the constitutional protection under s 53(5)(e).

The requirement that before the administrator could declare any waste and vacant or ownerless land as Crown land, he or she had to be satisfied that such land was not "used or required or reasonably likely to be required by native-born Papua New Guineans for building, agricultural or other industrial purposes",[167] was tested in *Tolian v The Administration (Re Vulcan).*[168] Minogue J said that the administrator's decision as to the ownerless appearance of land was examinable. Accordingly, he said that the court had the power to look behind the Order in Council declaring the land, known as Vulcan land, to be ownerless.

In *First Assistant Secretary, Department of the Administration v The Administration,*[169] Minogue CJ adhered to the view which he expressed in *Re Vulcan*, that:

(a) a proclamation declaring land to be waste and vacant was open to examination;

(b) the natives could show that the proper conditions did not exist for the making of a proclamation;

(c) there was appearance of ownership over the land at the time of the making of the proclamation;

(d) good cause was in fact shown against the vesting of the land in the administration within the time limited by the proclamation; and that

(e) no further steps were taken by the administration to disclaim ownership.

In contrast, Prentice J, with whom Clarkson J agreed, was willing to apply the presumption of regularity to the making of a proclamation that was clearly an official public act, unless there was an apparent defect on the face of it. On the basis of the facts of the case, he found no material evidence to show the inaccuracy of the recitals in the proclamation or establishment of good cause to the contrary within the meaning of s 11 of the *Land Ordinance* 1922 (New Guinea). In the circumstances, Prentice J was of the view that it was unnecessary to consider and decide upon the issue as to the circumstances and extent to which the courts can go behind proclamations in an attempt to show their invalidity. The implication of this finding is that the court could go behind a proclamation to determine whether or not it was properly made.

In *Guba Doriga v Administration of the Territory of Papua and New Guinea,*[170] only Frost SPJ in the Full Court of the Supreme Court answered the question of whether a waste and vacant declaration could be challenged on the ground that the land was required, or reasonably likely to be required, by native-born Papuans for building, agricultural or other industrial purposes. He was of the opinion that "the issue whether the land answered the statutory description as declared in the Order in Council, is a matter which is not to be canvassed once it appears that the formal conditions for vesting are present". His Honour distinguished *Re Vulcan* on the grounds that it was based on different legislation.[171] The rest of the judges apparently assumed, for the purposes of argument, that it was possible to look behind the statement of the administrator to ascertain whether the land answered the statutory description. They disposed of the argument on the ground that there was a lack of evidence on the matter.

---

167 See s 23 of the *Crown Lands Ordinance* 1890 and s 11 of the *Land Ordinance* 1906.
168 *Tolian v The Administration (Re Vulcan)* [1965-1966] PNGLR 232.
169 *First Assistant Secretary, Department of the Administration v The Administration* (1974, FC 55).
170 *Guba and Doriga v Administration of the Territory of Papua and New Guinea* (unreported, FC18)
171 Ibid at 99-100.

Finally, in *Arthur Agevu v The State*,[172] the court, when considering the effect of a declaration under s 83 of the *Land Act* 1962 (as amended), expressed a general principle that the statutory provisions were merely regulatory, and did not create or extinguish any authority or right of the Crown to such lands, because, by virtue of the proclamation of the protectorate and subsequent annexation of Papua, the ownership of all waste and vacant land effectively vested in the Crown as Crown land. Thus, unless land is customary land, such land is, for all purposes, state land.

One thing that is apparent from the judgment, is that the judges appear to be loathe to substitute their 20th century ex post facto opinion on the question of whether the land was required or reasonably likely to be required by native-born Papua New Guineans, for the contemporary opinion of the administrator.

Most of the government land has been acquired under this method, a method that has been the source of bitter contention. As will be seen later, the Commission of Inquiry into Land Matters (CILM) established that this power was abused during the colonial era in PNG. It recommended return of such land not being used by the government to the original owners or their descendants (if any) or to land-short people for subsistence and/or economic development purposes.

The power to declare land waste and vacant or ownerless is now contained in s 5 of the present *Land Act* 1996. It gives the Minister the power to declare any land, which appears to the Minister not to be customary land, to be state land, unless good cause is shown to the contrary within three months. There can be possible constitutional implications where land that is customary land is declared not to be customary land under s 5 of the Act. This can be so especially where customary owners fail to object to the declaration within the statutory time limit due to circumstances beyond their control. Section 53 of the *Constitution* protects property rights as special rights of citizens, and allows acquisition under very limited circumstances.[173] Acquisition in this instance, therefore, has to meet the criteria in s 53 of the *Constitution*.[174] It must be noted, however, that s 53(5)(e) permits acquisition of ownerless or abandoned property other than customary land. The difficulty here is in the use of the term “ownerless”. On the authority of the principle expressed in *Arthur Agevu v The State*, such land is not customary land but state land. The land, therefore, does not fall within the constitutional protection under s 53, unless, of course, it can be established that the land is customary land.

The waste and vacant or ownerless land acquisition power was not always strictly observed and, as a result, cases were reported where the power was abused during the colonial administration. For instance, with its monopoly on acquisition of land, the New Guinea Company acquired large areas of land without proper investigations to ascertain whether or not the land was occupied.[175] When the German Imperial Government assumed administrative responsibility from the New Guinea Company, the acquisition procedures were streamlined to ensure greater protection for native landowners. However, despite the streamlining of the procedures, the German

---

172 *Arthur Agevu v The State* [1977] PNGLR 99.

173 See further discussions below in this chapter.

174 See Muroa, “Constitutional Constraints on Power of Eminent Domain” (1995) 23 MLJ at 95-118, for discussions on the criteria for acquisition of land under s 53.

175 Failure to institute proper investigations prior to acquisition of native lands in this case was contrary to the directions regarding the procedures for the acquisition of land by the company in the colony. See Sack and Sack, op cit n 71, for the directions given to the company. The New Guinea Company's actions with respect to native lands in this instance have been largely responsible for the subsequent land shortage faced by Papua New Guineans in many parts of the country, as discussed later in this chapter. It has been highlighted, however, that land was never equally distributed among the people or groups in different parts of the country in the first place, and alienation was also heavier in some parts than in others. Thus, there are groups who, even now, have more land than they can utilise. There are others whose traditional land holdings are, irrespective of alienation, inadequate for present needs. There are also groups who have lost most, or even all, of their land through alienation. See Sack, op cit n 68, p 206; Fingleton, “Land Policy in PNG” in Weisbrot, Paliwala and Sawyerr (ed), *Law and Social Change in PNG* (Butterworths, 1982), pp 105-125 for further discussions on this subject.

administration failed to adequately safeguard the native land rights. As a result, in some areas people lost most of their arable lands through waste and vacant or ownerless declarations.[176] Furthermore, early officers of the administration declared waste and vacant or ownerless any land from which they could not see smoke rising.[177] According to James, numerous communities and their leaders have questioned many of the waste and vacant or ownerless declarations over their traditional hunting, fishing and grazing lands.[178]

3.9.1 Commission of Inquiry into Land Matters (CILM) recommendation

The colonial governments of PNG had acquired a total of 308,000 hectares of land under this process.[179] Some freehold and leasehold titles have been granted over parts of it. Some towns have been built on such land. However, much of it remains undeveloped. The acquisition of these lands has been a source of contention.[180] The CILM treated the declaration of rural waste and vacant or ownerless lands, for which no payments of any kind were made to traditional right-holders, as a special case. It recommended that undeveloped rural waste and vacant or ownerless land should be returned under registered customary leasehold title to people living on or near it, according to need. Any remaining land was to be used for general leasing to anyone with compensation to traditional owners or their descendants.[181] However, where traditional owners are acutely short of land for cash or subsistence cropping purposes, developed rural waste and vacant or ownerless land should be recovered by the government and returned to them. The present freeholders and leaseholders should be compensated for unexhausted improvements on the land. Where traditional owners are not acutely short of land, developed land under these circumstances should not to be returned, but right-holders should be compensated for the land itself and given additional compensation for the loss of gardening, hunting, fishing and gathering rights.[182]

The CILM recommended that where there are big areas of virgin forestland and only a small population, the government should declare some parts of the land which it believes, after investigations, have not been used for agricultural purposes, to be national land.[183] The criteria to decide if land should be declared national land is whether the land has been used for any form of agriculture in the last 20 years.[184] If it has not been so used and the government requires it for public purposes or for purposes it thinks will benefit the nation, then it should declare the land to be national land. However, if it is established that although people have not been exercising agricultural rights, they have been exercising non-agricultural rights, such as hunting and gathering on the land, these rights should be preserved and marked as encumbrances on the government's title. If these rights are not preserved or extinguished, the customary right-holders must be compensated for the loss of these rights. However, only those rights that are being

[176] Such areas are Gazelle Peninsula in the East New Britain Province, and around Madang township in the Madang Province: Sack, op cit n 125, p 114; Fingleton, op cit n 158, p 106. It is said that, in Lae, 11,721 acres of land were acquired in this manner. The native owners tried to claim their land back from the administration, but the law and the administrative action were heavily loaded against them. Land in a number of areas is still *subjudice* as a consequence of claims by original owners and/or their descendants. Oram, "Urban Expansion and Customary Land" in Sack (ed), op cit n 51, p 171.

[177] See *CILM Report*, p 46; Chatterton, op cit n 124, p 14. In many cases, there were villages on the land, and in other cases, it was hunting and gathering land or contained "pies masalai". "Pies masalai" is a Papua New Guinean pidgin English phrase meaning sacred place. See also Kaputin, "Indefeasibility and Justice" in Sack (ed), op cit n 51, pp 159-163; Kambipi, "Cash-Cropping and Population Pressure" in ibid.

[178] For details, see James, op cit n 19, Ch 4.

[179] *CILM Report*, p 63. See also Antoninus, "The Tolai Land Case" in *Appendices to Land Tenure in PNG* (UPNG, 1976), p 106.

[180] See James, op cit n 19, Ch 4; The *CILM Report*, Ch 4.

[181] The *CILM Report*, p 63.

[182] Ibid, p 66.

[183] Ibid, Recommendation 55.

[184] Ibid.

exercised at the time of the declaration are to be preserved.[185] If a dispute arises as to whether or not people have been exercising agricultural rights over the land, the courts should deal it with.

It should be noted that the power here is to be used mainly in sparsely populated areas and only where the land is presently needed.[186] Thus, land cannot be acquired in a sparsely populated area, even though it has not been utilised within the last 20 years, unless there is a present need for the land. Clearly, the CILM believed the power of waste and vacant or ownerless declarations, as applied in the colonial era, was too wide, and that the test of "use in the last 20 years" would limit its scope. This would ensure greater protection of the customary land rights, while at the same time enabling the government to take lands that are not required by the owners for productive use, rather than leaving them fallow.

3.10 CONSTITUTIONAL PROTECTION

The successive post-independence governments (national government) of PNG, just as their predecessors during the colonial period, need land to carry out development programs effectively and efficiently. However, they have been mindful of the abuse of power on the part of the colonial administrations in the past, which led to general shortage of land in many parts of the country, and which has been exacerbated by the population increase in recent years as a result of improved health services throughout the country. They have also been concerned with the fact that these problems have led to increased resentment among nationals – a situation that has been demonstrated by hostile reactions against foreign plantation owners. This resentment is further kindled by the strongly held view that many of the acquisitions carried out during the colonial period were unjust.[187] Accordingly, the criteria used by the successive national governments to determine the amount of land the state should own in PNG today are those based on "necessity", viewed in the context of public purpose, and not one of "desirability".[188]

In order to tackle the land shortage and related problems associated with alienated lands, the property rights of Papua New Guineans were accorded constitutional protection as an integral part of the basic human rights provisions. The provision is contained in s 53 of the *Constitution*, which provides that "possession may not be compulsorily taken of any property, and no interest or right over property may be compulsorily acquired except" where acquisition, inter alia, is for a public purpose. The protection of property rights is necessary to prevent the perpetuation of the status quo regarding land rights of customary landowners.[189]

---

185 Ibid, Ch 6.

186 Ibid.

187 See *Papua New Guinea Proposals to Australia for a Joint Scheme for Settlement of Alienated Land Problems* (mimeo, Port Moresby), p 1. See also Fingleton, op cit n 158, pp 110-115; The *CILM Report*, Ch 4.

188 James, op cit n 19, p 65.

189 Other measures instituted to deal with the land shortage situation were: (a) the compulsory acquisition and redistribution of alienated lands owned by foreigners to land-short citizens; and (b) the return of unutilised state lands to the original owners, or to land-short citizens generally, with a view to dealing with land shortages in the country. See Muroa, op cit n 33.

The provision of s 53, as part of the individual's fundamental rights and freedoms, operate, inter alia, as a legal restraint on the power of the government of the day to expropriate property, especially land. However, the right under s 53 is a qualified right and, as such, the property of citizens can be acquired by the government from time to time, provided it meets the requirements of s 38 of the *Constitution.* This section provides that any restriction or regulation of the exercise of any qualified right or freedom must be necessary, taking into account the National Goals and Directive Principles and the Basic Social Obligations, for the purpose of giving effect to any of the public purposes set out under that provision. Where acquisition is permitted, compensation must be made on just terms as determined by the government.[190]

There are several reasons why the property rights of citizens are protected in the *Constitution* of the country. Among other things, most of the land in PNG is still owned by the people. People throughout the country regarded the protection of these rights in the *Constitution* as a matter of high priority.[191] In addition, if the property rights are contained in ordinary legislation, like the *Human Rights Act* 1971,[192] they can be easily changed in the same way (by a simple majority vote) as any ordinary legislation, at any time, by the government of the day to suit its own interest. On the other hand, if they are incorporated in the *Constitution*, it is difficult for the government to change, and they are, therefore, better protected.[193] The decision to incorporate property rights into the *Constitution* was a direct consequence of the experience people had during the colonial days when the compulsory acquisition power was abused. The constitutional protection of the land rights of the people was necessary to prevent the repetition of those abuses. Therefore, in the post-independence era, compulsory acquisition is governed strictly by constitutional provisions.

190 See *Constitution*, s 53(2). See also Muroa, "Constitutional Constraints on Power of Eminent Domain" (1995) 23 MLJ 97, for more detailed discussions on compensation under s 53(2).

191 See Constitutional Planning Committee, *Final Report* (Port Moresby, 1974), Ch 5.

192 Protection of property rights was one of the 11 basic human rights previously contained in the 1971 Act.

193 Constitutional Planning Committee, op cit n 174, Ch 5.

CHAPTER 4

FORESTRY LAW

*Eric Kwa**

4.1 INTRODUCTION

Papua New Guinea (PNG) has a total land area of 463,000 km^2 and a population of just over 4 million people. Seventy-seven percent of its land mass is covered by tropical rainforest, which represents about 1.5 percent of the world's tropical rainforests.[194] The forest consists of more than 2,000 species of trees, of which 400 species are of commercial value.[195] In 1979, it was estimated that 15 million hectares of forest were accessible and viable for commercial development.[196] A study in 1992, by the Australian International Development Assistance Bureau (AIDAB), estimated that only 7 million hectares were available for commercial utilisation.[197]

The contemporary exploitation of forest resources in PNG is recorded as early as 1884, when Europeans settled in PNG. The economic utilisation of forests in the early period of colonisation was slow, and was generally restricted to meeting domestic needs. It was not until the 1930s that timber production soared as a result of mining activities in the Wau-Bulolo areas.[198]

Over the years, the forestry sector has contributed its share of revenue to the economy. Exports of forest products expanded from A$257,000 in 1951-1952, to K36,400,000 in 1979.[199] The table below shows the growing importance of the sector to the national economy.

Royalties collected from timber operations rose from K208,000 in 1958-1959, to K2,500,000 in 1979.[200] By 1990, export earnings reached K62 million,[201] and by 1992 they reached K100 million, ranking third after minerals and agricultural produce.[202]

The important role that the forestry sector plays in the development of PNG, and the environmental consequences of this sector, cannot be understated. This chapter examines the law on forestry, beginning with the historical development of forestry legislation and policy in PNG. The position of resource owners, local-level governments, provincial and national governments in the development of forestry resources, in the context of the provincial governments reformed under the *Organic Law on Provincial Governments and Local-Level Governments* (OLPGLLG), will also be examined. A brief discussion on the relationship between the environmental law and forestry development projects will also be made.

---

* Dean, School of Law and Business Studies, UPNG.

194 *A Blueprint for Sustainable Use of PNG's Forests: Definition and Indicators of Progress* (CSIRO, Canberra, 1992), p 3.

195 Ibid.

196 Brown Bai, "Foreign Assistance for Developing Forests in Papua New Guinea: Past, Present and Future" in Shepherd and Richter (eds), *Forestry in National Development: Production Systems, Conservation, Foreign Trade and Aid* (Australian National University, Canberra, 1979), p 189.

197 This figure is cited in Nadarajah, "Now What? Proposed Forestry Guidelines for Papua New Guinea" (1993) 8 *Pacific Economic Bulletin* 51 at 53.

198 See generally, Lane-Poole, *A Report of the Goldfields of New Guinea: Together with Recommendations Regarding a Forest Policy for the Whole of the Territory* (RNB Agriculture Series (SI), Sydney, 1935).

199 *Department of Forests; Facts and Figures* (Department of Forests, Port Moresby, 1980), p 12.

200 Ibid.

201 Thompson, *The Forests of Papua New Guinea: The Dilemma of Development* (Murdoch University, Perth, 1992), p 4

202 *A Blueprint for Sustainable Use of PNG's Forests: Definition and Indicators of Progress* (CSIRO, Canberra, 1992), p 1.

Volume, value, and revenue contribution of PNG's log exports, 1978-1999

Year	Export volume ('000 m3)	Export values (K million)	% share of domestic export values	Log export Taxes (K million)	% share of non-grant revenues
1978	421	11.8	(02.3)	–	–
1979	476	20.9	(03.0)	–	–
1980	618	30.0	(04.7)	–	–
1981	749	31.5	(05.8)	–	–
1982	1,063	49.6	(09.1)	–	–
1983	1,003	43.2	(06.5)	4.7	(01.1)
1984	1,278	69.9	(08.7)	12.4	(02.6)
1985	1,158	58.4	(06.5)	12.6	(02.3)
1986	1,299	68.0	(07.0)	13.7	(02.5)
1987	1,450	103.0	(09.3)	16.5	(02.5)
1988	1,348	90.5	(07.4)	15.6	(02.3)
1989	1,349	90.0	(08.6)	11.4	(01.4)
1990	990	65.2	(06.2)	12.2	(01.6)
1991	1,062	81.2	(06.2)	17.7	(02.2)
1992	1,601	140.0	(08.0)	25.0	(02.7)
1993	2,375	400.2	(16.3)	70.9	(06.3)
1994	2,944	483.1	(18.1)	131.3	(10.2)
1995	2,513	436.7	(12.8)	127.6	(08.6)
1996	3,000	564.0	(16.9)	144.0	(09.6)
1997	3,090	605.6	(19.3)	146.9	(09.7)
1998	3,180	648.7	(18.5)	149.9	(09.9)
1999	3,280	695.4	(19.8)	152.8	(09.5)

Sources: Bank of PNG, *Quarterly Economic Bulletins*, for all actual figures to 1995; 1996 Government of PNG Budget Papers (Tables 2.2, 2.3, 4.1), for 1996-1999 projections.[203]

[203] Taken from Filer, "A Statistical Profile of Papua New Guinea's Log Export Industry" in Filer (ed), *The Political Economy of Forest Management in Papua New Guinea* (Monograph 32, Port Moresby, 1997), p 209.

Land tenure and forestry ownership

Land tenure in PNG is complex and, for the most part, difficult to mobilise and use for economic and other related purposes.[204] The reason for this is that there are two land tenure systems, namely, customary land tenure and alienated land in PNG. Chapter 3 exposes the tensions between these two different systems. The focus of this part of the chapter is to ascertain the link between land ownership under custom and forestry resources ownership.

The issue of land ownership is crucial to an understanding and appreciation of the use and management of natural resources in PNG. The determination of forestry resources utilisation is really a question of land use. It is, therefore, imperative that we begin our discussion by addressing the issue of land ownership and land use rights. The premise of this chapter is that customary owners have exclusive ownership of forestry resources located on their land.

The importance of land to the people of PNG has been described as:

> *Land is the only thing worth living for*
>
> *Land is the only thing worth working for*
>
> *Land is the only thing worth fighting for*
>
> *Land is the only thing worth dying for*
>
> *For land is the only thing that lasts forever and ever.*[205]

Land is the source of life, and is also the resting place of the dead.[206] To give up land ownership and control means death, and to hold on to land means life. There can be no better way of describing the importance of land to the people of PNG than the illustration given above.

Customary land transfer

Land alienation to persons from outside the clan or society[207] under custom is rare or uncommon.[208] If a portion of land is transferred to an outsider in breach of customary rules, the clan members would regard the transaction as void and of no effect. Arrangements[209] could be made between clans from the same society for the use of each others' land, either for short or longer periods. Where an arrangement is in place between two clans of the same society for the transfer of land, the members are required to utilise the land only for the purposes specified by the arrangement.[210] If there is a dispute in relation to the ownership of the land, a disputing party

---

[204] Such related purposes include national parks, conservation and amusement areas, which may be declared under the *National Parks Act, Conservation Areas Act* and the *Fauna (Protection and Control) Act.*

[205] *Report of Emergency Committee Relating to the Declaration of a State of Emergency* (Five Highlands Provinces, Port Moresby, 23 July 1979), cited in Haynes, "Succession to Land in Papua New Guinea" (Paper presented at the Australian Universities Law Schools Association Conference, Macquarie University, Sydney, 1981), p 1.

[206] Ibid.

[207] Land alienation to individuals within the same clan or society was unknown, because the land was communal property.

[208] Due to the flexibility of custom and the introduction of the monetary economy in PNG, customary land near the cities and towns is being sold outright to outsiders for cash. This is particularly evident in the Highlands: Haynes, "The Land Mobilisation Program and Customary Law" in Aleck and Rannells (eds), *Custom at the Crossroads* (Law Faculty Publication Unit, Port Moresby, 1995), p 129.

[209] Arrangements mean oral agreements.

[210] Under custom, transfer of use means that other members of a clan would use the land belonging to another clan of the same society, for instance, gardening for a specific period without claiming title to the land. This is different from alienation. Alienation of land means that land title and other rights attached to the land are surrendered to the person or clan to whom the land is transferred.

cannot transfer its interest to another party under a contract without first resolving the ownership issue. This point was made in *Golpak v Kali.*[211] In this case, the defendants, claiming to be the landowners of the land in dispute, temporarily transferred their rights to the customary land to a foreign logging company that was logging in their area. The applicant sought orders in the National Court to declare the transfer invalid, as it was contrary to custom. The court declined to make the declaration, but instead referred the matter to the Local Land Court to determine the issue of ownership.

The concept of alienation under custom is significant, given the relationship between natural resources located under, on, above and adjacent to the land. Because alienation of land was very rare and exceptional under custom, it is suggested that mineral and forestry resources on, under, and adjacent to customary land were unalienable. This argument may be regarded as obsolete in relation to the mineral and petroleum resources, as they belong to the state by virtue of s 5 of the *Mining Act* 1992 and s 3 of the *Oil and Gas Act* 1998. However, for the forestry sector the concept as applied under custom is very important. This issue is addressed later in the chapter.

PNG has a total land area of 46.2 million hectares. Of this, some 78 percent (36.2 million hectares) is covered by tropical rainforest, and around 15 million hectares were deemed suitable for commercial forestry.[212] The question is, who owns these forestry resources, and what is the basis of this ownership? Is it the customary landowners who own the forestry resources?

The dictum *cujus est solum ejus est usque ad coelum* ("his whose is the soil, his is also the heavens"), is very much a reality in PNG.[213] Customary law in PNG deems that customary landowners are the true owners of the forestry resources.[214] Their participation in the development of these resources is, therefore, crucial.

The role of forests is vital to the people of PNG, especially those in the rural areas. A landowner expressed the relationship of his people to the forest by saying that "[t]he most important plant in the world is the tree."[215] To the rural communities, the forest has an intrinsic value. It is an important source of food, fruits, building materials, herbal medicines, wild animals and birds.[216] Brown described the relationship of the PNG Highlanders to their forest as follows:

> "[T]he New Guinea highlanders know and appreciate the resources of their locality. Forest and bush is never wasted."[217]

This is also true for the other areas of the country. Transfer of the forest and its resources were unknown under custom. The rationale was that what grew on the land was a part and parcel of the

---

211 *Golpak v Kali* [1993] PNGLR 491.

212 *Catalyst: Development and the Environment in PNG* (Special Issue: The Steinberg Report) (Melanesian Institute for Pastoral and Socio-Economic Services, Goroka, 1990). The figure of 15 million hectares has now been declared obsolete. Recent estimates put the figure at 7 million hectares of operable forests: Nadarajah, op cit n 4.

213 Artihulawa describes the situation with reference to the Siane as "whatever grows above and below the land belongs to the owner of the land"; Carson, *Forestry and Forestry Policy in Papua New Guinea* (Department of Forestry, Port Moresby, 1974), p 2.

214 *New Directions in Resource Management For Papua New Guinea* (Occasional Paper No 20, Law Reform Commission, Port Moresby, 1990), pp 5-10. See also *Stretim Nau Bilong Tumora: National Sustainable Development Strategy & 20th Waigani Seminar Recommendations* (Department of Environmental Science, UPNG, Port Moresby, 1993), pp 16-21.

215 Kaspou, "People, Money-lenders, Forests and Exploitation: An Inquiry into Forest Resources in the Marius Province" in Gladman, Mowbray and Duguman (eds), *From Rai to Rio: Environment and Development in Papua New Guinea* (UPNG Press, Port Moresby, 1996), Vol 3, p 189.

216 See the discussion on the use of forest by Pokanas, "The Value of Trees in Marius Province" in Morauta, Pernatta and Heaney (eds), *Traditional Conservation in Papua New Guinea: Implications for Today* (Monograph No 16, IASER, Port Moresby, 1980), p 169; also see Kube, *Tropical Lowland Rainforests: Some Possibilities for their Utilisation with Particular Reference to Guinea and with Special Emphasis on Agriculture* (Papua New Guinea Environmental Series No 2, Wau Ecology Institute, Wau, 1990), pp 24-28.

217 Brown (ed), *Fashion of Law in Papua New Guinea* (Butterworths, Sydney, 1969), p 113.

land. Land and forest were inseparable. This position was affirmed in *Vaniak v Muvamastrum Pty Ltd*.[218] The decision in this case is significant, because the court (Doherty J) declared that "timber is a thing growing on land and so is within the definition of land in the *Land Dispute Settlement Act* (Chapter 45)". The definition of "land" according to the court includes trees. Trees and land are therefore a single element under custom.

The difficulty of separating forest ownership from customary land was clearly observed by the colonial administration. This was evident in the first forestry legislation, which was introduced in British New Guinea in 1892. The *Indigenous Timber Ordinance* 1892 recognised and maintained the status quo.

Timber Rights Purchase

In 1909, the colonial administration, in an attempt to free forest resources from the hold of customary owners, introduced the Timber Rights Purchase (TRP) concept under the *Timber Ordinance (Consolidated)* 1909. The TRP concept was aimed at wresting forest ownership from the customary owners without disturbing the land ownership. Essentially, the device allowed the administration to purchase, as the name suggests, timber rights from the customary owners. The acquisition of these rights enabled the administration, through its agents (timber permit holders), to harvest the timber located on customary land. A trademark of the TRP arrangement was that customary owners were hardly actively involved in the negotiations for the sale of their timber rights.

The TRP concept proved very successful in transferring the timber rights of the customary owners to the colonial administration (and now the state). The rate of its success was such that successive governments have proudly nourished and cherished it, even after 25 years of independence.

There were two problems with the TRP process. First and foremost, it was (and to a certain extent still is) void under custom. This proposition is based on the premise that, under custom, transfer of forest ownership or rights was unknown *at that time*. It may be argued that such transfers were (and are) valid because of the flexibility of custom to change with new political and socio-economic values,[219] because, as Robert Cooter said, "custom is 'alive'".[220] It is suggested that the real issue is whether or not customary rules and principles are changing simultaneously with the political and socio-economic changes in a given period, to validate transactions occurring at a given time and space. The crucial factor is the timing of the change in customary law. Thus, the question is, was customary law compatible with the western socio-economic values at the time the TPR concept was introduced? The answer is, of course, in the negative.

The second problem that will be highlighted throughout this chapter is that the TRP process operated to the detriment of the forest resource owners. The general assumption was that the TRP process was the catalyst to change, and would bring about better development and benefits to the forest resource owners and their area. Unfortunately, as will be shown in this chapter, the contrary seems to be the order of the day.

---

218 *Vaniak v Muvamastrum Pty Ltd* [1994] PNGLR 425 (Doherty J).
219 Larmour, *Customary Land Tenure: Registration and Decentralisation in Papua New Guinea* (IASER, Monograph 29, Boroko, 1990).
220 Cooter, "Kin Groups and the Common Law Process" in Larmour (ed), ibid, p 38.

4.2 THE DEVELOPMENT OF THE FORESTRY POLICY

Colonial forestry policy

The evolution of the contemporary forestry policy in PNG has a long history dating back to 1951. Prior to 1951, the colonial administration had no formal forestry policy to direct the development of the sector in PNG. It has been said that:

> "Forestry is a long-term activity and needs unusual vision to determine over-all policies in advance of the pressure of events. This is particularly so in an underdeveloped country where basic information is lacking, machinery for implementing policy is non-existent or inadequate, and short term needs are given priority."[221]

Unfortunately, as will be shown below, the development of a coherent forestry policy in the colonial era was very disappointing. The rate at which the colonial administration exploited the timbers was much faster than its efforts in developing and promoting a sustainable forestry sector.

When the British introduced the *Indigenous Timber Ordinance* of 1892, there was no forestry policy in place to give direction to the law. No serious attempt was even made by the Australians to give some meaning to the law.

Some attempts were made to assess the potential of the forest of the Territory, initially in 1908, and later in 1923,[222] but no concrete measures were taken by the colonial administration to address the issue of policy. During this period, the forestry legislation underwent a lot of amendments,[223] but these changes lacked any policy initiative.

In New Guinea, the German New Guinea Company was more interested in the exploitation of the resources than long-term organisation of the Territory. The company did not have, nor did it introduce, any formal policy or law to regulate the utilisation and management of this natural resource. Even when the Imperial German Government took over control of the Territory, it maintained the status quo.

The absence of any forestry policy in the two territories during the early period of colonisation may be attributed to:

(a) the instability of government in the territories; and

(b) the low priority that the three different administrations gave to forestry due to the lack of data on the viability of different species of timber.

As Vatasan correctly pointed out, "[d]uring most of the colonial time Forestry was of a fairly low priority, the little administration needed being relegated to the Districts."[224]

The first signs of any policy initiative undertaken in the colonial period was in 1951, when the Minister for External Territories, the Honourable P C Spencer, made a statement on forestry to

---

221 *The Encyclopedia of Papua New Guinea* (Australian National University Press, Canberra, 1983), p 452.

222 *Forestry: Papua New Guinea* (Department of Territories, Canberra, 1961), p 1.

223 The first amendment was in 1903, and other amendments followed in 1908, 1909, 1917 and 1920.

224 Vatasan, "The Human Dimension of Forest Operations in Papua New Guinea: A Historical Perspective" in *Proceedings of the Huon Seminar '94: Workshop on Forestry Management* (The Papua New Guinea University of Technology, Lee, 1995), p 81.

the House of Representatives. In his speech, the Minister informed the house that the administration would:

(a) locate, assess and regulate availability of natural forest resources to bring them within reach of development;

(b) encourage investment of private capital for development of these resources; and

(c) ensure native participation in development.

This was the first attempt by Australia to introduce any kind of formal forestry policy in Papua New Guinea. The emphasis of this policy "was on the provision of sufficient local timber for construction and expansion by developing a timber industry".[225] This policy was to be "achieved by concentrating activity in areas of major European development and where timber lands were to be cleared for agricultural development, again, by Europeans".[226]

In 1957, the Minister for Territories, Mr Hasluck, made a further policy statement on forestry, which can be summarised as follows:

1. Acquisition and reservation of an adequate permanent forest estate of 4 million acres (1.6m hectares) of dedicated forest within ten years, and 10 million acres in 20 years.
2. Establishment of a forest training centre.
3. Establishment of a forest research institute.
4. Reafforestation program, including expenditure in the Highlands for grassland reclamation.
5. Timber utilisation research into natural durability and preservative treatments.
6. Botanical collections and identifications.
7. Encouragement of a timber industry.

This parliamentary statement marked a shift in policy and a firmer commitment by the colonial government to the forestry sector. In response to this policy, the colonial administration amended the forestry statutes to accommodate these new initiatives, established a new forestry college at Bulolo in the Morobe Province in 1962, and established a research institute in Lae, also in the Morobe Province.

In 1973, the government of Michael Somare purported to introduce its own forestry policy. The emphasis of the policy was on protecting and managing the forest estate as a national asset. It was aimed at establishing permanent forest processing industries, effective schemes of reafforestation, full local participation and protection of the environment.[227] This forestry policy was really a translation of the coalition government's eight-point improvement plan.[228]

In 1974, the government engaged a consultant to review the forestry policy and make appropriate recommendations to the government. In his report to the interim government, the consultant, Carson, noted that it was this policy statement, and its subsequent implementation through the

[225] *The Encyclopedia of Papua New Guinea* (Australian National University Press, Canberra, 1983), p 453.
[226] Ibid.
[227] Mossop, "Taming the Robber Barons? The Reform of Forestry Legislation in Papua New Guinea" (1992) 8 QUTLJ 113 at 115.
[228] The eight-point plan was the statement of the government's ideology during the run up to self-government. See Barnett, *Report of the Commission of Inquiry into Aspects of the Forestry Industry* (Commission of Inquiry, Port Moresby) (7 Interim Reports and Final Report, 1987-1989); (Interim Report No 1, 1987), pp 40-41 (referred to as the "Barnett Inquiry").

five-year program of 1968-1973, that provided the basis on which development had taken place in the forestry sector.

The consultant identified seven major objectives of the policy. These objectives were:

- declaration of forests as national assets;
- reafforestation of forests;
- forests conservation;
- development of permanent industries and customary owner participation;
- forest research;
- training; and
- effective regulation of the forestry sector.

This so-called "forestry policy" had a profound effect on the forestry sector. Commenting on the policy, Tak observed that the policy encouraged:

(a) the rapid depletion of viable timber stands;

(b) almost a total lack of reafforestation or other follow-up land use;

(c) industry domination by large foreign enterprises with every incentive for transfer pricing;

(d) excessive wastage in timber processing; and

(e) conflicting national development objectives surrounding the industry.[229]

These and other problems relating to the forestry policy were clearly envisaged by Carson, and he therefore insisted that to fully implement the national forestry policy, a draft White Paper, setting out the forestry policy and the directives required to implement it, was required.[230] However, as Commissioner Barnett found out:

> "[D]espite the known urgency of the situation the expected White Paper never materialised and despite critical comments and express directives from the National Executive Council, the forestry legislation has still not been revised".[231]

When assessing the government's forestry policy, Barnett sadly concluded that:

> "There is no clear written statement of policy in any single document and a study of all available documents, in an endeavour to piece together a sort of composite or aggregate policy, has not produced a satisfactory result."[232]

What had purportedly been the government's forestry policy was actually no policy per se. Commissioner Barnett described the existing forestry policy as a de facto forest policy.

---

229 Tak, *Evaluation of Achievements 1976-1987* (Discussion Paper No 35, Institute of National Affairs, Port Moresby, 1988), p 14.

230 Barnett, op cit n 35, p 41.

231 Ibid, p 46.

232 Ibid, p 17.

The forestry policy of 1979

Following Carson's report in 1974, there was no change in the forestry policy until 1979. In that year, the Department of Forests made an attempt to revise the "Forest Policy". A White Paper titled *Revised National Forest Policy* was presented and approved by the National Executive Council (NEC). The forest policy contained:

(a) proposals and guidelines for the formation and operation of PNG log exporting enterprises;

(b) guidelines for enterprises involved in timber processing;

(c) directions pertaining to foreign enterprises dealing in large log exporting and not processing within PNG; and

(d) directives aimed at foreign enterprises which were involved in limited log export and road construction.[233]

The guidelines envisaged by policy statement (a) and (b) were found to be of little encouragement in promoting PNG-owned enterprise or large scale domestic processing, because, as Mossop pointed out, "the emphasis of the Revised Forest Policy had shifted from one of onshore processing of logs to large scale exportation of logs".[234] Generally, Commissioner Barnett described the guidelines pronounced by the policy, saying:

> "the observer could be excused for believing that the guidelines were prepared for a different country. It became apparent that virtually none of these guidelines are being followed".[235]

After a thorough analysis of the government's forestry policy, the Barnett Inquiry left the Revised National Forest Policy in tatters by declaring that the commission could not find any document that would prove that there was a formal forest policy in operation in the country.[236] The Barnett Inquiry concluded that the existing forest policy was merely a de facto forest policy.

Commissioner Barnett recommended that the government should put all efforts into the formulation and approval of an appropriate forest policy as soon as possible. This was to be done with the participation of the NEC and relevant government departments, provincial governments and the forestry industry.

The Commission of Inquiry into Aspects of the Forestry Industry

At this juncture, it is important that a brief discussion be made of the "Commission of Inquiry into Aspects of the Forestry Industry" because of its profound effect on the forestry sector. The findings of the commission helped revamp the forestry sector, and elevated what was obviously a domestic issue into the global arena.

In 1987, "there was public war of words in the press and in Parliament over the competence of the Forest Industries Council in undertaking large scale marketing of logs".[237] On 29 April 1987, the Prime Minister of PNG, Mr Paias Wingti, responded by appointing a commission of inquiry

---

[233] Barnett, op cit n 35.

[234] Mossop, op cit n 34.

[235] Barnett Inquiry (Final Report, 1989), Vol 2, Appendix 1, p 43; Mossop, op cit n 34.

[236] Ibid.

[237] *The Barnett Report: A Summary of the Report of the Commission of Inquiry into Aspects of the Forestry Industry in Papua New Guinea* (Asia-Pacific Action Group, Hobart, 1990), p 9.

to investigate the Forest Industries Council. Mr Justice Barnett, a judge of the National Court, headed the commission. The Barnett Inquiry took two years to complete its investigations, and in July 1989 it presented its final report to the Prime Minister.

The commission was originally set up to investigate certain matters, relating mainly to the Forest Industries Council and its marketing activities. It was to investigate the process by which the Forest Industries Council became involved in the marketing of timber, and to ascertain the benefits obtained by PNG (if any) from the marketing operations of the Forest Industries Council. Its investigations ranged from the identification of national forest policy to the investigation of loggers and the benefits derived by customary owners and the government.

The Barnett Inquiry revealed "widespread transfer pricing, corruption throughout Government and Government agencies, destruction of timber resources and few benefits from resource exploitation flowing to either the landowners or the nation".[238] The Barnett Inquiry also revealed:

(a) an imbalance of power, between the Minister of Forests and the Department of Forests, that effectively gave the Minister of Forests total power over the allocation of concessions and licences;

(b) an imbalance of power between the national Department of Forests and the provincial Departments of Forests (once again, the central structure had right of veto, and the right to force through projects against the wishes of the local authorities); and

(c) a high level of corruption amongst parliamentary Ministers and, to a lesser degree, amongst the heads of the Department of Forests, the Forest Industries Council and provincial governments.[239]

The situation in the forestry industry was at its worst state. The forestry law had allowed the situation to deteriorate to a point where it was not serving the interests of the people for whom it was enacted. Justice Barnett pointed out that there was a substantial need for legislative reform, which should be based on a well-considered policy.[240]

Tropical Forest Action Plan – PNG (TFAP)

Another event worth mentioning is the World Bank-sponsored TFAP. The reckless destruction of the forest resources of PNG were not only felt locally, but also recognised internationally. In 1985, the World Bank, in collaboration with other international organisations, began organising a donors' meeting on the Tropical Forest Action Plan for PNG: "The initiative was designed to provide an international coordinating mechanism to help the world's tropical countries come to grips with deforestation."[241] In March 1990, the World Bank released its report titled *Papua New Guinea. The Forestry Sector: A Tropical Forestry Action Plan Review*.

The World Bank identified six major problems that required immediate attention by the government of PNG.[242] These were:

---

238 Mossop, op cit n 34, p 116.
239 See the summary of the commission's findings by The Asia-Pacific Action Group.
240 See generally Barnett Inquiry (Interim Report No 1).
241 Thompson, op cit n 9, p 12.
242 These points are also set out in a tabular form in Mossop, op cit n 34, pp 117-118.

1. PNG did not have adequate information on the growth etc of its timber resources. There was a need for this information to successfully deal with forestry problems.

2. There was a major breakdown in the effective management of resources. This was due to the lack of decision-making framework. Also, there was no link between the Forestry Department and the other appropriate government departments, such as the Department of Environment and Conservation.

3. There was a serious loss of revenue to the government due to poor control of resources and corrupt practices.

4. Forest products processing in PNG was poor and lacked competition.

5. There was a need for conservation and proper land use.

6. PNG lacked proper forestry institutions. It needed skilled labour and better forestry policies.

The underpinning of the report was that timber cutting was to be reduced to a sustained yield of 3.6 million cubic meters annually, from about 5.7 million cubic meters, with the loss of earnings to be compensated by the donors of up to $US15 million per year for five years.

However, the TFAP was criticised savagely for its:

> "failure to identify and specify the forces that pose a threat to the rainforests in Papua New Guinea [and that] the Review is deeply flawed by its failure to confront the fundamental contradiction between a money-based profit-orientated economic system and its values on the one hand, and wider national, global, environmental, ecological, customary, political and social needs on the other hand".[243]

Brunton also attacked the TFAP on other grounds, such as:

(a) its focus on industrial forestry development;

(b) the treatment of rainforests as a timber resource;

(c) the report being founded on the unproven and uncertain concept of "sustained yield";

(d) the report being premised on the maintenance of PNG as a supplier of unprocessed resources;

(e) the failure of the report to take into account the political and constitutional framework in which it was meant to operate;

(f) its failure to recognise the importance of customary landowners in the development process; and

(g) the inappropriateness of the World Heritage Area concept as a vehicle for conservation in PNG.[244]

---

243 Brunton, *Critique of the World Bank's Tropical Forestry Action Plan Review for Papua New Guinea* (Working Paper No 26, PNG Law Reform Commission, Port Moresby, 1990), p 4; see also the same line of arguments in Thompson, op cit n 9, p 13.

244 These points are paraphrased from Mossop, op cit n 34, pp 119-120.

The criticisms of the World Bank did little to deter it from intervening in the forestry sector. It continued to play a significant role in the formulation of the Forestry Policy 1990 and the *Forestry Act* 1991. The World Bank and its partners continue to participate actively in the sector through the current structural adjustment program.[245]

The forestry policy of 1991

The Barnett Inquiry and the TFAP showed that the management and utilisation of the PNG forestry resources were in a critical state. These two events created the impetus for the government to reassess its position pertaining to the forestry sector. Consequently, it introduced the *National Forest Policy* in 1991. The *National Forest Policy* is a comprehensive document, containing an introduction and seven parts. Essentially, the *National Forest Policy* comprises two main aims and supportive objectives. The main aims are:

1. Management and protection of the nation's forest resources as a renewable natural asset.
2. Utilisation of the nation's forest resources to achieve economic growth, employment creation, greater Papua New Guinean participation in industry and increased viable onshore processing.[246]

The Forest Authority hopes to achieve the first aim by conducting surveys in potential forest areas, and thereby classifying the forests into five categories, namely, production forests, protection forests, reserve forests, salvage forests and land suitable for afforestation.[247]

After a forest is classified, the ownership of the forest is then determined.[248] Where the forest is classified as a production forest, the Forest Authority can enter into negotiations with the customary owners with a view to purchasing their timber rights. This process will ensure the proper management of the forestry resources and the flow of benefits to customary owners. The Forestry Authority hopes to achieve the second aim through the participation and involvement of nationally owned enterprises and PNG citizens, and the encouragement of onshore processing of timber. The Forest Authority will also promote and market forest products to minimise transfer pricing, and will charge levies for forest products, which will be distributed to customary owners.

To enable it to achieve its two main aims, the Forest Authority will follow three strategies. The first strategy will be the collation of information and advancement of knowledge relating to the utilisation and maintenance of PNG's forest resources through forest research.[249] Based on this information, the Forest Authority will increase the acquisition of forestry resources, and disseminate skills, knowledge and information in forestry through education and training.[250]

---

245 For a detailed discussion on the role of the World Bank in the PNG forestry sector, see Filer, Dubash and Kalit, *The Thin Green Line: World Bank Leverage and Forest Policy Reform in Papua New Guinea* (Monograph 37, National Research Institute & Australian National University, Canberra, 2000); Dubash and Filer, "Papua New Guinea" in Seymour and Dubash (ed), *The Right Conditions: The World Bank, Structural Adjustment, and Forest Policy Reform* (World Resource Institute, Washington DC, 2000), p 29.

246 *National Forest Policy* (Ministry of Forests, Port Moresby, 1991), p 2.

247 Ibid, p 5. However, see the discussion about the difficulty of the application of the different categories of forests by Filer (ed), op cit n 7, pp 218-222 and Filer and Sekhran, *Loggers, Donors and Resource Owners* (International Institute for Environment and Development, London, 1998), p 163.

248 Customary owners are identified and encouraged to form themselves into landowning groups, which would then be incorporated under the *Land Groups Incorporation Act*. The Forest Authority can then deal directly with the registered land group: see *Forestry Act* 1991, s 57 and *Forestry (Amendment) Act* 1993, s 13.

249 *National Forest Policy* (Ministry of Forests, Port Moresby, 1991), Supportive Objective 1. This is an important area that contributes to the overall objective of attaining sustainability of forestry resources.

250 Ibid, Supportive Objective 2.

Under the third strategy, it will introduce effective strategies, including administrative and legal machinery, to manage the forest resource, incorporating national, provincial and local interests.[251]

The forestry policy continues to be reviewed by the government. Even after a decade of operation, there are still suggestions that the forestry policy of 1991 is inadequate, as it does not cover certain facets of the sector, such as resource owners' mobilisation, royalty distribution and monitoring of loggers and their activities. The World Bank has identified these and other defects. It has, therefore, demanded, as one of its conditions to releasing much needed funds to the cash-strapped country, that the government agree to undertake a review of the forestry sector.[252] The review of the policy and law are still continuing.

4.3 THE EVOLUTION OF THE FORESTRY LAW

In this part of the chapter, the development of forestry law in PNG will be considered. To appreciate the evolution of forestry law in the country, its development under the different regimes will be examined. This approach is also useful because it sheds light on the current practices in the forestry sector and identifies the origins of some of the provisions in the *Forestry Act* 1991.

4.3.1 Colonial forestry law

Colonial forestry law: Papua

The move to develop and manage the forestry resources of PNG has a long history, which began in the early part of the 1900. A few years earlier, the Imperial Government had set up a Royal Commission to investigate and report on the peoples of the Western Pacific and their cultures.[253] In the case of British New Guinea, the commission found that the indigenous people cultivated their land and were very jealous of their proprietary rights.[254] There was, however, no inventory of the timber resources in the Territory at that stage.

When the first forestry legislation was introduced in British New Guinea in 1892, it lacked substance. The legislation, the *Indigenous Timber Ordinance*,[255] was short, and contained only 14 sections. The primary aim of the Ordinance was "to regulate the cutting of indigenous timber".[256] Customary owners were allowed to cut and sell timber on their land. They were, however, not allowed to harvest protected timber.[257] Customary owners could also supply timber growing on their land to any persons, provided they entered into a contract with those persons and a timber inspector approved the contract.[258] It was ironic that the customary owners were required to enter into a contract of sale in order to supply timber to any person of their choosing. As James correctly pointed out, at that time customary owners were incapable of concluding a valid contract.[259]

---

251 Ibid, Supportive Objective 3.
252 Dubash and Filer, op cit n 52.
253 The Imperial Government appointed the Royal Commission in 1884.
254 *Report of the Royal Commission appointed by the Imperial Government to inquire into the working of the Western Pacific Orders in Council, etc 1884*, cited in Lalor, "Land Law and Registration" in Brown (ed), op cit n 24, p 137.
255 *Indigenous Timber Ordinance* (No 7 of 1892).
256 Ibid, preamble.
257 Ibid, s 11.
258 Ibid, s 12.
259 James, *Land Law and Policy in Papua New Guinea* (Monograph No 5, PNG Law Reform Commission, Port Moresby, 1985), p 114.

The requirement that indigenous Papuans must enter into a contract in order to sell their timber has remained a permanent feature of forest utilisation ever since. Over the years it has taken on different names, the two most notable being "Native Timber Authority" provided under regs 17-18 of the *Forestry Regulation* 1974, and the "Timber Authority" spelt out under ss 87-90 of the *Forestry Act* 1991. The Native Timber Authority concept has been very manipulative and destructive to the customary owners and their environment. However, the court, in *Rainbow Holdings Pty Ltd v Central Province Forest Industries Pty Ltd*,[260] commenting on the *Forestry Regulation*, said that:

> "[T]he aim of the *Forestry Regulations,* 16 to 18 is to prevent customary owners being exploited".

However, a few years later the Barnett Inquiry exposed that this was not the case. This grim scenario has been attributed to the lack of management control with greater emphasis on the quantity of timber that was to be purchased.[261]

The *Indigenous Timber Ordinance* was not enforced effectively, as there was no Forest Service in place to implement it at that stage.

Aside from its shortfalls, the *Indigenous Timber Ordinance* did make one important contribution to the forestry industry. The Ordinance laid the foundation for three fundamental practices that have now become synonymous with the forestry sector. These were the declaration of protected areas, the declaration of protected species of timber, and the recognition of customary ownership of forestry resources.

Protected areas could be declared on any land, whether it was customary, freehold or Crown land. Later forestry statutes specifically stipulated that protected areas could only be declared on Crown land.[262] Logging of timber in these areas was prohibited. Only two areas were declared as protected areas: one in 1905, and the other in 1920. These were the township of Port Moresby[263] and the vicinity of Sapphire Creek and Laloki River.[264]

The first initiative to assess the timber potential of the Territory was taken in 1908. In that year, the Papuan administration engaged the services of Gilbert Burnett, the District Forest Inspector of Queensland, to conduct an assessment of the timber potential of the Territory. The assessment was not very successful due to the lack of transport facilities. Burnett's report, however, resulted in the passing of the *Timber Ordinance (Consolidated)* of 1909.[265]

---

[260] *Rainbow Holdings Pty Ltd v Central Province Forest Industries Pty Ltd* [1983] PNGLR 34 at 36 (Bredmeyer J).

[261] Carson, *Forestry and Forestry Policy in Papua New Guinea* (Department of Forestry, Port Moresby, 1974), pp 6-8.

[262] *Timber Ordinance* 1909-1920, s 6; *Forestry Ordinance* 1936, s 10; *Forestry Act* 1974, s 6; *Forestry Act* 1991, s 3.

[263] The area was declared a Protected Area on 11 October 1905 (*Government Gazette* No 18, 1905). This declaration was repealed and redeclared on 19 October 1919 (*Government Gazette*, 29 October 1919).

[264] The area was declared on 31 March 1920 (*Government Gazette*, 7 April 1920).

[265] *Timber Ordinance (Consolidated)* 1909 (No 28 of 1909). This statute consolidated the former forestry statutes and the *Sandalwood and Rubber Ordinance* of 1907.

The *Indigenous Timber Ordinance* was repealed and replaced by the *Timber Ordinance* of 1903. This 1903 Ordinance was, in turn, amended by the *Timber Ordinance* of 1908.[266] In 1909, the Legislative Council enacted the *Timber Ordinance (Consolidated)*, which came in force on 6 October 1909. It was aimed at encouraging timber utilisation. Timber utilisation was to be achieved through the infamous Timber Rights Purchase process, which was stipulated under s 2 of the Ordinance. The Ordinance also introduced a new provision on the declaration of timber reserves. Under s 9, timber reserves could be declared on Crown land and land which was the subject of a TRP agreement. Timber in reserved areas could only be harvested by permit and licence holders.

The *Timber Ordinance (Consolidated)* 1909 was amended twice; first in 1917,[267] and again in 1920.[268] In 1909, the *Timber Regulations* 1909 were enacted. The regulations were amended in 1914 and again in 1918. They related to the fees charged for timber permits, and the amount of royalties payable to the administration.

A decade after the first attempt to assess the timber potential of Papua, the Australian government engaged the Commonwealth Forestry Adviser, Mr Lane-Poole, in 1923, to explore and assess the forest botany of the two territories.[269] In his report to the Australian government in 1925, Lane-Poole recommended, among other things, the establishment of a Territory Forest Service responsible for the implementation of the forestry legislation. The colonial government did not implement the recommendations until after 1936.

The *Timber Ordinance* 1909-1920 continued in force in the Territory until 1950, when it was repealed and replaced by a new forestry statute. The new statute, the *Forestry (Papua) Ordinance* 1950,[270] applied the provisions of the *Forestry Ordinance* 1936-1937 of the Territory of New Guinea to the Territory of Papua. Section 4(1) of the *Forestry (Papua) Ordinance* stipulated that:

> "The provisions of the *Forestry Ordinance* 1936-1937 of the Territory of New Guinea as in force at the date of commencement of this Ordinance, and the provisions of the *Forestry Regulation*, made under that Ordinance, at that date, shall be in force in the Territory of Papua as if contained in this Ordinance."

A year later, the *Forestry (Papua) Ordinance* was amended by the *Forestry (Papua) Ordinance* 1951. A new section, relating to the declaration of an administration land as a special area, was inserted into the Ordinance. The *Forestry (Papua) Ordinance* 1951 remained in force until 1974, when the two pieces of legislation were amalgamated under the *Statute Law Revision (Amalgamation of Laws) Act* 1973.[271] The amalgamation of these two statutes was made without any alteration to the provisions of the *Forestry Ordinance* 1936-1937.

Colonial forestry law: New Guinea

The development of forestry law and, in fact, the forestry sector in New Guinea, was not regarded as a significant issue by the Reich and the German New Guinea Company. This was evident by

266 *Timber Ordinance* 1908 (No 16 of 1908).
267 *Timber Ordinance* 1909-1917 (No 1 of 1918).
268 *Timber Ordinance* 1920 (No 3 of 1921).
269 Lane-Poole, *A Report of the Goldfields of New Guinea: Together with Recommendations Regarding a Forest Policy for the Whole of the Territory* (RNB Agriculture Series (SI), Sydney, 1935).
270 *Forestry (Papua) Ordinance* 1950 (No 7 of 1950).
271 *Statute Law Revision (Amalgamation of Laws) Act* 1973 (No 2 of 1974), s 3.

the lack of regulation and control of forestry in the Territory. The German New Guinea Company had exclusive power and authority to achieve its economic interests in the Territory. Forestry utilisation and management was, therefore, seen within the ambit of the general policy of maximum commercial exploitation of the protectorate's resources. The absence of any forestry legislation in the Territory persisted even after Germany was defeated in World War I.

The *Timber Ordinance* 1922 was the first forestry legislation to be introduced into the Territory and was similar to the *Timber Ordinance* 1909-1920, which was in force in Papua. The *Timber Ordinance* 1922 was quickly amended in the same year,[272] and later in 1926 by the *Timber Ordinance* 1922-1926.[273] The *Timber Ordinance* 1922-1926 was eventually repealed in 1936.

In 1935, Lane-Poole again took a trip to the two Territories and conducted an extensive exploration around the goldfields of Wau and Bulolo, Rabaul and Laloki.[274] In the course of his survey, Lane-Poole discovered that, under the *Timber Ordinance* 1922, a few licence holders were already operating in the Territory of New Guinea. These licence holders were mostly individuals, and operated on the island of New Britain. The term of their licences ranged from five to 15 years, and the timber that they harvested was most probably used for domestic purposes. Commercial logging was mainly concentrated in the goldfields of Wau and Bulolo, which had four commercial mills.[275]

Again, Lane-Poole recommended that a Forest Service be established for the two Territories.[276] He also recommended that the Forest Service staff should consist of a Conservator of Forests who would operate from the headquarters at Rabaul, a District Forester and a Forest Overseer who would be based at Wau.[277] Attached to his recommendations was a draft Forestry Ordinance, which was later enacted in 1936. A Forest Service was eventually established in 1938.

A real desire in both the logging and export of timbers and the appreciation of the need for a professional controlling organisation in the Territory, led the Legislative Council to implement Lane-Poole's recommendation by enacting the *Forestry Ordinance* 1936.[278] The Ordinance was influenced mainly by the activities at the Wau and Bulolo goldfields. However, as Lane-Poole pointed out, "this law and the regulations appended to it should meet not only the conditions that have arisen in the goldfields but any timber cutting in other parts of the Territory".[279] In 1937, the *Forestry Ordinance* 1936-1937 was introduced. It incorporated the *Forestry Ordinance* 1936 with the *Forestry Ordinance* 1937. A new *Forestry Regulation* was also enacted at the same time.

The purpose of the *Forestry Ordinance* was to repeal the *Timber Ordinance* of 1922-1936, and to provide for the conservation[280] and management of forests and other purposes.[281] The administration hoped to conserve the forest through the dedication of Territory forests[282] and the declaration of timber reserves.[283] The management of the forests was to be achieved through the

272 *Timber Ordinance* 1922 (No 2 of 1922). At that stage there was no Legislative Assembly for the Territory, so all territorial statutes were ordained by the Governor-General of the Commonwealth of Australia with the advice of the Federal Executive Council.
273 *Timber Ordinance* 1922-1926 (No 9 of 1926). The Act came into force on 6 May 1906.
274 Lane-Poole, op cit n 76, p 1.
275 Ibid, p 20.
276 Ibid, p 8.
277 Ibid, p 17.
278 *Forestry Ordinance* 1936 (No 46 of 1936).
279 Lane-Poole, op cit n 76, p 17.
280 The term "conservation" here relates to the conservation of forest for future use: Personal communication with Allan Ross (an officer of the PNG Forest Authority), 26 June 1994.
281 This was spelt out in the preamble of the Ordinance.
282 *Forestry Ordinance* 1936, s 10.
283 Ibid, s 11.

purchase of timber rights from the customary owners,[284] and the control and supervision of timber permit[285] and timber licence[286] issuances. The legislation was to be administered by a secretary appointed by the administrator.[287] The secretary was to be assisted by forest officers[288] and forest inspectors,[289] who were to be appointed by the administrator.

The *Forestry Ordinance* of 1936 continued in force in the Territory until 1974. It is generally believed that this statute is the cornerstone of the present forestry law in PNG.[290] This view is misconceived for two primary reasons. First, this Ordinance did not introduce any new concepts into forestry management. It essentially adopted and developed the *Timber Ordinance* of 1909-1920.[291] Secondly, this was not the first forestry legislation introduced in New Guinea, or for that matter, Papua. Thus, to maintain the premise that the *Forestry Ordinance* of 1936 is the foundation of PNG's forestry law is a grave distortion of fact and history.

Colonial forestry law: Papua and New Guinea

In direct response to the forestry policy on capital investment in forestry resource utilisation enunciated by Mr Spencer in 1951, new legislation was introduced in the Australian Parliament aimed at encouraging large-scale development of forest resources in PNG. The legislation, known as the *New Guinea Timber Agreement Act*,[292] was to approve an agreement made between the Australian government and Bulolo Gold Dredging Limited with respect to the formation of a company known as Commonwealth-New Guinea Timbers Limited ("Timber Company"). The aim of the Timber Company was to acquire timber rights in the Territories of Papua and New Guinea for the purposes of harvesting logs, the sawmilling of timber, the peeling of timber and manufacture of plywood.[293] These forest products were to be exported to Australia. Under the legislation, the Timber Company was required to harvest 100 million super feet of Hoop and Kliniki pine on administration land covering 15,000 acres in the Bulolo Valley in the Morobe Province.[294] The term of the agreement was ten years, with an option for renewal for a further ten years.[295] The Timber Company was also accorded a wide range of privileges, including the recouping of a certain rate of subsidy from the Australian government upon the exportation of timber products to Australia.[296] The company was also exempted from the operations of the *Timber Ordinance* 1936-1937.

The *Forestry Ordinance* 1936-1937 continued to apply in the Territory up to 1971, when it was amended by the *Forestry (New Guinea) (Amendment) Ordinance* 1971. The aim of the new statute was:

> "To amend the *Forestry Ordinance* 1936-1937 of the Territory of New Guinea for the purpose of clarifying the rights of native owners of land who have disposed of the right to remove timber from that land, to provide for the adjustment of the purchase price of timber

284 Ibid, s 9.
285 Ibid, ss 14, 15, 18 and 19.
286 Ibid, ss 14, 17, 18 and 19.
287 Ibid, s 6.
288 These officers were required to be holders of a degree or diploma in forestry: *Forestry Ordinance* 1936, s 7.
289 An officer of the Public Service of the Territory or a European member of the New Guinea Police Force was eligible for this post: *Forestry Ordinance* 1936, s 8.
290 Mossop, op cit n 34; Yauieb, "Land Tenure and Forestry in Papua New Guinea: Problems and Solutions" in Shepherd and Richter (eds), *Forestry in National Development: Production Systems, Conservation, Foreign Trade and Aid* (Australian National University, Canberra, 1979), p 24.
291 Look at, for instance, the Timber Rights Purchase concept, timber reserves, territory forest and the issuance of timber permits and timber licences.
292 *New Guinea Timber Agreement Act* (No 40 of 1952).
293 Ibid, Sch, cl 4(1)(a).
294 Ibid, Sch, cl 10.
295 Ibid, Sch, cl 12.
296 Ibid, Sch, cl 14.

rights in certain circumstances, to remove out of date provisions, to provide for reafforestation, to provide for advisory services to be made available by the Administration to stimulate economic development in certain areas, and for related purposes."[297]

This was a very important piece of legislation for the following reasons:

1. The "timber reserve" concept was replaced with the "timber rights purchase area" concept, which, when defined, meant an area of native land over which the administration had acquired the rights of felling, cutting, removing and disposing of timber under s 9 of the *Forestry Ordinance* 1936-1937. The change of concept meant that the administrator was prevented from declaring a TRP area as administration land. This change worked in favour of the customary owners, because, unlike in the past when they also indirectly lost control of their land, the revised TRP concept guaranteed them continued control of their land even though they had disposed of their timber rights.
2. For the first time since the introduction of the TRP concept, the legislation required that all future TRP agreements were to be in writing. Unwritten TRP agreements were made void by s 5(d) of the Act.
3. All TRP agreements were required to operate within a given period. In the past, there was no specific period in which the administration would exercise its rights in a TRP area. This Ordinance gave certainty to customary owners, in that they knew when they would exercise their rights in their land after the cessation of the TRP agreement.
4. For the first time, the law obliged the administration to set out in detail the breakdown of the financial benefits that the customary owners would gain. The administration was also required to inform the customary owners of the particulars of any timber permit that was to be consequently granted by the administration in respect of the TRP area.
5. The Ordinance buried the practice of declaring timber reserves in the TRP areas.
6. The right of permit and licence holders to erect sawmills or other buildings in the TRP areas was put to an end. The Ordinance prohibited the erection of such buildings in the TRP area. These changes were influenced by the prohibition on declaring areas as administration land.
7. The legislation introduced the concept of reafforestation. The Ordinance introduced a new section that required that in areas of major forest activity, reafforestation would follow soon after the harvesting of timber in that TRP area.

These drastic changes were a reflection of the introduction of the forestry policy in 1957 by Mr Hasluck. It had finally dawned on the colonial administration that, as the customary owners were the true owners of the forestry resources, they also had an unequivocal right in determining the utilisation and management of those resources.

[297] *Forestry (New Guinea) (Amendment) Ordinance* 1971, preamble.

There were no significant changes to the legal framework until 1971, when the House of Assembly enacted the *Forestry (Private Dealings) Ordinance* 1971.[298] The Act, the brainchild of Mr (later Sir) Julius Chan, the Member for Namatanai, was to be incorporated and read as one with the *Forestry Act.*[299] It was accompanied by a regulation known as the *Forestry (Private Dealings) Regulation.* In 1991, during the debate on the new Forestry Bill, Sir Julius Chan proudly informed Parliament that:

> "For the first time, even before independence, I saw the anomaly (*in the Forestry Act 1936-1971*) and introduced the *Private Dealings Act* which gives the right to the owners of the land to form their own companies to negotiate conditions, harvest timber and infrastructure."[300] [Emphasis added.]

The purpose of the Act was to enable customary owners of timber to dispose of their timber to any person, subject to certain safeguards, and for related purposes.[301] Mossop suggested that the Act was introduced to "overcome the extremely centralised and cumbersome administration of the *Forestry Act*".[302]

Under the *Forestry (Private Dealings) Act*, the customary owners were required to form themselves into a body corporate, which was to be certified by an authority appointed by the Minister for Forests. The customary owners would, through customary land owning groups, apply to the Minister for Forests[303] to declare their area as a Local Forest Area under s 4 of the Act. Where the Minister approved the application, s 5 of the Act empowered the customary owners to sell or otherwise dispose of their timber to any person of their choice. Such arrangements were, however, subject to the Minister's approval by virtue of s 6 of the Act.[304]

These administrative procedures were to be carefully complied with. Their breach could result in a judicial review of the process, as illustrated in *Manus Provincial Government v Tarsicus Kasou* [1990] PNGLR 3. In this case, the Manus Provincial Government sought a judicial review of various administrative steps taken by an authority appointed under the Act before the commencement of logging. The provincial government argued that the defendant, who was appointed by the Minister for Forests as an authority to certify customary owner groups in the Manus Province, had acted unreasonably in certifying the customary owners of the West Coast Local Forest Area. The provincial government sought to have the defendant's decision quashed. The court (Ellis J) held that the defendant acted on bias. However, the court fell short of striking down the Minister's decision.[305]

The *Forestry (Private Dealings) Act* provided a means for customary owners to dispose of their timber to whoever they wished, provided:

(a) the interests of the owners were protected;

(b) there was no conflict with national interest;

---

298 *Forestry (Private Dealings) Ordinance* 1971 (No 107 of 1971).
299 *Forestry (Private Dealings) Act*, preamble.
300 *Hansard*, 16 July 1991.
301 Carson, op cit n 20, pp 7-8.
302 Mossop, op cit n 34 at 114-115.
303 Under the Regulation, they only had to pay $50 with their application: *Forestry (Private Dealings) Regulation*, s 2.
304 See the case studies on the impact of the legislation on various Local Forest Areas in the country in Filer (ed), op cit n 7.
305 See the history of the case in Ghai and Regan, *The Politics and Administration of Decentralisation in Papua New Guinea* (Monograph 30, National Research Institute, Port Moresby, 1992), pp 328-331.

(c) prospects for economic development were considered; and

(d) the administrator's assent in relation to the above had been obtained.[306]

No environmental controls were inserted into the Ordinance, and no restrictions on the size of the area covered by the Local Forest Areas were provided. The Forest Department interpreted the Ordinance as allowing the sale of small forest areas. However, as the Barnett Inquiry found, this was not the case. In fact, large tracts of forest areas were being harvested illegally through this process.

4.3.2 Post-independence forestry law

Forestry Act (Ch 216)

The main objective of the *Forestry Act* 1974 was to encourage customary owners to sell their timber rights to the government. The government could then, through a selection process, grant logging permits to developers to harvest the timber located in the timber rights purchase area.

The PNG Government readily adopted the Act after independence. Even though the legislation contained many loopholes that were capitalised on by the forest resource developers, as exposed by the Barnett Inquiry, no changes were made to the Act to suit the circumstances of the newly independent nation. Even after the Barnett Inquiry, logging companies continued to breach the *Forestry Act*, as illustrated in *Central Pomio Logging Corporation Pty Ltd v The State* [1992] PNGLR 20. This case shows a clear breach of the Act by the logging company, when it failed to have its logs graded before being shipped. The Act and its accompanying Regulation remained in force until 1991, when they were repealed by the *Forestry Act* 1991.[307]

Forestry (Private Dealings) Act (Ch 217)

The aim of the *Forestry (Private Dealings) Act* was to enable customary owners to dispose of their forestry resources to any developer who was willing to pay them a certain amount of money. There was very limited government control.

This pre-independence legislation was adopted without any alteration. In 1989, the constitutionality of this Act was challenged by the Manus Provincial Government in *Supreme Court Reference No 3 of 1989; Re Forestry Act (Private Dealings) Act* (Ch 217) [1990] PNGLR 222.[308] The Manus Provincial Government argued that the Act breached s 53 of the *Constitution*, which precludes the compulsory taking of private property. It argued that the method of declaring Local Forest Areas under the Act, which allowed customary owners to dispose of their timber rights to any person, was an infringement of s 53 of the *Constitution*. The court ruled that the provisions of the Act were validly enacted, and were therefore valid.

Like its counterpart, the *Forestry (Private Dealings) Act* continued in force until it was repealed by the *Forestry Act* 1991. This Act was the more controversial of the two forestry statutes, as it contained several deficiencies that the developers, Ministers[309] and the forestry officials

---

306 Barnett, *Report of the Commission of Inquiry Into Aspects of the Forestry Industry* (Commission of Inquiry, Port Moresby), p 44.

307 *Forestry Act* 1991 (No 30 of 1991).

308 This case has a long history and is discussed succinctly in Ghai and Regan, op cit n 112, pp 328-331.

309 *Mcdui Development v Genia* [1990] PNGLR 50. In this case the Forests Minister (Mr Genia) revoked Mcdui's licence to log in the Lako Imala Local

capitalised on to satisfy their greed. Its repeal in 1991 brought great relief to those who were concerned with the interests of customary owners and the wanton destruction to the forests.

The Forestry Act 1991

Acting in response to the Barnett Inquiry Report and the TFAP, the government eventually passed new forestry legislation in July 1991. The *Forestry Act* came into force on 25 June 1992. Its date of commencement, almost a year later and a few weeks before the national elections, was shrouded in controversy.[310]

The Act is very comprehensive, and sets up a complex administrative structure and procedure for control and regulation of all forestry operations throughout the country, including the allocation of timber permits.[311] The legislation is an important law and, according to the Supreme Court in *Supreme Court Reference No 7 of 1992; Re Forestry Act 1991* [1992] PNGLR 514 at 515, is law concerning a matter of national interest.

The major elements of the legislation are:

(a) the creation of a National Forest Board and the Provincial Forest Management Committees to be involved in the administration of the Act;

(b) the introduction of a legislative basis and procedure for forestry planning; and

(c) the reform of resource allocation procedures, including the repeal of the *Forestry (Private Dealings) Act.*

During debate on the Bill, Sir Julius Chan told Parliament that the Bill was taking the power away from the Cabinet and giving it to bureaucrats with the establishment of the authorities.[312] He warned that this was a move that Parliament would regret later.[313] This view was very shallow and lacked insight. The creation of the Forest Authority indicated the corporate nature of the Forests Department. Additionally, the inclusion of the Provincial Forest Management Committees in the administrative structure signalled the seriousness of the government in fostering the participation of provincial governments and customary owners in the decision-making process.

The Act also retains the four old practices that were established by its predecessors. First, under s 3 of the Act, national forests (formerly Territory forests) can be declared. Secondly, certain trees or species of trees can be protected under s 4. Thirdly, customary ownership and rights to forests are facilitated under ss 46 and 56(3). Fourthly, timber reserves can be declared over Forest Management Agreement (formerly TRP) areas. The core of the legislation is Pt III, which forms the basis for the management and development of forest resources and the procedure for forestry planning. It contains provisions dealing with forest plans, forest protection, resource acquisition and allocation. It provides the mechanism for the utilisation of the forestry resources through the Timber Authority and the Forest Management Agreement process.

Section 136 of the Act repealed the *Forest Industries Council Act*, the *Forestry Act* and the *Forestry (Private Dealings) Act.* Part X contains the saving and transitional provisions. Section 137 saved the existing permits, agreements and registrations that were granted under the former

---

Forest Area (Central Province), so that his company could go in and log the area.

310 Filer and Sekhran, op cit n 54, pp 147-150.

311 For a detailed understanding of the mechanics of this Act, see the discussions in Mossop, op cit n 34.

312 *Hansard*, 16 July 1991.

313 Ibid.

Acts. In 1993, the logging giant Rimbunan Hijau,[314] in collaboration with the PNG Forest Resources Association, launched an attack against the government, claiming that the Act was anti-customary owners and developers.[315] In order to substantiate their claim, they engaged a Queen's Counsel (QC) from Australia to review the Act and make recommendations for changes. The QC reviewed the Act, and recommended that various parts of the Act be amended to reflect the views and aspirations of the customary owners and the developers.[316]

The involvement of Rimbunan Hijau in the debate angered many people. Others, including Sir Michael Somare, called for the deregistration of the company. The review by the Australian QC was also criticised. Some argued that his recommendations were faulty because he lacked "understanding of or experience with customary or other land laws, an important and fundamental aspect to the whole debate", and that "he is detached from the reality of PNG".[317]

The final point about the Act is that it has now been declared by the Supreme Court, in the case *Supreme Court Reference No 7 of 1992; Re Forestry Act 1991*, to be "an exhaustive law in the field of national forestry control and development throughout Papua New Guinea and is a matter of national interest". In this case, the Supreme Court was asked to determine whether the East New Britain provincial forestry legislation, the *Forestry Operations Control Act* 1992, was unconstitutional on the grounds of inconsistency with the national forestry legislation. Applying the "cover the field" test, the Supreme Court ruled that the provincial forestry legislation was invalid. The importance of this case is that provincial governments were estopped from enacting their own forestry legislation to regulate forestry activities in their respective provinces.

Forestry (Amendment) Act 1993

The *Forestry (Amendment) Act* was enacted in 1993. It corrects and changes many of the typological and terminological errors in the principal Act,[318] and brings into perspective the role of the PNG Forest Authority as a corporate body. It also reduced the number of the board members from 11 to six, and provided the board with temporary powers to extend the terms of existing timber permits or licences and to grant timber authorities.[319] The attack on membership of the board has been a contentious issue, which has resulted in two amendments to the same provision; one in 1996 and another in 2000.

4.3.3 Forestry Guidelines 1993

In 1993, the Forest Authority, through the Forests Minister, the Honourable Tim Neville, introduced a document titled "National Forestry Development Guidelines".[320] When introducing the National Forestry Development Guidelines ("the Guidelines"), the Minister stated that "these Guidelines provide a prescription for remedying" a sub-sector which the Barnett Inquiry described as "out of control".[321] The Guidelines introduced "tougher checks and procedures governing new project entrants and a new forest revenue system which will ensure that customary

[314] In 1993 it was estimated that Rimbunan Hijau controlled about 86 percent of the timber concessions in the country: *The Times* (PNG, 29 July 1993).

[315] *The Times* (22 July 1993). See also the discussion about Rimbunan Hijau in Filer (ed), op cit n 7, pp 212-217.

[316] The sections of the Act which were recommended for change included Pt II, Div 2, ss 21, 42, 47, 49, 56 and 61.

[317] *The Times* (5 August 1993).

[318] For example, the term "Director-General" under the principal Act was changed to "Managing Director".

[319] Nadarajah, *The Sustainability of Papua New Guinea's Forest Resource* (Discussion Paper No 76, National Research Institute, Port Moresby, 1994), p 16.

[320] For a detailed discussion on the background to this document, and the consequent controversies of its impact on the sector, see Filer and Sekhran, op cit n 54, pp 203-222.

[321] Neville, *National Forestry Development Guidelines* (Department of Forests, Port Moresby, 1993), p i.

owners and the nation as a whole receive their full and just share of economic rent from timber that is harvested".[322]

The Guidelines set out a program for forest resource development based on sustainable production. Requirements for reafforestation and afforestation during and after the cessation of a timber project were also set out. The Guidelines also provided for industrial development in the forestry sector, training, localisation and forest research. A vital element of the Guidelines was the provision relating to the distribution of forest revenue.[323]

The introduction of the new forest revenue system was to ensure that customary owners received shares from timber production of their forests. The revenue system was to be introduced as soon as possible. Under the new system, no export duties would be paid on logs. Instead, stumpage would be payable in respect of all timber which was harvested or scaled. Miscellaneous charges and levies under the forestry arrangements were no longer going to be payable. This system was a revolutionary aspect of the Guidelines and was seen as fair to all the parties involved in the forestry sector.

The most crucial element of the revenue system was the stumpage. In its simplest form, "stumpage" meant "you pay for what you cut". The Guidelines stipulated two forms of stumpage. These were the minimum stumpage and the additional stumpage. The minimum stumpage comprised three charges payable at a rate per cubic meter of timber harvested. These charges were:

(a) royalties – K5 (payable to customary and other owners of harvested timber);

(b) provincial levy – K1 (payable to the provincial government of the Province in which the timber is harvested); and

(c) forest administration levy – K14 (payable to the state, as represented by the Forestry Authority).

The additional stumpage would be payable to a representative body appointed by the customary owners in each project area.

The stumpage system had two advantages. First, it ensured that the customary owners gained fairly in the distribution of the forest revenue. As Mr Neville pointed out, "resource owners would earn about K12.9 million in direct revenue and an additional K30 million in premiums which are going to the developers".[324] Secondly, it discouraged wastage of forest logs. Because the system required the logger to pay for every log that was cut, the developer would not be inclined to rush in and bulldoze every tree. The revenue system, therefore, encouraged proper management of the forest environment. One can easily be misled into believing that because of the friendly nature of the Guidelines to the customary owners and the environment, they had no shortcomings.

The introduction of the Guidelines, however, was marred with controversy. These controversies centred on the new revenue system. The strongest opposition to the Guidelines came from developers and, sadly enough, customary owners, through the PNG Forest Resources Owners

---

[322] Ibid, p ii.
[323] Ibid, p 20-24. The revenue system originates from Pt VI of the *Forestry Act* 1991.
[324] *Post Courier* (6 August 1993).

Association (FROA).[325] The developers and the FROA waged a vigilant attack on the Guidelines, claiming that their interests were not adequately covered by the Guidelines.[326]

Even though the Forests Minister had earlier stated that the Guidelines were there to stay,[327] the government bowed to these pressures and deferred the implementation of the Guidelines for a month. Eventually, the revenue system was suspended indefinitely, while the whole Guidelines were brought into operation in April 1994. A new revenue system was introduced through the budget in 1996. Under the new revenue system, there were to be no stumpage charges on all logs harvested, landowners were to receive a substantially higher royalty payment, and landowners were to be entitled to a project development levy.[328] By not introducing the new revenue system earlier, the government and the resource owners suffered greatly, with revenue losses of about K200 million within the four years from 1992-1995.[329]

4.4 DEVELOPMENT OF FORESTRY RESOURCES

The forestry resources in PNG are utilised in three ways. These methods are the Forest Management Agreement (FMA) process, the timber authority process, and the timber licence process. Each method has its own distinctive attributes. This section of the chapter examines these forest utilisation methods, with the objective of ascertaining the degree of participation by the parties involved in these processes, and the benefits derived by these players.

4.4.1 Registered forestry industry participants

Before a person can participate in the forestry sector, he or she has to be registered with the PNG Forest Authority. Section 105 of the *Forestry Act* states that a person shall not engage in any activity under the Act unless that person is registered as a forest industry participant or a consultant. A registered forest industry participant or a consultant may be a natural person or a corporation. A person who carries out an activity under the Act without being registered is liable to a fine of up to K100,000.

A person who intends to engage in the forestry industry has to apply to the Managing Director for registration as a forest industry participant. The application must be in the prescribed form, specify the particulars of the applicant, state the kind of work to be undertaken and be accompanied by the prescribed fee. Where the applicant is a corporation, it has to be registered under the *Companies Act*. The *Forestry Act* does not distinguish between a national and a foreign company. If the applicant is a foreign company which is registered under the *Companies Act*, the applicant has to take into account the requirements imposed on foreign companies by the *Investment Promotion Act* 1992.[330] A breach of the *Investment Promotion Act* can result in prosecution and hefty fines, as realised by a logging company.[331]

---

325 The PNG Forest Resources Association was formed in 1992 to represent the customary owners and the landowner companies engaged in the forestry industry.

326 See *Post Courier* (20 July 1993; 20 January 1994; 18 February 1994; and 3 March, 1994).

327 *The National* (7 February 1994).

328 Filer and Sekhran, op cit n 54, p 209.

329 Ibid.

330 The *Investment Promotion Act* (IPA) was enacted in 1992 to replace the *National Investment and Development Act* (NIDA), which was regarded by many in the private and government sectors as very cumbersome and an impediment to economic development. NIDA was aimed at controlling foreign investment in PNG. It restricted foreign investment to only certain activities. The IPA's main thrust is to encourage greater investment and faster economic growth. However, it still maintains restriction of foreign investment to certain enterprises.

331 The Malaysian logging company, Niugini Lumber Merchants Pty Ltd, was fined K30,000 by the National Court for breaching the *Investment Promotion Act* 1991: *Post Courier* (24 December 1993).

A registered forestry industry participant is defined under s 104 of the Act as:

(a) a person (whether natural or corporate) carrying out or intending to carry out any activity for which a timber permit, timber authority or licence is required under this Act; and

(b) any person (whether natural or corporate) engaging in, or intending to engage in, the forestry industry as a contractor, buyer or processor.

This section explicitly prohibits a registered forest consultant from engaging in activities that require a timber permit, timber authority, or as a contractor, buyer or processor.

After considering the application, the Managing Director is to refer the application, with any recommendation, to the Forest Board. The board can approve or reject the application. If the board approves the application, the board will direct the Managing Director to register the applicant as a registered forestry industry participant or a consultant.

Section 98 of the Act makes it mandatory for all registered consultants and registered forestry industry participants to deposit a "performance bond" at a bank nominated by the Managing Director before conducting an activity permitted by the Act. The performance bond is a security held by the government to ensure that the consultant or the registered forestry industry participant satisfies all the conditions of the licence, permit or timber authority. A forest consultant and a registered forestry industry participant can thereafter engage only in specific forest activities. These activities are categorised into three groups, namely those that require a licence, those requiring a timber authority and those requiring a timber permit.

4.4.2 The Forest Management Agreement process

The Forest Management Agreement (FMA) process is a very important tool established by the *Forestry Act* 1991, which enables the government to access forestry resources located on customary land. The process is set out in Div 4 of the Act (ss 54-60). For the government to exploit a forestry resource located on customary land, it is required under s 56 to acquire those rights to harvest, plant, grow and manage timber from customary resource owners. It must, through its agent, the National Forest Authority, enter into a Forest Management Agreement with the landowners. The FMA concept is the offspring of the TRP process introduced by the *Timber Ordinance (Consolidated)* 1909.

Before entering into a contract with the government, the resource owners are required to organise themselves into land groups recognised under the *Land Groups Incorporation Act.* The government then concludes an FMA with the customary owners. The agreement is usually a pro forma document with blank spaces that are to be completed by the landowners. Section 56(1) of the *Forestry Act* 1991 expressly stipulates that the FMA shall contain "such terms as are agreed between the customary owners and the Authority". It has been argued that the completion of the pro forma document by the customary owners without any formal negotiations is a violation of s 56(1).

After the conclusion of the FMA, the board or its agent proceeds to conduct a feasibility study into the forest area with the objective of developing the forestry resource. This requirement is in line with the National Forest Policy.[332] Under s 62(2) of the *Forestry Act* 1991, a feasibility study is not necessary for the harvesting of forest plantations, for salvage logging, or where the proposed annual allowable cut of a forest development project does not exceed $5000m^3$. This requirement enables the government to conduct a feasibility study of the project so that it becomes aware of the possible environmental and social impacts of the project.

When the feasibility study is completed, the Provincial Forest Management Committee (PFMC) established under s 21 of the Act, in consultation with the customary owners and the provincial government concerned, is required to prepare draft project guidelines for the proposed forestry project. The draft project guidelines are submitted to the board, which must review them and then issue final guidelines for the project. This requirement is an innovative feature of the Act. It encourages the national government, the provincial governments, the developers, and customary owners to work together.

When the final guidelines of the project have been issued, the project is advertised pursuant to s 64, and expressions of interest are sought from registered forestry industry participants for the development of the forestry project. The advertisement must be published in PNG. However, the advertisement can also be published overseas. Only registered forestry industry participants may apply.

While the government is processing the expressions of interest, a registered forestry industry participant can apply to the Managing Director for permission to enter the project area and conduct feasibility studies, appraisals of the forest resources and other preparatory work relating to the project. The activities are restricted only to the conduct of feasibility studies, appraisals of the project and other preparatory work related to the project. A registered forestry industry participant may also make project proposals, which are to be lodged with the Managing Director.

Sections 66-72 of the *Forestry Act* 1991 provide a meticulous method of processing the developer's project proposals. It involves the Forest Authority through the board, the committee and the Minister. These authorities are required to cooperate in determining the development of the project. This is another innovative feature of the Act, which encourages the participation of all the parties involved in the development of the forestry resources. Its aim is to limit the use of discretionary powers by the Forests Minister, and ensures fair allocation of timber permits.

The Act allows the board to advertise a forest development project for tender. A registered forestry industry participant can respond to this advertisement by lodging its interest with the Managing Director within the time specified in the advertisement. A successful applicant must comply with s 66 of the Act, which requires that a registered forestry industry participant must lodge project proposals with the Managing Director.

Where the board accepts the project proposals, the registered forestry industry participant proceeds to enter into negotiations with the committee with the aim of concluding a project agreement. The project agreement is then submitted to the board for consideration pursuant to s 71. After considering the project agreement, the board shall recommend to the Minister to grant

[332] *The National Forest Policy* (Ministry of Forests, Hohola, 1991), p 16.

a timber permit to the registered forestry industry participant. The Minister may then issue a timber permit to the registered forestry industry participant.

The attributes of a timber permit are that it must:

(a) specify the description of the project area;

(b) specify the amount of the allowable cut;

(c) specify the rate of royalties, levies and charges to be paid;

(d) make provisions for the construction and/or use of roads, bridges and other infrastructural requirements;

(e) state the amount of performance bond; and

(f) state any other conditions consistent with the project.

The procedure for the application of a timber permit is complex and takes time. As noted above, this process is scrutinised by both the committee and the board before it reaches the Minister who issues the timber permit. This mechanism reduces the opportunity for bias and corrupt dealings, because under the old *Forestry Act* the Minister had a lot more discretion and was able to deal directly with the applicant for a timber permit. The Act encouraged the potential for ministerial bias. This was clearly illustrated in *Tonolei Development Corporation v Lucas Waka – Minister for Forests*[333] and *Mcdui Development v Genia.*[334]

The term of a timber permit is ten years. However, where the forest development project is large, the term may exceed ten years. A timber permit exceeding ten years must contain provisions for review by the board after the expiration of the first ten years and on the expiration of every successive five-year period. A timber permit may be renewed or extended.

Before proceeding with a forest development project, the permit holder must lodge with the board a project statement, a five-year working plan and an annual logging plan. When the board has approved these documents, the developer can proceed with the project. The project statement must also contain a follow-up land use plan. A new five-year working plan must be submitted to the board three months prior to the expiry of each five-year period. The annual logging plan must be lodged with the board one month prior to the end of each year, and must be based on the methods and procedures specified in the current five-year working plan. A developer whose annual logging plan conforms to the methods and procedures described in the five-year working plan, is issued with a certificate by the National Forest Service to that effect.

The developer is also mandated, under s 120(6) of the *Forestry Act* 1991, to lodge monthly statements about the operation with the Managing Director. During the course of logging, the developer is required to identify all logged areas, and to measure and brand logs according to the specifications given by the Managing Director.[335] Forest inspectors randomly check the logged timbers to ensure that the loggers do not falsify the documents. A classic example of falsifying such information was revealed in the case of *The State v Asaoka Kouji of Rabaul.*[336] The exercise is to ensure that all royalties, charges and other fees payable to the customary owners are proportionate to the volume and quantity of the timber felled.

---

333 *Tonolei Development Corp v Lucas Waka – Minister for Forests* (unreported, N404L, 1982).
334 *Mcdui Development v Genia* [1992] PNGLR 50.
335 *Forestry Act* 1991, s 103, Timber authority holders are also bound by this section.
336 *The State v Asaoka Kouji of Rabaul* [1976] PNGLR 292.

4.4.3 The timber authority process

The timber authority process dates back to 1892. It was first introduced in a rather rudimentary fashion under the *Indigenous Timber Ordinance*. The scope of a timber authority is less than that of a timber permit, but greater than that of a licence. The timber authority process has taken on different names, but its objective has remained intact. Pratt J, in *Rainbow Holdings v Central Province Forest Industries Pty Ltd,*[337] declared the aim of the timber authority as:

> "to protect customary owners being exploited. The Timber Authorities provide that the customary owners can only sell their logs to non-natives on terms and conditions which the Government considers fair".

Under the *Forestry Regulations*, which were made pursuant to the former forestry legislation, any person, with the authority of a forestry inspector, could purchase forest produce from a customary owner for his or her domestic use.[338] The timber authority was only issued to applicants who intended to purchase barks, gums, rattans, nipa and other species of palm, bamboo, nuts, plants, flowers, leaves, roots, ferns, timber for firewood, posts, rails, mine laths, or any other timber for which a royalty of an amount not exceeding K20 was payable. The timber authority process continued to apply in PNG after independence in 1975.

The timber authority concept has been entrenched in the *Forestry Act* 1991. Its scope and application has been broadened by the legislation. The Act has delegated the task of administering the timber authority process to the provincial government through the Provincial Forest Management Committee (PFMC).

The PFMC consists of six members who represent the provincial government, the National Forest Service, the local or community governments, the customary owners and the non-government organisations. The functions of the committee are spelt out in s 30. These include:

(a) to provide a forum for consultation and co-ordination on forest management between national and provincial governments, forest resource owners and special interest groups;

(b) to undertake continuous consultation with the provincial Minister responsible for forestry matters on matters relating to acquisition and allocation of forest resources;

(c) to assist the provincial government in preparing forest plans and forest development programs, consistent with national and provincial programs; and

(d) to make recommendations to the provincial Minister on the issue of timber authorities.[339]

Functions (a), (b) and (c) are restricted only to a consultation process, while function (d) is directed at advising.

Section 49 of the *Forestry Act* requires provincial governments, in consultation with the committee members, to draw up provincial forest plans, which must conform to the National Forestry Development Guidelines. They must also contain Provincial Forestry Development Guidelines and a five-year rolling forest development program. This provision gives the

---

337 *Rainbow Holdings v Central Province Forest Industries Pty Ltd* [1983] PNGLR 34 at 36.

338 *Forestry Regulations*, regs 16-18.

339 *Forestry Act* 1991, s 30(1).

provincial governments an opportunity to effectively participate in the development of their forestry resources. The PFMC is required to assist in the early identification and resolution of disputes involving customary owners in a forestry resources project area. The PFMC is further required to ensure that the environment within, and in the vicinity of, the forestry project is protected.

A vital role of the committee is to make recommendations to the provincial Forests Minister on the issue, extension, renewal, transfer, amendment and surrender of timber authorities. The procedure for applying for a timber authority is similar to that of the licence. The distinction between the timber authority procedure and the licence process is that only a registered forestry industry participant can apply for a timber authority, and the application is considered by the committee (with the consent of the board) and approved by the provincial Forests Minister.

Section 88 of the *Forestry Act* clearly suggests that before an application for a timber authority is lodged with the Managing Director, the applicant must be able to produce documentation concerning the ownership of the forest, the subject of the application and the consent of the customary owners. The implication here is that timber authorities are only issued for activities as specified in s 87 of the Act where the land involved is customary land. This section is defective, because it allows customary owners and a registered forestry industry participant to conclude their own contract without the national and provincial government's participation. The provincial government, through the PFMC, is only engaged during the screening process. Section 88 of the *Forestry Act* leaves a lot of room for corrupt practices – the very problem that the government is aspiring to eradicate in the forestry industry.

Section 88 of the *Forestry Act* is a compromise provision. It compromises the practice of declaring Local Forest Areas under the *Forestry (Private Dealings) Act* and the timber authority concept in the old *Forestry Regulations.* It is composed of certain Local Forest Area and timber authority attributes. This proposition finds support in the statement of Sir Julius Chan to Parliament in July 1991. When supporting the Forestry Bill, he said:

> "I think the present Minister and the previous Minister looked at the *Forestry Act, Private Dealings Act* and have come up with a good comparison. One aspect of the Bill which I like is that it incorporates the *Private Dealings Act.* I am the father of the *Private Dealings Act.*"[340]

The current timber authority is a vain attempt by the government to rectify the unscrupulous nature of the Local Forest Area and the timber authority under the former forestry statutes. The current timber authority has two conflicting objectives. On the one hand, it tries to expand the scope of the former timber authority so as to accommodate the Local Forest Area. On the other hand, it attempts to eliminate the problems encountered by the same two processes. In either way, the timber authority process will not achieve its purpose. It is my view that the Act only creates a bigger problem than was anticipated.

The provincial Forests Minister issues timber authorities to registered forest industry participants in the following cases:

(a) where:

  (i) the amount of timber to be harvested annually does not exceed 5000m^3 and

[340] *Hansard*, 16 July 1991.

(ii) the timber to be harvested is for domestic processing only; or

(b) for purposes of:

(i) the removal of trees on areas designated for agriculture or other land use by the relevant authorities where the … [is] less than 50 hectares; or

(ii) the removal of trees on areas designated for a road by the relevant authorities where the road line would not exceed 12.5 kilometres outside the area covered by the Forest Management area; or

(c) for the purposes of harvesting of other forest produce to an amount specified in the timber authority.[341]

This section has expanded the scope of the timber authority to cover a wide range of activities over large areas of land. The timber authority authorises the holder to carry out operations specified therein. Section 87(4) of the *Forestry Act* prevents the transfer of the timber authority. Unlike the applicants for a timber permit, the applicants for a timber authority do not need to conduct a feasibility study of the proposed project. They do not need to adhere to any guidelines relating to the project or any other obligations imposed by ss 61-65 inclusive.[342]

4.4.4 The licence process

The third method of forest utilisation is through the licence process. A registered forestry industry participant or a consultant can apply for a licence under the *Forestry Act*. The application must be submitted in the prescribed form to the Managing Director. It must contain particulars of the applicant, specify the proposed activity, and be accompanied by the prescribed fee.

The proposed activities are restricted to those specified in s 91(1). These are:

(a) harvesting of timber;

(b) transport of timber;

(c) sale or purchase of timber;

(d) marketing of timber;

(e) processing of timber;

(f) grading of timber; and

(g) other activities (other than those which require a timber authority or timber permit) which, in the opinion of the board, require a licence relating to forest produce.

A registered consultant also requires a licence to engage in consultancy work. The term of a licence must not exceed 12 months and is renewable. Only the Minister can grant an extension of the licence.[343] The term of extension must not exceed 12 months. A licence cannot be transferred or amended.

---

341 *Forestry Act* 1991, s 87(1) as amended by the *Forestry (Amendment No 2) Act* No 27 of 1996.

342 Ibid. The obligations under ss 61-65 are mandatory, and have to be satisfied by an applicant of a timber permit before a forest development project can commence.

343 *Forestry Act* 1991, s 95. Where a condition of the licence has been breached, the licence will not be extended.

4.5 PROVINCIAL AND LOCAL-LEVEL GOVERNMENTS AND FORESTRY

The Constitutional Planning Committee envisaged that the provincial governments should co-ordinate all government activities and act as agents of the national government in the execution of national government policies and laws.[344] The *Organic Law on Provincial Governments* (*Organic Law*) set the stage for participatory government at the provincial level. The *Organic Law* became the vehicle for partnership between the national and provincial governments and a channel for the empowerment of the people.

The *Organic Law* empowered the provincial legislatures to enact laws for certain primarily "provincial" subjects and "concurrent" subjects of legislative activity. There were nine subjects, set out in s 24, which were primarily provincial subjects. These were:

(a) the control by licensing of mobile traders (other than mobile banks);

(b) primary schools (including community schools and village self-help schools) and primary education other than curriculum;

(c) the sale and distribution of alcoholic liquor;

(d) the control by licensing of public entertainments and of places of public entertainment;

(e) housing (other than housing owned, or to be owned, by the state);

(f) libraries, museums, cultural centres and Cultural Councils (but does not apply to libraries, museums, cultural centres and Cultural Councils established and conducted, or to be established or conducted, by the state);

(g) sporting activities;

(h) to the extent provided for by s 39, Village Courts; and

(i) subject to s 1871 (local and village governments) of the *Constitution*, local, community and village governments and other local-level governments.

The exercise of these powers, however, did not extend to the imposition of taxation, except as specified in the *Organic Law*. Provincial governments could also pass legislation regarding subjects that were deemed "concurrent". In this arena, provincial governments and the national government could enact laws on the same subject, the only condition being that the provincial legislation was not inconsistent with an Act of the Parliament on the same subject. Thus, provincial government could pass laws on such things[345] as agriculture and livestock, fishing and fisheries, forestry, wildlife protection, parks and reserves, town planning and health. Provincial governments and the national government were required, by s 85 of the *Organic Law*, to consult each other in relation to major project developments affecting a province.

In pursuance of their powers under s 27 of the *Organic Law*, two provincial governments, namely Manus and East New Britain, enacted their own provincial forestry legislation. In 1989, the Manus Provincial Government enacted the *Manus Provincial Forest Management Act* 1988-1989. This provincial Act was designed to supplement the national forest legislation, and was aimed at protecting the province's forests. The provincial Act set a maximum volume of timber to

---

[344] Goldring, *The Constitution of Papua New Guinea* (Law Book Co Ltd, Sydney, 1978), pp 73 and 153.

[345] The list was provided in s 27 of the *Organic Law on Provincial Governments* and covered 24 subjects.

be harvested annually in the province by logging operators. In 1989, a logging operator in the province was successfully prosecuted by the provincial government for breaches of the provincial Act: *Jaha Development Corporation Pty Ltd v Ilagi, Secretary for Department of Manus* (unreported, Ap No 242 of 1989, 1990). However, the defendant appealed to the Supreme Court against its conviction. Before the Supreme Court could deliver its judgment, a member of the bench died. The appellant argued that its case should be reopened because, firstly, a member of the bench who was hearing the appeal had died, so a new panel had to be established, and secondly, because of the Supreme Court decision in *Supreme Court Reference No 7 of 1992.* Thus, in *Jaha Development Corporation v Ilagi,*[346] the Supreme Court ruled that a new Supreme Court panel should be established to consider the appeal.

In 1992, the East New Britain Provincial Government enacted the *Forestry Operations Control Act* 1992. This provincial Act required a timber permit holder under the *Forestry Act* 1991 to submit a Forestry Operations Development Plan to the provincial executive for its approval.[347] In the same year, the East New Britain Provincial Government, in *Supreme Court Reference No 7 of 1992; Re Forestry Act 1991,*[348] sought the Supreme Court's opinion under s 19(3)(eb) of the *Constitution* regarding the validity of the provincial forestry legislation.

The Supreme Court, after considering the arguments, held that the provincial Act was inconsistent with the *Forestry Act* 1991, because the *Forestry Act* was an exhaustive law in the field of national forestry control and development in PNG, and dealt with a matter of national interest. This decision essentially prohibits the provincial governments from enacting their own forestry legislation.

The arrangements discussed above under the *Organic Law on Provincial Government* were repealed and replaced by the *Organic Law on Provincial Governments and Local-Level Governments* (OLPGLLG) in 1995. The OLGLLG was introduced as a vehicle to speed up the delivery of goods and services to the rural areas.

In respect of the mobilisation of natural resources, the OLPGLLG provides a number of inroads that were non-existent under the old *Organic Law*. However, these provisions are also complex and, in most cases, contradictory. The relevant provisions of the law are ss 42, 44, 98, 115 and 116.

The first two provisions relate to the legislative powers of the provincial and local-level governments respectively. Provincial governments are expressly empowered to enact legislation on forestry and agro-forestry. At first glance, one would be led to think that this provision is very generous, given the Supreme Court's decision in *Supreme Court Reference No 7 of 1992.* However, the court's decision is reaffirmed by s 41(2), which provides that on matters of "national interest" an Act of Parliament overrides a provincial law on the same subject. It is therefore clear that, on account of s 41(2) and *Supreme Court Reference No 7 of 1992*, provincial governments have no legislative powers over forestry matters.

---

346 *Jaha Development Corp v Ilagi* [1995] PNGLR 76.

347 *Forestry Operations Control Act* 1992, s 3(1).

348 *Supreme Court Reference No 7 of 1992; Re Forestry Act 1991* [1992] PNGLR 514.

However, it may be argued that given that there are no national laws on small-scale logging or walkabout sawmilling, the provincial governments may exercise their forestry powers to regulate these forestry activities.

As for the local-level governments, their legislative powers are enumerated under s 44 of the OLPGLLG. This provision empowers local-level governments to legislate on two matters that have a bearing on forestry matters. First, they can make their own laws on the local environment and the flora and fauna, and secondly, they can legislate on sacred sites. In the pursuit of development of forestry resources, national and provincial governments and loggers have to be mindful of these local laws. However, where there is a dispute as to inconsistency of laws on the same subject, a provincial or a national law will prevail over the local laws.

Participation of provincial and local-level governments in the development of natural resources, including forestry, in the provinces, is guaranteed by s 115 of the OLPGLLG. This provision makes it mandatory for provincial and local-level governments to be consulted by the national government and developers before any natural resources development projects can commence within their locality. Unfortunately, s 115 is circumvented by s 116, which states that s 115 cannot be implemented unless and until an Act specifying the manner of participation is enacted. At the time of writing, and after five years of operation, s 116 has not yet been implemented.

The final provision, s 98 of the OLPGLLG, elevates the current practices in the forestry and mining and petroleum sectors to a constitutional level. This provision makes it a duty for a developer of a natural resource within a province to pay project development levies, for the use of the provincial and local-level governments, into a trust account. The compulsory levies are the infrastructural development levy, the economic and land use development levy, the community and social development levy, and other levies as agreed to by the parties.

The concept of project development levies is not new in Papua New Guinea. It is found throughout the natural resources sector under various heads of agreements. In the forestry sector, these levies are usually stipulated in the logging and marketing agreements that are concluded between the developer and the landowners through their landowner companies.[349]

The application of the provisions is temporarily frozen by s 98(6), which stipulates that "an Act of the Parliament shall make provisions for the rates, management, sharing arrangement, and application of the development levies". As there is no such legislation in place, s 98 cannot be implemented yet.

In the final analysis, it is instructive to note that the spirit and intent of the *Forestry Act* and the OLPGLLG on participation is in unison. Both laws encourage and promote openness and transparency of the decision-making process at the local level. It is unfortunate that, at this stage, the relevant instruments to fully implement the provisions of the OLPGLLG are not yet in place. When such legislation is enacted, the interests of customary owners will be constitutionally entrenched.

---

[349] *A Blueprint for Sustainable use of PNG's Forests: Definitions and Indicators of Progress* (CSIRO, Canberra, 1992), p 1; Leedom, "Private Dealings: A Social History of The Hawaiian Local Forest Area, East Sepik Province" in Filer (ed), op cit n 7, pp 34-66.

4.6 CONCLUSION

Forestry plays an important role in the lives of the people of PNG in two ways. First, it is a source of food and materials for the people of rural PNG. Secondly, it is a major contributor to the economy. Forest products rank third in the economy, after minerals and agriculture.[350] The forest is also home to most of the flora and fauna species found in PNG.[351]

Most of the forestry resources of PNG are owned by customary landowners, who also own the land.[352] The forests, like the land, are the very heart of PNG's traditional society. This truth has been unfettered since the dawn of colonialism in PNG.[353] The involvement of the customary landowners in the development of their forestry resources is crucial to the success of a forestry development project.

However, since the first European settlement of PNG in 1884, the forests have been exploited for economic purposes. The non-economic values of the forests have usually taken the back stage. This is probably the saddest part of PNG's forestry history.

The most lethal tool for forestry resource developers has been the TRP process, which was introduced in 1909 under the *Timber Ordinance (Consolidated)*. The TRP process was both anti-environment and anti-customary owners. Through the TRP process, the colonial administration, and later the independent government, utilised large areas of forests. It was initially introduced as a vehicle for forest resources and land exploitation. In the early 1970s, the emphasis of the TRP process was shifted to being a device for enhancing the living standards of the customary owners of the forestry resources.

At the height of the Barnett Inquiry, it was common knowledge that the TRP process, and the other forestry resource utilisation mechanisms under the *Forestry (Private Dealings) Act*, had caused more harm than benefit to the customary owners of the forests and their environment.

The forestry industry reforms introduced by the government with the enactment of the new forestry legislation, the introduction of a comprehensive forestry policy and guidelines in 1991 and 1993, are encouraging. However, there are two main problems with the *Forestry Act* 1991. First, the new forest rights acquisition model, the FMA, is not a new concept. With the exception of its forest management attribute, it still retains many of the characteristics of its predecessor, the TRP process. The FMA is intended to promote the sustainable development of the forestry resources.[354] However, it lacks the necessary framework to attain this objective. This is particularly true of the issue of future rights over forest plantations and land-use rights over forest plantation lands. There is still confusion in this area of the legislation.

The other problem with the *Forestry Act* 1991 is with the timber authority process. It has been shown that the timber authority process is a compromise proviso. It is an offspring of the Local Forest Area process under the former *Forestry (Private Dealings) Act* and the timber authority process under the *Forestry Regulations* made pursuant to the *Forestry Act* 1974. Like the TRP,

---

350 Sem, *Environmental Management in Papua New Guinea* (East-West Centre, Hawaii, 1983), p 1.

351 Carson, op cit n 20, p 2.

352 Unlike other resources, such as gold, copper, silver and petroleum, which were declared as Crown property and are now owned by the state, forestry resources have always remained the property of the customary owners.

353 *The Barnett Report: A Summary of the Commission of Inquiry into Aspects of the Timber Industry in Papua New Guinea* (Asia Pacific Action Group, Hobart, 1990), pp 18-19.

354 The Forest Management Agreement encourages the wise management of forest resource use, and encourages the use of forestry plantations.

these two processes were applied to the detriment of the customary landowners and with disregard of the environment.

These two shortfalls reflect the attitude of the government, which is keen on reforms but is too weak to try out new and progressive ideas. The government's lack of foresight not only encourages the continuation of the former devious forestry practices, but also sanctions them under new legislation.

The forestry policy and law are continuously being carved in the hope that the best picture will be revealed through a vibrant and forward-looking policy and law. In the light of these reviews, if the existing difficulties identified in this chapter are also considered and acted upon positively, we may see a better picture.

It is obvious that all the necessary policies and legislation are in place to attain sustainable forestry development in PNG. What is required is a more concerted effort by the government to implement these policies and legislation, instead of paying lip service to them. This is especially true for the OLPGLLG. The relevant provisions of this law need to be supplemented by the necessary legislation to encourage and promote transparency in the forestry sector.

REFERENCES

Aleck and Rannells (ed), *Custom at the Crossroads* (Law Faculty Publication Unit, Port Moresby, 1995).

Asia Pacific Action Group, *The Barnett Report: A Summary of the Commission of Inquiry into Aspects of the Forestry Industry in Papua New Guinea* (Asia Pacific Action Group, Hobart, 1990).

Barnett, *Report of the Commission of Inquiry Into Aspects of the Forestry Industry* (7 Interim Reports and Final Report) (Commission of Inquiry, Port Moresby, 1989).

Brown (ed), *Fashion of Law in Papua New Guinea* (Butterworths, Sydney, 1969).

Brunton, *Critique of the World Bank's Tropical Forestry Action Plan Review for Papua New Guinea* (Working Paper No 26, PNG Law Reform Commission, Port Moresby, 1990).

Carson, *Forestry and Forestry Policy in Papua New Guinea* (Department of Forestry, Port Moresby, 1974).

CSIRO, *A Blueprint for Sustainable use of PNG's Forests: Definitions and Indicators of Progress* (CSIRO, Canberra, 1992).

Department of Environmental Science – UPNG, *Stretim Nau Bilong Tumora: National Sustainable Development Strategy & 20th Waigani Seminar Recommendations* (Department of Environmental Science – UPNG, Port Moresby, 1993).

Department of Forests, *Facts and Figures* (Department of Forests, Port Moresby, 1980).

Department of Territories, *Forestry: Papua New Guinea* (Department of Territories, Canberra, 1961).

Dubash and Filer, "Papua New Guinea" in Seymour and Dubash (ed), *The Right Conditions: The World Bank, Structural Adjustment, and Forest Policy Reform* (World Resource Institute, Washington DC, 2000).

Filer (ed), *The Political Economy of Forest Management in Papua New Guinea* (Monograph 32, National Research Institute and International Institute for Environment and Development, Port Moresby, 1997).

Filer and Sekhran, *Loggers, Donors and Resource Owners* (International Institute for Environment and Development, London, 1998).

Filer, Dubash and Kalit, *The Thin Green Line: World Bank Leverage and Forest Policy Reform in Papua New Guinea* (Monograph 37, National Research Institute & Australian National University, Canberra, 2000).

Ghai and Redan, *The Politics and Administration of Decentralisation in Papua New Guinea* (Monograph 30, National Research Institute, Port Moresby, 1992).

Gladman, Mowbray and Duguman (ed), *From Rai to Rio: Environment and Development in Papua New Guinea* (Vol 3, UPNG Press, Port Moresby, 1996).

Goldring, *The Constitution of Papua New Guinea* (Law Book Co Ltd, Sydney, 1978).

Haynes, "Succession to Land in Papua New Guinea" (Paper presented at the Australian Universities Law Schools Association Conference, Macquarie University, Sydney, 1981).

James, *Land Law and Policy in Papua New Guinea* (Monograph No 5, PNG Law Reform Commission, Port Moresby, 1985).

Kube, *Tropical Lowland Rainforests: Some Possibilities for their Utilisation with Particular Reference to Guinea and with Special Emphasis on Agriculture* (Papua New Guinea Environmental Series No 2, Wau Ecology Institute, Wau, 1990).

Lane-Poole, *A Report of the Goldfields of New Guinea: Together with Recommendations regarding a Forest Policy for the Whole of the Territory* (RNB Agriculture Series (SI), Sydney, 1935).

Melanesian Institute for Pastoral and Socio-Economic Services, *Catalyst: Development and the Environment in PNG* (Special Issue: The Steinberg Report) (Melanesian Institute for Pastoral and Socio-Economic Services, Goroka, 1990).

Ministry of Forests, *National Forest Policy* (Ministry of Forests, Port Moresby, 1991).

Morauta, Pernatta and Heaney (ed), *Traditional Conservation in Papua New Guinea: Implications For Today* (Monograph No 16, IASER, Port Moresby, 1980).

Mossop, "Taming the Robber Barons? The Reform of Forestry Legislation in Papua New Guinea" (1992) 8 QUTLJ 113.

Nadarajah, "Now What? Proposed Forestry Guidelines for Papua New Guinea" (1993) 2 *Pacific Economic Bulletin* 53.

Nadarajah, *The Sustainability of Papua New Guinea's Forest Resource* (Discussion Paper No 76, National Research Institute, Port Moresby, 1994).

Neville, *National Forestry Development Guidelines* (Department of Forests, Port Moresby, 1993).

PNG Law Reform Commission, *New Directions in Resource Management For Papua New Guinea* (Occasional Paper No 20, Law Reform Commission, Port Moresby, 1990).

Sem, *Environmental Management in Papua New Guinea* (East-West Centre, Hawaii, 1983).

Shepherd and Richter (ed), *Forestry in National Development: Production Systems, Conservation, Foreign Trade and Aid* (Australian National University, Canberra, 1979).

Tak, *Evaluation of Achievements 1976-1987* (Discussion Paper No 35, Institute of National Affairs, Port Moresby, 1988).

The Encyclopedia of Papua New Guinea (ANU Press, Canberra, 1983).

The Papua New Guinea University of Technology, *Proceedings of the Huon Seminar '94: Workshop on Forestry Management* (The Papua New Guinea University of Technology, Lae, 1995).

Thompson, *The Forest of Papua New Guinea: The Dilemma of Development* (Murdoch University, Perth, 1992).

CHAPTER 5

FISHERIES RESOURCE DEVELOPMENT AND MANAGEMENT IN PAPUA NEW GUINEA: LAW, BIOLOGY AND ECONOMICS

Billy Manoka and Ursula Kolkolo***

5.1 INTRODUCTION

The fishing industry in Papua New Guinea (PNG) remains highly undeveloped, despite the fact that the country is endowed with extensive fishing grounds. These fishing grounds are characterised by PNG's islands and the large extent of ocean within its 200-mile exclusive economic zone (EEZ). The island chains form inshore lagoon systems, fringing and barrier reefs, shallow banks and, in the Bismarck Sea, the volcanic arch from which the islands have been formed, deep submarine vents of lava flows support abyssal micro-organic life forms. Estimates of the coastal habitats include 46,000 square kms of estuaries, bays, lagoons and coral reefs, of which estuaries are about 6,000 square kms, and the balance is reef, bays and lagoons. The total area within the 200-mile exclusive economic zone is 2.4 million square kms, which are the fisheries waters of PNG (see Figure 1 below).

This chapter analyses the effect of the *Fisheries Management Act* 1998 on the sustainable development of the fisheries resource from the legal, biological and economic perspectives. This legislation caters for only the management of commercial and industrial fisheries. Subsistence and artisanal fisheries, involving the majority of Papua New Guineans, remain largely unregulated, unmanaged and unsupported. While this chapter focuses on the management issues of the resource since the inception of the first *Fisheries Act* in 1984, it also provides a brief historical overview of the fisheries resource, including a discussion of the problems that have plagued the industry. It also briefly summarises the enforcement and monitoring mechanisms provided under the legislation.

---

* Billy Manoka (PhD, Resource and Environmental Economics), Economics Strand, School of Law and Business Studies, UPNG.

** Ursula Kolkolo (MAQ, Aquaculture), Biology Strand, School of Natural and Physical Sciences, UPNG.

FIGURE 1: FISHERIES WATERS OF PAPUA NEW GUINEA

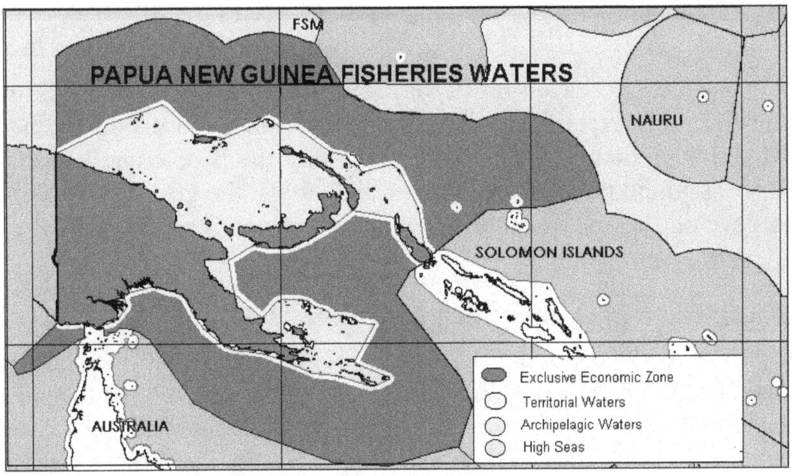

Overview of the fisheries sector

In Papua New Guinea, fishing has always been both a hunter-gatherer activity to supplement traditional diet, as well as a trading tool in traditional Melanesian barter systems. In inland areas, villagers fished for freshwater eels, freshwater molluscs and macrobrachium prawns. In the coastal areas, estuarine catfish, barramundi, mud-crabs, prawns, shellfish and mullet were the main food fishes. In coral reef systems, various reef food fishes, molluscs, octopuses and squids were regular food items. In deeper waters, deep-bottom hand-lining developed, and fishing for deepwater snappers and carangids is commonly practised. Coastal pelagics, like rainbow runner, Spanish mackerel and tuna, are trawled for and caught in special fish traps designed for such fish. Fishing to eat and trade is a tradition.

The focus of these traditional practices changed with the inception of the cash-based economy. The traditional barter system changed, in that now money is exchanged rather than other goods. Artisanal fishing developed rapidly as the economy changed to rely on money as the source of buying power, domestically and internationally.[355] Artisanal fishing by both genders is one of the sources of rural income. Conservative estimates in the mid-1990s placed the production from this sector at about 30,000 tonnes annually, generating overall incomes of well over K1,000,000. This sector is unrecorded and unmonitored by the National Fisheries Authority (NFA). The main reason for the lack of licensing and monitoring is that enforcement costs are very high. As well as that, the land tenure systems in PNG are such that traditional communities declare ownership and rights to utilise what they see as their natural resources. The general perception was that management authorities had no right to charge villagers fees for management costs, thus they were free to fish and earn an income from their own resources.

Irrespective of this and other traditional perceptions, government policies during the 1960s and 1970s were geared towards fulfilling the government's role as a provider of goods and services. Thus, the government established coastal fisheries stations throughout the country to fulfil its obligations. These facilities were constructed, refrigerated units were established and fish

[355] While the medium of exchange is now money, artisanal fishing is sustained because of the requirement to meet needs. Once needs, such as school fees, bride-price payments or feasts, are met, the utility curve stops, and fishing is suspended until a future need arises.

collector vessels were bought. These stations were in various parts of the country to provide both market outlets for, and transportation of, fish.

The Fisheries Department envisioned that these facilities would develop into viable fishing businesses to be owned and managed by Papua New Guineans. This vision did not materialise. The lessons learnt from this experience in the 1970s and 1980s led the government to introduce new policies and activities that were aimed at mobilising the people and harnessing the sector. One of the main shifts in the policies was that, in the 1990s, the government began to allow the private sector to develop the fisheries sector, while the government acted as the facilitator and regulator of the sector.

The government has also embarked on a number of initiatives to target specific areas of the fisheries sector. The recently enacted *Fisheries Management Act* 1998 empowers the NFA to facilitate industrial and commercial development of traditional commercial fisheries (tuna, prawn, lobster, trochus, beche-de-mer (sea cucumbers), pearl shells and reef associated fisheries) and to pursue the development of new fisheries. Industrial tuna fishery is another example. The national government policy to domesticate the industry did not succeed in the last 20 years. However, the *Fisheries Management Act* 1998 and the National Tuna Management Plan have provided the legal framework to achieve this aim.

5.2 Fisheries Resources of Papua New Guinea

PNG's coastal deltaic mangrove forests and sea-grass beds are important as nursery and breeding grounds for a wide variety of reef and pelagic fish, prawns and crabs. The estuaries support a wide range of artisanal fisheries for barramundi (*Lates calcarifer*), threadfin salmon (*Polydatcylus sheridani*), mullet (*Lisa spp*), mud crabs (*Scylla serrata*), penaeid prawns (*Penaeus merguiensis, Peneaus monodon*) and a range of molluscs. Coral reefs dominate in various coastal areas and island archipelagos. Milne Bay Province has 1.3 million ha of reef, which is 32 percent of the total reef area of the country. The Warrior reefs of Western Province have one million ha (26 percent of the total reef area), and Oro Province has 517,000 ha (13 percent of the total reef area).

The oceanographic features of the Bismarck Sea and northern PNG are shaped by the nature of the geology of the area. The Pacific and Australian plates meet on southern New Britain, forming upwellings and terrestrial sediment transport systems within the Vitiaz basin, which drains into the Bismarck Sea. The Bismarck Sea, at 2000 metres in its greatest depths, is the major oceanic system supporting the industrial tuna fishery for skipjack (*Katsuwonus pelamis*), yellowfin (*Thunnus albacares*) and bigeye tuna (*Thunnus obesus*).

PNG's extensive and diverse habitat supports a wide range of tropical coastal fishery resource bases, generated by its productive declared fisheries zone (DFZ) over 2.4 million square kms (see Figure 1 above). These resources support a number of fishing activities, including an industrial tuna fishery largely fished by distant water Korean, Philippine, Taiwanese and Vanuatu tuna purse-seiners, small domestic commercial longline vessels targeting yellowfin tuna, a domestic based Philippine company, operating purse-seiners that land skipjack and other pelagics for canning and exports, domestic tuna boats targeting yellowfin tuna and commercial boats targeting penaeid prawns (*Penaeus merguiensis, Penaeus monodon,* and *Metapenaeus ensis*). Coastal artisanal fisheries target estuarine stocks of mullet, threadfin salmon, mud crabs, prawns and various molluscs. In the islands, artisanal fishers fish for *lethrinids, lutjanids* and a wide variety of reef fish and deepwater snapper. They also troll for coastal near-shore pelagics, rainbow runner (*Elagatis bipinnulatus*), small tuna (*Euthynnus affinis*), Spanish mackerel (*Scomberomorus commersoni*), carangid species and belonidae. A wide variety of sedentary species supports artisanal fishing for trochus (*Trochus niloticus*), beche-de-mer (several *Holothuria* spp, *Actinopyga* spp, *Thelenoca* spp), pearl shell (black-lip *Pinctada margaritifera*), goldlip (*Pinctada maxima*) and green snail (*Turbo marmorata*).

5.2.1 The fishable resource bases

The fishable resource bases in the entire range of habitats are:

1. **Estuarine stocks:** This category is dominated by *Mugilidae* (mullet), *Polynemidae* (threadfin salmon), *Ariidae* (catfish), *Lobotidae* (triple tails), *Atherinidae* (silversides), *Sciaenidae* (jewfish and croakers), *Lutjanidae* (snapper), *Hemirhamphidae* (garfish) and *Centropomidae* (barramundi). Production potential is 11,000 tonnes per annum.

2. **Reef and lagoon fish:** These are abundant and diverse, and there are well over 2,000 different species. The shallow reef habitats support a diverse range of food fishes. *Lutjanidae* (snapper), *Mugilidae* (goatfish), *Siganidae* (rabbit fish), *Haemulidae* (sweetlip), *Scaridae* (parrot fish), *labridae* (wrasses), *Serranidae* (rock cod and groupers), *Holocentridae* (squirrelfish), *Acanthuridae* (surgeonfish), *Apogonidae* (cardinal fish) and *Pomacentridae* (damselfish) dominate the fish fauna. Potential yield is estimated at 80,000 tonnes.

3. **Sedentary marine resources:** These are important components of the subsistence and artisanal fisheries in PNG. These include shells (trochus, mother of pearl shell and green snail), sea cucumber (which has 23 different commercial species processed into beche-de-mer), six species of giant clam, a wide range of edible molluscs, ornamental shell species, precious corals and seaweed. The potential is estimated at 2,000 tonnes.

4. **Crustacea:** The important crustaceans of export value are penaied prawns and lobsters (*Panulirus ornatus*). Locally based prawn trawlers harvest prawns. Lobsters are caught by commercial local divers and processed by private companies operating freezer boats to process lobster tails. Mud crabs and other reef dwelling lobsters (*Penicillatus* spp) are caught for subsistence and artisanal fishers. The potential is 3,000 tonnes.

5. **Coastal pelagics:** This covers a wide range of reef-associated and oceanic stocks of rainbow runner, trevally and queenfish (*Carangidae*), dolphin fish (*Coryphaenidae*), longtoms (*Belonidae*), garfish (*Hemirhamphidae*), anchovies (*Engraulidae*), small tuna, skipjack, yellowfin, bigeye (*Scombridea*), Spanish mackerel (*Scombridae*), squids (*Loliginidae*) and cuttlefish (*Sepiidae*). The potential is around 58,000 tonnes.

6. **Coastal sharks, sawfish and rays:** The elasmobranhcs common in PNG's waters include tiger sharks, blacktip, whitetip, silvertip, bullsharks, speartooth sharks, silky sharks and whaler sharks (*Carcharinidae*), catsharks and epaulette sharks (*Hemiscyllidae*), weasal sharks (*Hemigaleidae*), hammerheads (*Sphyraenidae*), sawfish (*Pristidae*), rays (*Rhynchobatidae, Rhinidae, Dasyatididae, Gymnuridae, Rhynopteridae, Myliobatididae*) and guitar sharks (*Rhinobatidae*). The potential production is 6,000 tonnes.

7. **Offshore fishery resources:** Seven main species of tuna are found in PNG's waters. These are skipjack tuna, yellowfin tuna, bigeye tuna, albacore tuna (*Thunnus alalunga*), longtail tuna (*Thunnus tonggol*), small tuna (*Euthynnus affinis*) and frigate tuna (*Auxis thazard*). Of these, the most important commercial species are skipjack, yellowfin, albacore and bigeye tuna.

8. **Skipjack tuna:** Regional tuna tagging and ecological studies by the South Pacific Commission (SPC) tuna program over the last 30 years estimate annual resource potential to be between 200,000 to 600,000 tonnes as a sustainable harvest tonnage for the PNG EEZ. Current reported catches are about 200,000 tonnes, indicating room for growth.

9. **Yellowfin tuna:** Regional SPC studies indicate maximum sustainable yield levels at 300,000 tonnes per annum. Annual reported catches of yellowfin are about 70,000 tonnes.

10. **Albacore tuna:** This species has not received much population dynamic study, hence, the resource sustainable levels are poorly known. NFA reports of Albacore catches by tuna long-liners for the period 1990 to 1999 ranged from 1,149 tonnes to 99,000 tonnes.

11. **Bigeye tuna:** Like Albacore tuna, this species is also poorly known, but is taken in purse-seine surface fishing operations. Annual catches reported to the NFA ranged from 25 tonnes to 1,095 tonnes (1990-1999). The rest of the tunas (frigate, small tuna and longtail tuna) could yield up to 1,600 tonnes.

12. **Demersal stocks:** Deepwater (approximately 300 meters deep) stocks include families represented in inshore reef areas, and include *Lethirnidea, Lutjanidae, Serranidae* and other deepwater families like moray eels (*Moridiae*), whiptails, rattails and grenadiers (*Macrouiridae*) and deep-sea armourheads (*Pentacerotidae*). The potential resource estimate is 65,000 tonnes per annum.

13. **Sharks and billfish:** The other remaining offshore groups are the deep-sea sharks and billfish. The main shark species include tiger, white tip, mako, blue porbeagle and bronzewhaler sharks (*Carcharhinidae*). The main billfish are blue marlin, striped marlin, sailfish, spearfish (*Istiophoridae*) and swordfish (*Xiphiidae*). The estimated resource potential is 14,000 tonnes per annum.

14. **Deepwater shrimp:** The deeper waters of PNG harbour a range of deepwater shrimp and scampi. Potential production is 1,000 to 2,000 tonnes per annum.

15. **Freshwater resources:** The fish resources of inland waters are generally poor, due to the recent geological history of the country. The native species include macrobrachium prawns, freshwater eels (*Anguilla* spp), freshwater catfish (*Ariidae*), freshwater yabbies (*Cherax* spp) and introduced species (*Tilapia mossambica, Tilapia rendalli, Carpio carpio, Oncorhynchus mykiss, Tor putitora, Puntius gonionotus, Prochilodus margavii,* chocolate and golden mahseers).

While a number of resources have had research done into the dynamics of the stock, and potential estimates have been derived, the sustainable levels of most freshwater and marine fishery resources are unknown. Also, the wide range of artisanal and subsistence production of marine resources is poorly recorded and reported. Localised over-fishing in some stocks may have occurred. The tuna fisheries are an interesting case study of resource assessment. First, the stock is part of an overall western tropical pacific stock being fished by various other countries such as the Philippines, Indonesia, Palau, Tuvalu, the Federated States of Micronesia and the Solomon Islands. Tuna stock estimates have to be considered in light of those countries and international laws relating to straddling stocks. Within the fishery industry, various tuna species are caught by different gear. The interactions of surface gear (purse-seine) and deep-water gear (longline) for yellowfin is poorly known, hence estimates have to be treated with caution. Perhaps there is localised over-fishing in the inshore reef fisheries. Generally, the standing stock of most artisanal and commercial stocks for lobster, reef food fishes, trochus, beche-de-mer, pearl shell and barramundi has not been assessed in recent years. Using the 1995 figures, it is estimated that, overall, a figure of 680,000 tonnes of fish and crustacea resources are available for harvest from PNG's waters.

5.2.2 Fisheries production

Fish production, as recorded by the NFA from the artisanal, commercial and industrial sectors from 1997 to 1999, is shown in Table 1 below. The data in Table 2 provides actual production figures from each of the major resource groups that were monitored by the NFA in the same period. The subsistence sector is not monitored, however, an estimate of production is approximately 30,000 tonnes annually. This estimate was done in 1994, but the figure may have increased or decreased since that time.

TABLE 1: QUANTITY AND VALUE OF MARINE PRODUCTS FROM 1997-1999[356]

Year	Quantity (kg)	Total Value(US$)	Total Value (Kina)
1997	7,809,364.62	24,828,385.88	37,148,169.77
1998	38,989,006.34	64,610,172.18	136,754,997.70
1999	32,527,307.33	42,369,824.12	110,173,972.12
Total	**79,325,678.29**	**131,808,382.18**	**284,077,139.59**

The above figures clearly show that the fisheries sector contributes a significant amount of revenue to the various players in the sector. The quantity and value of fish production has risen significantly from 1997 to 1999.

[356] Source: National Fisheries Authority, *Annual Report* (1999).

TABLE 2: FISH AND MARINE PRODUCT EXPORTS 1999 FROM THE FORMAL SECTOR[357]

Product	Quantity (kg)	Total Value (US$)	Total Value (Kina)
Beche-de-mer (dried)	370,128.25	3,880,049.80	10,252,373.08
Crab (frozen)	1,456.00	6,556.34	15,907.77
Crab (live)	58.50	234.00	92.56
Fish (canned)	35,779.00	58,942.89	148,219.40
Fish (fresh chilled)	3,679.30	6,968.30	17,517.97
Fish (frozen)	33,460.00	209,148.08	579,107.70
Fish (live)	6,214.41	31,003.78	86,894.00
Fish (oil)	18,620.00	25,137.00	69,439.23
Lobster (frozen)	92,430.70	2,080,862.97	5,422,243.22
Shark (jaws)	52.00	421.71	1,245.45
Shark (fresh chilled)	72.50	65.81	176.90
Shark (frozen)	1,118,515.00	836,647.30	2,154,214.97
Sharkfin (frozen)	9,065.11	425,438.90	1,161,887.69
Shell (whole)	61,634.00	807,939.50	2,041,114.57
Shell (button)	224,198.00	980,671.39	2,479,570.59
Shell (meat)	24,094.00	837,447.00	2,144,559.30
Prawns (frozen)	8,126.00	113,865.75	287,948.08
Tuna (canned)	808,588.30	7,025,874.05	18,058,529.29
Tuna (meal)	5,587,333.56	10,552,200.08	27,270,924.99
Tuna (fresh)	260,000.00	122,393.32	318,303.15
Tuna (fresh chilled)	543,865.20	1,604,906.01	4,070,173.44
Tuna (frozen)	23,319,937.50	12,763,050.14	33,593,173.43
Total	**32,527,307.33**	**42,369,824.12**	**110,173,972.12**

The table above clearly highlights the value of the fisheries sector to the national economy. The volume and value of fish products in a single year as shown above is very significant.

[357] Ibid.

5.3 PROBLEMS IN THE FISHING INDUSTRY

The issues and challenges of the fishing industry in PNG can be addressed according to the nature of each of the sectors contributing to the industry, namely, *subsistence, subsistence and artisanal, commercial* and *industrial.* The challenges of the industry are also compounded by the inadequacies of the *Fisheries Act* 1984, the *Fisheries Act* 1994, the *Fisheries Management Act* 1998 and the lack of infrastructure and policies supporting each sector.

5.3.1 Sectoral problems

The 2000 census places the total population of PNG at 4.5 million people. Of this total number, the subsistence sector is made up of approximately 80 percent of the population. The issue facing this sector, and especially those communities that depend on the fisheries and marine resources, is the diminishing fish resources in lakes, rivers and estuaries.

The second group of users of fish resources is the subsistence and artisanal users, who depend on the fish resources for subsistence and income. The issues for this sector are population growth, transport, marketing of rural produce and food quality standards for fresh sales. The main marketing infrastructures available to the people engaged in this sector are roads, seaports or wharves. The current transport infrastructure is not appropriate or is unavailable to the fishing communities, thus they are not able to benefit from the sale of their fish products.

The third category of fishers is the purely artisanal fishers, involved largely in lobster, trochus, reef-fisheries and beche-de-mer fishing. This sector relies on private sector transport and marketing systems to support the utilisation of these resources for rural income.

In the beche-de-mer and trochus fisheries, local villagers fish in groups according to clans and/or family groups. The semi-processed products are brought to buying centres using motorised crafts, fibreglass dinghies or canoes, and are sold. In many cases, the buyers of the fish products provide transport or dories that have store goods on board as well as freezer and/or storage space for bringing back product for re-processing, packaging and export. In the reef-fisheries and deep-water snapper operations, local fishers work with private sector buyers with freezers and packaging facilities. Fish are bought and processed for export and/or domestic sales. This sector needs strengthening, particularly in the area of training locals.

The commercial fishing sector covers the domestic prawn and tuna long-lining operations. These are owned by PNG nationals who operate commercial prawn trawlers and tuna long-liners. They are PNG-based, and almost all their product is for the export market.

The final category is the industrial sector, and currently, in PNG, it is based on tuna stocks of the Bismarck Sea. This sector comprises locally based but foreign-owned industrial tuna fishing and canning out of Madang, and the completely foreign-owned and foreign-port-based tuna purse-seiners and long-liners from Korea, Taiwan, the Philippines, Indonesia and Vanuatu. Some of these operations have nationals as their agents for sorting out access agreements and port call requirements.

5.3.2 Legal problems

Prior to 1984, the fisheries sector existed as a sub-sector of the then Department of Agriculture and Livestock, which later became the Department of Primary Industry. In 1984, Parliament, for the first time, enacted specific fisheries legislation in the form of the *Fisheries Act* 1984. The *Fisheries Regulation* supplemented this legislation. Following the enactment of the legislation, the government, again for the first time, created the Department of Fisheries and Marine Resources (DFMR) as the implementing agency for the fisheries policy and the law.

The DFMR was vested with the power to conduct research for resource identification, development and management. Under the organisation, key sections, such as scientific research and surveys into fish stocks, resource development programs in downstream processing, fishing gear technology, marketing studies and international access negotiations, were initiated.

Over the ten years in which the *Fisheries Act* 1984 was implemented, a number of problems emerged. These included:

- corruption in the issuing of fishing licences;
- a lack of clarity in the law about the sustainability of the sector;
- a lack of scientific and economic analysis of the viability of the sector;
- large dependency on foreign aid;
- the fact that the Act did not define the manner and method of calculating and disbursing derivation grants from fisheries resources to the maritime provinces;
- the fact that there was disparity in the law, in that there was no linkage between the fisheries law and other natural resources legislation and the environmental laws; and
- a lack of enforcement of the fisheries law by the DFMR and the PNG Defence Forces.

The deficiencies in the law led to a review of the *Fisheries Act* 1984 in 1990. The aim of the legislative review was to identify possible solutions to overcome most of the problems inherent in the sector. Three important proposals that eventually emerged were, first, the proposal to corporatise the DFMR, and secondly, the establishment of a National Fisheries Authority (NFA). The second proposal was in line with the trend in the forestry sector.[358] The third proposal was to repeal the *Fisheries Act* 1984 and replace it with a new legislation. The three proposals were collectively achieved under the *Fisheries Act* 1994.

To overcome the problems identified above, the *Fisheries Act* 1994 established a number of mechanisms. These included:

- vesting the power to issue fishing licences in the National Fisheries Board;[359]
- the development of resource management guidelines by the NFA. The NFA was required to develop fishery plans. Fishery plans provided for measures such as access restrictions to PNG's fisheries waters (enforced through licensing, access agreements and cooperative arrangements), regulation of fishing practices (for example, gear restrictions,

[358] In the forestry sector, the Department of Forestry was abolished in 1991 under the *Forestry Act* 1991 and replaced by the National Forest Service. This change was necessary to achieve the government's policy of corporatisation of some of its service departments. The National Forest Authority handles the management of the sector.

[359] *Fisheries Act* 1994, s 43. Under this provision, the Minister had the power to issue fishing licences.

boat size etc) and the establishment of catch limits through the use of total allowable catches (TACs);[360]

- a requirement of the Act for scientific and economic research into the sector to establish its viability;[361]
- the justifications of derivation grants to maritime provinces were to be contained in the fishery plans required under the Act. Records were to be kept for the purpose of determining derivation grants. If the resource harvested in one province was sold or exported in another province, it was required that the originating province be declared for the purpose of determining derivation grants; and
- the NFA was to employ vessel monitoring systems, which allowed daily tracking by the NFA of boat fishing patterns via a satellite and computer inter-phase system. The government was very rigorous on defaulters, particularly those who were fishing in PNG's fisheries waters without valid fishing licences.

One would have thought that with the enactment of the 1994 legislation the problems associated with the sector would have been overcome. However, problems began to emerge even after the enactment of the *Fisheries Act* 1994. These were both legal and administrative problems, and needed to be addressed adequately under any reform. Some of these problems were:[362]

- inadequate institutional linkages between the various departments, organisations, institutions and interest groups;
- overfishing;[363]
- inadequate incentives and the lack of a suitable administrative machinery to stimulate commercial activities;
- insufficient resources to permit the development of sound fisheries management policies, including the lack of effective systems to monitor the status of stocks currently being exploited;
- the need for more research on biological, economic and social aspects, and insufficient fisheries data to enable the formulation of sound management and investment policies;
- the need for a more effective fisheries surveillance system to ensure compliance with fisheries legislation;
- the lack of effective inspection services to ensure that fish and fish products meet international standards;
- the lack of professional and technical skills due to insufficient training and lack of motivation for those involved in the fisheries sector;
- the need for more effective extension and transfer of appropriate technology for development and management of a sustainable local industry;
- the need to stimulate development opportunities through careful identification, preparation and economic analysis of investment projects;

---

360 *Fisheries Act* 1994, s 39. To facilitate the preparation of the fishery plans, s 40 required operators and licence holders to furnish "all relevant data and information, including fishing time and effort, landing, processing, sales and other related transactions".

361 See *Fisheries Act* 1994, s 41(1)(e).

362 See generally the *Corporate Plan for the Papua New Guinea National Fisheries Authority* (National Fisheries Authority, Port Moresby, 1996).

363 What was required was appropriate management and control of fishing activities combined with effective environment programs.

- the need for licensing guidelines that provide yardsticks against which to evaluate licence applications; and
- the need for increased technical, managerial and financial resources.[364]

The NFA identified most of the above problems as the issues inhibiting the development and management of the fisheries sector in PNG. These problems have been addressed under the *Fisheries Management Act* 1998. However, real issues remain with the implementation of the legislation.

5.3.3 The gaps in the Fisheries Management Act 1998

The 1994 Act was implemented over a period of three years. Over those three years, substantial changes occurred. Fishery plans now became fishery management plans and were written and approved for implementation. Fishing licences were being thoroughly assessed prior to board approvals. Fisheries management measures, such as access restrictions, regulation of fishing practices and TACs, continued under the 1998 legal regime. However, they continued to be based on ensuring maximum sustainable yield strictly in the biological sense. *Economic sustainability*, as implied under s 25(c) of the *Fisheries Act* 1994, was never pursued.

The exclusion of the subsistence and artisanal sector in the *Fisheries Management Act* 1998 [365]continued, despite its huge potential.[366] The 1984 and 1994 Acts included requirements for the NFA to develop the subsistence and artisanal sectors. The rationale for excluding this sector in the 1998 legislation was that the *Organic Law on Provincial Government and Local Level Government* (OLPGLLG) was to cater for artisanal and subsistence fisheries development. The NFA was simply to make money available to finance the artisanal and subsistence sectors.[367] There are, however, no institutional linkages between the 1998 Act and the OLPGLLG to implement the subsistence and artisanal sectors.

The main drawback of the law has been the complete disregard by the fisheries legislation over the years for assessing the *economic* factors to complement the *biological* factors in fisheries management.

Under the 1998 legislation, the NFA's natural resource scientific assessment capabilities have been diminished, despite the fact that this was an area identified as a critical need. This aspect of fisheries management will now be contracted out. This may be problematic. If private companies have the scientific capabilities to challenge and refute, as non-scientific, the TACs set by the NFA, these companies may wish to "hike up" the TACs based on their own assessments. In this situation, the NFA has no capacity to independently counteract such private company scientific assessments.

In the organisational structure to implement the *Fisheries Management Act* 1998, it was considered appropriate for the NFA to become a commercial entity. Labour was reduced and various sections under the 1994 legislation were made redundant. For example, in abolishing

---

364 These are critical factors if the National Fishing Authority is to provide adequate support for development programs, plans and policies.

365 It is argued that there is no nexus between the 1998 legislation and the *Fisheries (Torres Strait Protected Zone) Act*. It would have been legally sound if these two were harmonised. The problems of duplicity, inconsistency and the enforcement and management of these two statutes are inherent given this scenario.

366 Mungkaje, *Coastal Fisheries Development in Papua New Guinea: An Opportunity for Economic Development in Coastal Communities* (Development Bulletin No 50, October 1999) notes the huge potential in coastal fisheries for coastal communities.

367 This is provided under *Organic Law on Provincial Government and Local-Level Government*, s 42(1)(l).

basic functions such as stock assessments and economic assessments, capacity building in fisheries is no longer possible. In addition, the 1998 legislation failed to establish linkages with other resource-based and environmental legislation. Under the 1994 legislation, fisheries development was placed in the hands of the NFA. However, the NFA was financially restricted by having all its funds deposited back into the Treasury Department. The NFA was given funds only to maintain its recurrent expenditure. Consequently, the NFA was not able to initiate new projects and activities.

At the provincial level, it was assumed that the traditional role of resource development for the provinces was adequately covered by the OLPGLLG. Thus, the main thrust of the *Fisheries Management Act* 1998 is to develop the commercial and industrial sectors, leaving the subsistence and artisanal sector in the hands of the provinces. The provinces are, however, ill-equipped for this task, because the 20 years of monopoly by the Department of Fisheries have left most provinces technically poorly resourced.[368]

The *Fisheries Management Act* 1998 is solely focused on commercial and industrial fisheries development. The question of "authority on all fish resources management" has not been addressed by the Act.

5.4 APPROACHES TO FISHERIES MANAGEMENT

There are essentially four ways in which fisheries resources can be managed and the problems caused by open access in marine fisheries can be overcome. These approaches include:

(a) restricting access;

(b) regulating fishing practices, and setting catch limits by establishing:

(c) total allowable catches (TACs); and

(d) individual transferable quotas (ITQs).

The first three approaches to fisheries management are usually referred to as regulatory approaches, while ITQs are a market incentive type policy that permits individual quota holders in a fishery to trade quotas amongst themselves.

The *Fisheries Management Act* 1998 and the *Fisheries Management Regulation* 2000 provide for approaches (a), (b) and (c), and generally reflect the highly undeveloped nature of the fisheries sector, the recognition of territorial use rights to fisheries (TURFs) of customary landowners beyond the shoreline, and how fishing licences are issued in PNG. The *Fisheries Management Act* 1998 also incorporates the requirements of the *International Law of the Sea* as it relates to fisheries and access to the fisheries zone of PNG. The management arrangements for the fisheries zone are maintained in the drawing up of the National Tuna Management Plan.[369]

---

368 However, in recent times (1997-1999), the Momase provinces have made a comeback through the German Development Coastal Fisheries Project, and are now actively buying fish from local fishers.

369 Part III of the Act provides for "fisheries management, conservation and development" issues. Section 28 provides for fishery management plans. Fishery management plans basically give effect to most of the provisions in the Act, in particular s 25 (Management Objectives and Principles), s 26 (Customary Resource Ownership), s 27 (Total Allowable Catch) and s 29 (Records, Returns and Other Information). The fishery management plans also cover matters such as prohibition of fishing, and related activities such as the use of poisons or explosives, access agreements, fisheries management agreements with other sovereign states and the provisions relating to the granting of licences and the terms and conditions of those licences.

5.4.1 Access restrictions

One of the most common ways to overcoming the problem of open access is by excluding would-be encroachers to a fishing territory through the use of informal and formal TURFs. Informal TURFs have been in existence for centuries in countries with maritime areas, and PNG is no exception. For example, along the coast of the Central Province, villagers have sought to define territorial rights to fishing boundaries and have defended them by excluding outsiders. Section 26 of the *Fisheries Management Act* 1998 recognises customary resource ownership rights. Informal TURFs work well for sedentary species (beche-de-mer, clams, oysters etc), because particular coral reefs, lagoons, bays, etc can be defended. However, TURFs are really site specific and not resource specific and, as such, are not as useful for migratory species like tuna.

Recently, the idea of TURFs (excluding outsiders) has been formally adopted worldwide by sovereign nations. National jurisdiction over waters and resources was extended from three miles (12 miles in a few cases) from the shore to the offshore limits of 200 miles. The push for extended jurisdiction was initiated and pursued in the 1960s and early 1970s. The 200-mile exclusive economic zone (EEZ), as it is known today, still poses problems of open access and overfishing, particularly for countries with extensive sea areas and ineffective management institutions. PNG adopted the EEZ in March 1978.

In PNG, customary territorial fishing rights are recognised in s 26 of the *Fisheries Management Act* 1998. Section 26 states:

> "The rights of the customary owners of fisheries resources and fishing rights shall be fully recognized and respected in all transactions affecting the resource or the area in which the right operates."

However, in practice, s 26 actually applies to the commercial harvesting of fish (for example, beche-de-mer and prawns) in a defined area. In other words, customary resource ownership and fishing rights are recognised only to the extent that a fishery, for the purpose of commercial harvesting in a defined area, has a fishery management plan (FMP) as provided for in s 28.[370] The importance of other fisheries, such as reef fisheries, to the traditional resource owners, particularly within the three-mile limit, is recognised in the FMPs to the extent that the designated fishery activity does not adversely affect the environment or the livelihood of traditional resource owners.[371]

In effect, for the fishery and fishing areas not covered by an FMP, the localised groups of people themselves, while recognised, can only defend traditional rights. In other words, the Act does not provide for legal recourse against intruders in the case of informal TURFs. This is hardly a weakness of the Act, as it would be administratively and politically impossible to physically map out fishing boundaries for each and every coastal community, let alone enforce and monitor access restrictions. Community enforcement of localised TURFs is administratively efficient.

Fishing licences and access agreements essentially enforce formal TURFs, as represented by the EEZ. In the case of prawns, lobsters and tuna, licences are issued only to vessels wholly owned by Papua New Guineans and registered in PNG, and to foreign-owned vessels based in PNG. The

---

[370] For example, the New Ireland Province Beche-de-Mer Fishery Management Plan (FMP) and the Gulf of Papua Prawn FMP.

[371] For instance, prawn operators in the Gulf of Papua Prawn FMP are required to submit to the National Fisheries Authority (NFA) catch and effort data on the by-catch, including non-fish species and the recording of all by-catch. All live mammals and turtles caught shall be returned to the sea, while the dead ones may be retained and recorded. Removing fins from sharks and returning them to sea alive is prohibited.

beche-de-mer fishery is restricted only to Papua New Guineans. This is also in line with the government's objective of maximising returns from the fisheries resource to Papua New Guineans. Part IV Div 1 of the Act deals with the granting and issuing of licences, applications for licences, terms and conditions of licences, appeals and the issuing of foreign fishing licences by an authorised administrator. Division 2 deals with illegal fishing and other unlicensed activities.

Section 33 of the *Fisheries Management Act* 1998 provides for access agreements between the government of PNG, foreign states, regional economic integration organisations, any fishing associations or similar bodies, publicly incorporated companies, or individuals. Section 33(2) stipulates that:

> "No foreign fishing vessel shall be used for fishing in the fisheries waters except pursuant to an access agreement and in accordance with a valid and applicable license issued under Section 41 or Section 44."

The conditions of access agreements are outlined under s 35. Under s 37, the NFA may also enter into fisheries management agreements, arrangements or treaties with other states. The main purpose of such agreements is for co-operation in, or co-ordination of, fisheries management initiatives with the other states.[372] Section 33(2)(a)-(d) states:

> "Fisheries management agreements may, at the Authority's discretion, include the following provisions:
>
> (a) authorization of a person, body or organization to perform functions required by an access agreement, including but not limited to the allocation, issuance and denial of fishing licences valid in the region or part thereof, including the exclusive economic zone;
>
> (b) an observer program;
>
> (c) fisheries monitoring, control and surveillance;
>
> (d) any other matter relating to fisheries management."

The *Fisheries Management Act* 1998 does not cover the waters under the Torres Strait Treaty with Australia. A separate Act, the *Fisheries (Torres Strait Protected Zone) Act*, provides for the management of the shared stocks between the two countries. This treaty has defined a protected area in which traditional communities of Australian nationality, the Torres Strait Islanders and Papua New Guineans within the boundaries of the Torres Straits Protected Zone continue their traditional customary practices in fishing and social obligations. The treaty, however, governs the fisheries resources of the area, in that the Minister of Fisheries of either country may grant commercial fishing licences.[373]

5.4.2 Regulating fishing practices

The regulation of fishing practices is a tool that is used in specific fisheries to protect different life stages of a particular target species or fishable stock from being harvested, and/or minimising

---

[372] The *Fisheries Management Plans for Fisheries in the Torres Strait Protected Zone* of July 1998 is one such agreement between PNG and Australia. The fisheries affected are prawns, Spanish mackerel, dugong, turtles, pearl shells and lobsters

[373] Ibid. Torres Strait Treaty, Art 22.

the catch of non-target species. These regulations include restrictions on the type of gear that is to be used, the timing and closing of fishing seasons to protect both spawning and juvenile stocks, the size of vessels that are allowed in various fisheries and, in applying the *International Law of the Sea*, restrictions of foreign vessels to fish within the archipelagic waters of PNG.

In applying the *Investment Promotion Act*, sedentary and inshore fish resources are, by law, to be fished by PNG nationals only. In the waters of the Torres Straits, the Torres Straits Protected Zone is managed under the Torres Straits Treaty. The nature of the shared stocks between PNG and Australia, and the economic disparity between the two countries, means that the fishing practices applied in the commercial fisheries listed under the treaty have to be agreed upon regularly to avoid international disputes and unsustainable fishing practices.

The ornate lobster (*Panulirus ornatus*) fishery in the Torres Straits Protected Zone is simply managed as a dive fishery. Prior to 1983, the fishery was both a dive and trawl fishery. The trawl fishery was in the Papua New Guinean part of the fishery in the Gulf of Papua, where, in the off-season for prawns, prawn trawlers would simply trawl waters of about 60 metres and thereby land large volumes of lobster. While this was beneficial for PNG in generating revenue, in the longer term stock sustainability was becoming an issue. Consequent fishery management meetings between PNG and Australia led to changes in fishing practices to be agreed to and enforced by both countries as a dive fishery. To further protect the stock, it was also agreed that, in the licensing arrangements for prawn trawlers, licensed boats are required to throw overboard any live lobster that is unintentionally caught, whether in the Gulf of Papua or the Torres Straits prawn fishery.[374]

In the industrial tuna fishery, fishing practice, as it relates to gear restrictions and vessels types, is not managed and/or dictated by the NFA. The nature of the fishery and fishing operation makes it impractical. Most tuna vessels are foreign-based and only enter PNG waters under access agreements that allow them to fish but not land catch onshore. Licensed vessels submit regular catch reports and, while in the EEZ, they submit daily reports of catch on board. In recent years, the NFA has designated ports of call where NFA inspectors can board these boats and crosscheck the catch on board. In addition, all the foreign-based tuna boats have vessel-monitoring systems established on the boats, so that the NFA can computer-track their fishing patterns in the EEZ.

For domestic-based boats, catch reporting and onshore operations makes inspection easier. Various long-line and purse-seine boats operate from various ports in PNG. Domestic purse-seine boats are foreign-owned but locally based in Madang. These boats operate under a domestic licence and fish exclusively in the Bismarck archipelagic waters. The long-liners also provide catch reports and regularly take fishery observers to inspect operations.

The management of all tuna vessels is outlined in the National Tuna Management Plan.[375] In other fisheries, such as beche-de-mer, harvesting is restricted only to free diving. Underwater breathing apparatus (Scuba and Hookah), and underwater or surface lights at night, are banned from being used in the FMP area for the purpose of fishing for any sea cucumber species.[376] This type of direct control on fishing practices is essentially outlined in FMPs for fishery and fishing

374 Other fisheries managed using fishery management plans are Torres Straits Protected Zone Fisheries, Gulf of Papua and Orangerie Bay Prawn Fisheries, Beche-de-mer fisheries in Manus, New Ireland, Milne Bay and Western and Torres Straits Fisheries and the National Lobster Management Plan to cover any other lobster than the ornate lobster in the Torres Straits Protected Zone.

375 See the *Fisheries Management Act* 1998, the National Tuna Fishery Management Plan and the *National Gazette* (No G35, 8 March 1999).

376 See, eg, s 6(c)(i)(ii) of the New Ireland Province Beche-de-mer Management Plan, which was gazetted in the *National Gazette* (No G1, 2 January 1997).

areas that have FMPs. There are two major problems with this type of approach. First, fishing is made much more costly than it should be. Economic efficiency requires that the optimal yield and fish stock is arrived at, or achieved with, the minimum expenditure of scarce resources, that is, at minimum opportunity cost.[377] The second disadvantage with placing direct control on fishing practices is that it can never be complete. Placing an upper limit on boat size may not hinder fishers from shifting to boats with larger engines. Limiting horsepower, in turn, may encourage fishers to increase the number of trips each year.

5.4.3 Total allowable catch

Catch limits are necessary tools in natural resources management systems, because the unit stock is a living entity, being part of a living biological system. The catch limits on the Gulf of Papua prawn fishery are derived from surplus production modelling and independent research information on the stock. The tuna fishery is modelled on yield per recruit. Catch limits on the rest of the commercial fisheries on which catch limits have been set and gazetted (Torres Straits lobsters and prawns, all the beche-de-mer fisheries and all lobsters other than the Torres Straits lobster), are set using past fishing records and applying a precautionary approach in deciding what the catch limit is to be. In applying catch limits in the PNG fisheries sector, the usual approach is to set a total allowable catch (TAC) for the entire boundary of the stock. TACs are provided for under s 27 of the *Fisheries Management Act* 1998. For example, in sedentary resources like beche-de-mer (or sea cucumbers), the TAC is set for each of the provinces that have a fishery. This is because, in the absence of scientific evidence that all sea cucumbers within PNG's fisheries waters consist of a unit stock, the NFA has decided that, in operational terms, it is much easier to enforce TACs in this fishery by province. In such instances then, the more appropriate term is *allowable catch* (AC), since the NFA is unsure about the spawning boundaries of sea cucumbers. In the prawn fisheries, the stocks in the Torres Straits, the Gulf of Papua and Orangerie Bay consists of two separate stocks, hence, when the TACs are applied, it makes sense, as each fishery is separate. In the tuna fishery, the stock is a straddling stock, being fished by several countries in the South-western Pacific.

The concept, establishment and enforcement of TACs are a recent phenomenon in PNG fisheries, and represented a strategy of the 1990s.[378] In the past, all resource management strategies were based on knowledge about what the commercial catch rates and quantities were, and deciding the number of licensed boats to take the catch. As monitoring systems were developed in the prawn and tuna fisheries, these information systems were computerised, and further analysis and independent research took place. Through these developments, it is now possible for the NFA to set TACs based on more reliable resource information.

Table 3 below outlines the TACs and the number of operators and licence holders for the fishery management plan that were available.

---

[377] See generally Field, *Natural Resource Economics* (McGraw-Hill, New York, 2000).

[378] This was first incorporated in the *Fisheries Act* 1994, and has been retained by the present *Fisheries Act*.

TABLE 3: TOTAL ALLOWABLE CATCHES AND NUMBER OF OPERATOR AND LICENCE HOLDERS

Name of Management Plan	Annual TAC	Number of Exporters and Buyers
New Ireland Province Beche-de-mer Management Plan, 2 January 1997	80 tonnes	Maximum of 5 exporters, 5 buyers to each exporter
Manus Province Beche-de-mer Fishery Management Plan, 2 January 1997	54 tonnes	Maximum of 4 exporters, 5 buyers to each exporter
Western & Torres Strait Beche-de-mer Fishery Management Plan, 2 January 1997	Initial TAC: 30 tonnes for sandfish, 10 tonnes for other species	3 exporters
Milne Bay Province Beche-de-mer Fishery Management Plan, 2 January 1997	60 tonnes	Maximum of 3 exporters, 6 buyers to each exporter
Orangerie Bay Prawn Fishery Management Plan 2 January 1997	35 tonnes	2
Gulf of Papua Prawn Fishery Management Plan, 2 January 1997	1200 tonnes	15
National Lobster Fishery Management Plan, 20 April 1998	TAC shall be set for each province or fishery based on the estimated maximum sustainable yield (MSY) as qualified by relevant economic or environmental factors, fishing patterns and related factors	The Minister, upon recommendation by the Authority, shall set the number. Restricted to citizen companies or individuals
National Tuna Fishery Management Plan, December 1998:	300,000 tonnes total	
Long-line Tuna Fishery	10,000 tonnes	80, PNG registered and flagged fresh chilled vessels 10, locally based foreign vessels 10, freezer vessels 100% nationally owned

Purse-Seine Tuna Fishery	132,000 tonnes	30, PNG registered and flagged vessels and locally based foreign vessels
	40,000 tonnes	40, Federal States of Micronesia Arrangement licences and US Treaty licences
	128,000 tonnes	30, Bilateral Agreement licences
Pole-and-Line Tuna Fishery	20,000 tonnes	30 to all categories

In PNG, TACs are monitored by analysing export data and other information provided by the operators and licence holders under s 29 of the *Fisheries Management Act* 1998. Operators and licence holders are required, under this provision, to furnish records, returns and other information to the NFA.

Table 4 below shows the allowable catches and the number of operators and licence holders for the Torres Straits Protected Zone.

TABLE 4: ALLOWABLE CATCHES AND THE NUMBER OF OPERATORS AND LICENCE HOLDERS FOR THE TORRES STRAITS PROTECTED ZONE FISHERIES ACT 1986[379]

Name of Schedule	Annual Allowable Catch	Number of licensed vessels / dinghies
Schedule A (1996-1999) Fishery in the Torres Straits Protected Zone for Prawns	1,200 tonnes for both Australia and PNG	Australia 10 PNG 3 with 7 PNG cross-border licences to take the 25% of the AC for Australia in Australian waters
Schedule B (1996-1999) Fishery in the Torres Straits Protected Zone for Spanish Mackerel	No TAC PNG has not developed this fishery since treaty ratification in 1985	No fishery on the PNG side, no boats licensed
Schedule C (1996-1999) Fishery in the Torres Straits Protected Zone for Dugongs	No TAC This fishery is considered a non-commercial fishery. Only traditional catches for ceremonies are allowed.	Traditional fishery using traditional canoes and fishing gear

379 These management arrangements are valid from 1996-1999. The arrangements will need to be reviewed.

Schedule D (1996-1999) Fishery in the Torres Strait Protected Zone for Turtles	No TAC This fishery is considered non-commercial	Traditional fishery using traditional canoes and fishing gear
Schedule E (1996-1998) Fishery in the Torres Strait Protected Zone for Pearl Shell	No TAC set, except that PNG and Australia will use the average catch for the last 5 years to set the TAC	Australia will license 5 boats PNG will license an appropriate number
Schedule F (1996-1999) Fishery in Waters Under PNG Jurisdiction Beyond the Torres Strait Protected Zone, for Tropical Lobster	No TAC	An artisanal fishery for ornate lobster occurs in Eastern Gulf Province up to Yule Island in Central Province
Schedule G (1996-1999) Fishery for Tropical Lobster	The TAC will be the average fishers' catch for the past 5 years	PNG licensed 6 freezer boats and associated dinghies, plus cross-border licences to some of these 6 vessels

In the other fisheries, such as for beche-de-mer, TACs were regularly exceeded in New Ireland, Manus and Milne Bay in 1998. Not only were TACs exceeded, but where socio-economic needs of the people were seen to be restricted by the enforcement of TACs by the NFA, provincial authorities would request the NFA to allow area or time closures to be deferred until such time that social needs were met, especially during Christmas and when school fees were needed.

5.4.4 Individual transferable quotas

Individual transferable quotas (ITQs) are based on TACs, in that, after a fishery sets a TAC, quotas can be allocated to individuals. Individuals who do not wish to go fishing are able to sell that quota to someone else. For obvious reasons, ITQs are not a system that is adopted and followed in PNG's fisheries. The fisheries sector in PNG is under-developed, and for a long time the costs of enforcement were large. Therefore, only practical strategies that the NFA can enforce prevailed for a very long time. ITQs were inappropriate and costly to enforce, especially as basic requirements for monitoring fisheries in the early development of fisheries, like the timely submission of commercial catch and effort data, was difficult. In addition, PNG did not really use the quota system until the 1990s. Therefore, ITQs may still be a system for the future. The other reason for the lack of use of ITQs was that a lot of corrupt deals might have resulted from such a system. It is clearly stated under the *Fisheries Management Regulation* 2000, Pt V, s 15(1) and (2), that a licence is not transferable for a fishing vessel or licensed premises. Similarly, licences cannot be held or transferred in respect of another vessel, premises or place.

5.4.5 Enforcement and monitoring

The enforcement provisions of the *Fisheries Management Act* 1998 are contained in Pt V of the Act. Two approaches are employed. The first includes the appointment and deployment of fisheries officers by the Managing Director of the NFA. Fisheries officers are vested with wide-ranging powers. These include stopping, boarding, entering, searching and staying on board (without a warrant) any vessel in the fisheries waters of PNG, any PNG vessel outside the fisheries waters of PNG, or any other vessel to which the Act and any international law or agreement applies.[380] The officer may also, without a warrant, enter and search any premises or place, other than premises used exclusively as a dwelling house.[381] Among other powers, the fisheries officer has the power to seize, take, detain, remove and secure items such as fish, fish products, vessels, gear, equipment, explosives, noxious substances, any logs, charts or other documents, and may make arrests.[382]

The second approach involves the appointment of observers by the Managing Director of the NFA[383] under the observer program in s 50 of the *Fisheries Management Act* 1998. After boarding a vessel, the main duties of the observers are to collect and report reliable and accurate information to the NFA for scientific, management, and compliance purposes.[384] The NFA is required, under s 54(1), to give reasonable notice to the operator or licence holder of the vessel of its intention to place observers on the vessel. In addition, the operator or licence holder of the vessel is required, under s 53(1)(2)(a)-(e), to provide the observer with food, insurance coverage, salary, allowances, all travel and associated expenses to and from the vessel, and other costs associated with management of the observer program at a level to be approved by the Managing Director of the NFA.

Offences committed against the Act, and the associated penalties and liabilities, are dealt with under Pt VI[385] of the Act. Such offences are prosecuted summarily before a Principal Magistrate in the District Court,[386] except where administrative proceedings are taken in accordance with Pt VII.

The fines under the current Act have been standardised basically for *two groups of offences*, compared to the 1994 legislation, where separate fines where specified for each offence. The first group of offences are those punishable under s 58(5)(a), (b) and (c).[387] The penalties that apply[388] are specified in s 58(5) as follows:

(a) in respect of a crew member, a fine not exceeding K5,000; and

(b) in respect of a natural person, a fine not exceeding K100,000; and

(c) in respect of a corporation, a fine not exceeding K1,000,000.

The levels of seriousness of the offences are reflected in the levels of fines set above compared to the penalties mentioned below. For example, s 58(1)(c) provides the penalty for a violation of s 32, which relates to the use of poisons or explosives. The fines are also applicable to vessels fishing without a licence in the fisheries waters of PNG as specified in s 46.

380 *Fisheries Management Act* 1998, s 49(2)(a)(i)(ii) and (iii).
381 Ibid, s 49(2)(b).
382 Ibid, s 49(2)(f) and (g).
383 Ibid, s 51.
384 Ibid, s 52.
385 Ibid, ss 58-60.
386 ibid, s 57.
387 These apply in respect of offences described in s 58(1)(b), (c), (d), (e), (f), (g), (h), (n), (p), (r), (x), (y), (z), (bb) and (cc) of the *Fisheries Management Act* 1998.
388 These penalties apply in respect of offences described in s 58(1)(a), (i), (j), (k), (l), (m), (o), (q), (s), (t), (u), (v), and (aa) of the *Fisheries Management Act* 1998.

The second group of offences that are punishable are provided under s 58(6) as follows:

(a) in respect of a crew member, a fine not exceeding K2000; and

(b) in respect of a natural person, a fine not exceeding K50,000; and

(c) in respect of a corporation, a fine not exceeding K100,000.

The violation of s 29(1) is an example of an offence that would command such a fine.

It is our view that the fines provided for under the Act are commensurate with the offences created under the legislation. The value of fines highlights the seriousness of the government in monitoring and managing the fisheries resources of the country.

Monitoring of fish stocks is also provided for under s 29, whereby operators and licence holders are required to furnish the NFA with records, returns and other information. Violation of this provision is an offence under s 58(1)(a) and is punishable under s 58(6).

The PNG government has been rigorous in enforcing the fisheries laws. For example, in *Pawut v Bee* [1996] PNGLR 26, the defendant was found guilty of operating a foreign fishing vessel for the purpose of fishing in PNG fisheries waters without any lawful excuse. This was an offence under s 57 of the *Fisheries Act* 1994. The corresponding section under the current Act is s 58(1)(d). In this case, the defendant, Bee, who was the master of a foreign boat, was found guilty by the District Court and fined K20,000 under s 57 of the *Fisheries Act* 1994. The state appealed to the National Court, arguing that the fine was insufficient. The National Court substituted the District Court decision by ordering the defendant to pay K250,000 and that his boat be forfeited to the state.

In another case in the same year, *Ada v Beau* [1996] PNGLR 172, the defendants were charged with 21 counts of breaching the *Fisheries Act* 1994. The main provision of the Act relied upon by the state was s 55.[389] At first instance the District Court struck out the charges and discharged the defendant and his colleagues. The state appealed the decision to the National Court. The National Court considered the appeal and remitted the matter to the District Court for a rehearing.

5.5 CONCLUSION

The value of the fisheries sector to PNG cannot be underestimated. The sector plays, and will continue to play, a very important role in the economy of the country and lives of the people of PNG, especially those who depend on it for their livelihood. From the commercial perspective, the sector is still in its infancy in contrast to other sectors such as mining, forestry, and agriculture. Given the current nature of the fisheries sector within the context of the *Fisheries Management Act* 1998, and the commercial nature of the NFA, the following proposals are some examples of the avenues open to the sector.

First, provincial governments do not have the technical capacities to develop the artisanal fisheries sector. This sector could be readdressed through collaborative efforts between the provinces, the Department of Rural Development, the Rural Development Bank, the NFA and other relevant institutions and interest groups. The NFA could contribute to the sector by

---

[389] The corresponding provision in the *Fisheries Management Act* 1998 is s 58(1)(h).

transferring funds to the provinces for the construction of onshore infrastructures, such as fishing wharves and fish markets to serve both commercial and artisanal fishers.

Secondly, there is a need to review the *Fisheries Management Act* 1998 to incorporate institutional arrangements as envisioned by the OLPGLLG and the *Torres Strait Treaty Act*. There is also a need to create links between the *Fisheries Management Act* 1998 and other natural resource and environmental legislation.

Thirdly, there are other matters that could be considered in relation to the NFA, such as:

- the scope of the maximum sustainable yield (MSY) should be expanded to encompass social and economic factors consistent with s 25(c) of the *Fisheries Management Act* 1998;
- the NFA must cease contracting out its scientific stock assessment responsibilities; and
- the NFA should continue to maintain and strengthen its enforcement, surveillance and monitoring capabilities.

REFERENCES

Asian Development Bank, *Fisheries Management Project Feasibility Study* (Asian Development Bank, TA No 2258-PNG, Final Report, December 1995).

Field, *Natural Resource Economics* (McGraw-Hill, New York, 2000).

Mungkaje, *Coastal Fisheries Development in Papua New Guinea: An Opportunity for Economic Development in Coastal Communities* (Development Bulletin No 50, October 1999).

National Fisheries Authority, *Papua New Guinea National Fisheries Authority, Corporate Plan and Organizational Structure 1996-1998* (National Fisheries Authority, Port Moresby, 1996).

National Fisheries Authority, *Draft Annual Report 1999* (National Fisheries Authority, Port Moresby, 1999).

CHAPTER 6

WATER LAW

*Lawrence Kalinoe**

6.1 INTRODUCTION

The law on water resources management in Papua New Guinea (PNG) is largely based on the *Water Resources Act* 1982.[390] Essentially, it is under this legislation that water use rights are allocated and various other rights and obligations are imposed on the users of water and watercourses. The legislation also sets out water quality standards and employs criminal sanctions for enforcement of the various duties and/or obligations that it imposes, to oversee the successful implementation of its management processes and structures. The regulation of water extraction and the discharge and drainage of water focuses predominantly on a *permit system*. One of the main shortcomings of the Act is that it does not have any provisions dealing with in-stream flow and use. Neither does the Act have any provisions dealing with watercourse management.

This chapter presents the water resources management regime in PNG as it exists under the *Water Resources Act*,[391] including an explanation of the administrative process involved.

6.2 STATE CONTROL OVER WATER USE RIGHTS

The extent of the state's control over water use rights is restricted to the formal permit system. Use of water resources by customary water rights holders – the indigenous peoples of PNG in accordance with their customary uses and requirements – are left unregulated. Customary use is outside the formal permit system. This is clear from the operation of s 5 of the *Water Resources Act*, Ch 205. Section 5(1) of the Act merely declares that the right to the use and control of water in PNG is vested in the state. However, by s 5(2), the customary rights of local people to use water in accordance with their custom and traditional ways of life are exempted from the state's powers under s 5(1). Section 5(3) then provides further exemptions. It allows any person, either an indigenous or a riparian tenement holder, to extract or use water for any domestic and other prescribed purposes, including for recreational use. The extent and spirit of s 5(3) is further taken up by s 21. Section 21(1) provides:

> "A person may take water without charge for:
>
> (a) domestic purposes;
>
> (b) watering stock; or
>
> (c) fire fighting
>
> from a watercourse or lake to which the public has free access by road or from an area of land reserved for the use of the public."

---

* Lecturer in Law, Department of Law, UPNG.

390 *Water Resources Act* 1982 (No 8 of 1982). The pre-1982 *Water Resources Act* (Ch 205) was repealed and reinstated as Ch 205 in the Revised Laws of PNG.

391 For discussion on these and related issues, see Kalinoe, *Water Law and Customary Water Rights in Papua New Guinea* (UBS Publishers Distributors Ltd, New Delhi, 1999).

This, however, does not entitle one to extract water by erecting a permanent installation, either in or on the land adjacent to the watercourse. Any breaches of this nature are punishable with a fine of up to K200.[392]

Section 22(6) is significant, in so far as it relates to securing access to the watercourse or lake so that the rights of access given, for example under s 21(1), can be exercised. It provides:

> "A person who has a right to pass over land abutting on the bank of a watercourse or a lake, that is owned or occupied by another person, for the purpose of access to the watercourse or lake shall have, for the purpose of this section, the same rights as that other person, but must not place a permanent installation for taking water in or on the land adjacent to, the watercourse or lake.
>
> Penalty: A fine not exceeding K200.00."

Owners of riparian tenements are allowed, under s 22(1) of the Act, to take water for all domestic, stock watering and fire fighting purposes, either for themselves, their family members or their employees. However, in appropriate cases, the Director of Water Resources is empowered to set in writing a maximum allowable quantity of water for use under these circumstances.[393] If the Director of Water Resources has issued a written notice specifying the maximum allowable take of water, and the riparian owner fails to comply with such directions and takes water in excess of the set maximum allowable volume of water, such a person will be deemed to have committed an offence punishable with a maximum penalty of K200.[394]

While s 21(2) of the *Water Resources Act* allows any person to take water from a watercourse within public access, mainly for domestic, stock watering or fire fighting purposes, s 21(2) prohibits the use of permanent installations to take water under these circumstances. By contrast, owners of riparian tenements are entitled, under s 22(4), to extract or take water by using a permanent installation in or on the land adjacent to the watercourse or lake concerned. Such a permanent installation installed by a riparian tenement holder must not obstruct the flow of the watercourse or lake. Causing obstruction to the flow of the watercourse or lake under these circumstances may amount to an offence punishable with a fine not exceeding K200.[395]

The riparian tenement holder's right to take water under s 22(1) of the Act is, however, "subject to any rights granted under this or any other Act".[396] Accordingly, this clearly makes rights based on riparian tenements subject to statutorily acquired water use rights.

6.3 ADMINISTRATIVE ARRANGEMENT

The Water Resources Board, established under s 9 of the *Water Resources Act*, is the main regulatory body charged with all regulatory control and co-ordination functions pertinent to water use and conservation. Its powers and functions are spelled out under s 15 of the Act:

"(1) The functions of the Board are:

---

392 See *Water Resources Act*, s 21(2).
393 Ibid, s 22(2).
394 Ibid, s 22(3).
395 Ibid, s 22(4).
396 Ibid, s 22(5).

(a) to examine problems concerning and make plans in respect of:

(i) the allocation and quality of water; and

(ii) the control:

(a) of erosion on the banks of rivers and shores of lakes and coastal shores; and

(b) of flow and flooding in and from rivers and lakes; and

(iii) the conservation of water; and

(iv) the need of fisheries and wildlife and recreation of use of water;

and

(b) to advise the Minister on any question relating to the administration of this Act; and

(c) to co-ordinate all matters relating to water so as to ensure that this national asset is available to meet as many demands as possible and is used to the best advantage of the country and region in which it exists; and

(d) to consider all applications under Section 28 [applications for water use permits] and to carry out all duties as specified in this Act in connexion with such applications; and

(e) to control the damming, diversion, taking and use of water and discharge of anything into water so far as any such acts may affect the quality or availability of water for other purposes; and

(f) to guide and encourage research into matters relating to the investigation and use of water resources; and

(g) to demonstrate and encourage the development and use of efficient conservation of water resources; and

(h) to promote the best usage of water resources, including multiple users, and to allocate water resources between competing demands; and

(i) to consult with government bodies on maximum utilization of water resources in the national interest."

The Board has wide-ranging powers and functions to enable it to co-ordinate the management, conservation and utilisation of water resources in the overall national interest.

The Director of Water Resources, a position created by s 8 of the Act, is the chief executive officer in relation to water resources management, and is accountable to the Board.

6.4 STATUTORY WATER USE RIGHTS

There are few mechanisms employed by the *Water Resources Act* to issue water use rights. These mechanisms are used by persons who wish to conduct water works, extract water, discharge wastes into waterways or manage and utilise water in PNG. These mechanisms are:

- a declaration of a water control district, under Pt IV of the Act;

- a water use permit, through the process set out under Pts V, VI and VII of the Act;
- a water investigation permit, through the process set out under Pt VIII of the Act; and
- a control mechanism in a drought situation, as stipulated under Pt IX of the Act.

There is a curious deficiency in the *Water Resources Act*. While the Act specifies the water uses that do not require a water use permit etc, it does not specify the activities that require authorisation by way of permit etc. The legislation must be read as a whole to identify such instances.

There are separate considerations for each of these four mechanisms. There are also provisions for another type of control through a catchment management plan (CMP).

It must be noted that the Act does not provide separate regulatory mechanisms for the extraction and utilisation of ground water as opposed to that of surface water sources such as rivers, lakes and streams etc. This arises from the all-embracing nature of the definitions of "water course"[397] and "water source"[398] under s 2 of the Act. There is no distinction between surface and underground water.[399]

Water control district

The relevant Minister[400] may declare a water control district if an area is a catchment area of a river, lake, stream or underground water from which water is taken for sustaining the water supply for a particular community.[401] When such an area is declared a water control district, the following activities are prohibited:

- cutting or destroying trees;
- constructing or altering a drain, trench or channel;
- constructing, altering or removing an embankment against a watercourse or lake;
- constructing, altering or removing an embankment in order to alter, or cause to alter, the course of water;
- constructing, altering or removing an embankment in order to impede, or cause to impede, the flow or movement of surface water;
- constructing or sinking a well or water bore; and

---

397 "Water course" includes every river, stream, passage, and channel on or under the ground, whether natural or not, through which water flows, whether continuously or intermittently.

398 "Water source" includes watercourse, lake and any other water sources, whether on the surface or underground.

399 Interestingly, under the *Water Resources Act* 1967 (as amended by the *Water Resources (Amendment) Act* 1970), which became the initial *Water Resources Act*, when the pre-independence statutes were revised, "underground water" was separately defined, and any person who extracted underground water was required to obtain a specific water use permit pertinent to the extraction of underground water. The author has argued that in view of the ecological, geological and geophysical considerations in the extraction and utilisation of underground water, there ought to be specific regulatory and management mechanisms for underground water, distinct from those for surface water, to effectively and properly deal with it: Kalinoe "Water Resource Management in Papua New Guinea: Law Policy and Practice" (1994) 22 Mel LJ 23.

400 At the time of writing the relevant Minister is the Minister for Environment and Conservation.

401 See *Water Resources Act*, s 23.

- burning of trees, shrubs, plants, grass or foliage.

Any person found to be carrying on any of these prohibited activities is liable to a fine not exceeding K500.[402]

Furthermore, the Director of Water Resources may, by a written notice, require the owner or occupier of land within a water control district to:

- adopt, or refrain from using, certain agricultural or pastoral methods or practices;
- refrain from removing or clearing trees, shrubs, plants, grass or foliage; or
- take such action for preventing the erosion, drift or movement of soil or water or both.

Failure to comply with such a written notice is an offence punishable with a penalty of up to K500.[403] The Director of Water Resources may, however, by written approval, authorise any person to undertake any of those prohibited activities in a water control district for a specified period, in accordance with such conditions and restrictions specified in the written approval.[404]

Historically, the water control district mechanism was carried over from the 1962 Ordinance, where it was primarily designed to protect hydro dam catchments and water supply catchment environments. Available records show that the (Sirinumu) Laloki Catchment Area has been declared a water control district, and designated areas in the island of Daru (Western Province), Kwikila (Central Province), Lae (Morobe Province) and Rabaul (East New Britain Province) have been declared underground water control areas under similar provisions of previous legislation.[405] The current legislation neither provides for the annulment/repeal, nor specifically provides for the saving of these declared water control districts or underground water control areas. Given that, and in accordance with the general rules of statutory interpretation,[406] the declared water control district of Sirinumu, and the underground water control areas at Daru, Kwikila, Lae and Rabaul, as specified above, remain in force.

Since the current *Water Resources Act* (Ch 205) came into effect on 22 April 1982, the Water Resources Board has not initiated a water control district. The Board considers that the process and the implications of a declaration may amount to an unjust deprivation of property or an interest or right over property amounting to a conflict with s 53 of the *Constitution.* Since the *Constitution* is entrenched and, hence, supreme, any legislation that is inconsistent with it is, to the extent of such inconsistency, invalid and ineffective.[407] However, a water control district may be properly declared, provided that the enabling legislation is specifically enacted for that purpose

---

402 Ibid, s 24.

403 Ibid, s 27.

404 Ibid, s 25.

405 *Water Resources Regulations*, s 15 and, as specified under Sch 2 of the now repealed *Water Resources Act*, Ch 205 and related subsidiary legislation; Territory of Papua and New Guinea *Government Gazette* No 47 (27 August 1970), p 826; ibid No 49 (3 September 1970), p 482; ibid No 62 (28 November 1968), p 902; ibid No 59 (16 October 1969), p 787. The relevant previous Acts were the *Water Resources Ordinance* 1962, *Water Resources Ordinance* 1966, *Water Resources Ordinance* 1967 and the *Water Resources (Amendment) Act* 1970, which, when revised at independence, became the initial *Water Resources Act* (Ch 205).

406 See Pearce and Geddes, *Statutory Interpretation in Australia* (4th ed, Butterworths, Sydney, 1996), p 153.

407 Generally, s 53 of the *Constitution* guarantees protection from unjust deprivation of property by: (a) taking possession of any property compulsorily; or (b) acquiring and/or extinguishing an interest in, or right over, property compulsorily without compensation on just terms. In *Frame v Minister for Lands* [1979] PNGLR 626 on appeal to the Supreme Court [1980] PNGLR 433, it was held that compensation on just terms meant "full and adequate compensation for the compulsory taking".

and complies with other constitutional requirements.[408] This would bring it within the proviso to s 53(4) of the *Constitution* that compulsory acquisition or restriction on the use of property, or an interest in or right over property, can be made if such restriction is necessary for the preservation of the environment or the national cultural inheritance.

Water use permits

Any person who wants to use water for purposes other than domestic, customary or fire fighting use must obtain a water use permit. Equally, a permit must be obtained if a person wishes to discharge effluent or waste into any watercourse or to divert a normal flow of the watercourse.

An application for a water use permit must, in the first instance, be made to the Director of Water Resources in the prescribed form, together with the prescribed fee. The Director will then submit the application to the Water Resources Board for its consideration in accordance with ss 29 and 30 of the *Water Resources Act*.

In its considerations, the Board will, inter alia, consider whether an environmental plan under the *Environmental Planning Act* (Ch 370) is required, and then advise the Minister for Environmental and Conservation accordingly. In dealing with the application, matters that the Board is *required* to particularly consider include:

(a) any environmental plan where one is submitted;

(b) the data and any related information available on the water and water source;

(c) projected utilisation of the water and water source; and

(d) the adequacy of the water or watercourse for the proposed water works, the subject of the application.

The Board is also required to, inter alia, circulate notice of the application in the media and invite comments or submissions from community and interest groups on the proposed water use permit. It is required to take such submissions into account in its decision.

After careful consideration of the application and all other matters brought to its notice by public hearing, the Board makes a written recommendation to the Minister for Environment and Conservation for the granting or refusal of the permit. The Minister then makes the decision. Where a permit is granted, it may be interim or final. A permit is for a specified period, and attached with it are strict terms and conditions for the permit holder to observe.

Under s 42 of the *Water Resources Act* (Ch 205), a water use permit confers any of the following rights on the permit holder (depending on the nature of the application and the purpose for which it was obtained):

(a) the exclusive right of construction or protection of such water works, subject only to the Director of Water Resources' right of entry for inspection;

(b) the right to construct and maintain such water works in accordance with the approved plan;

---

[408] See ss 38 (general qualification or qualified rights) and 39 (reasonably justified in a democratic society) etc of the *Constitution* and *The State v NTN Pth Ltd and NBN Ltd* [1992] PNGLR 1; [1987] SPLR 205.

(c) the right to take water at the rate and for the purpose specified in the permit;

(d) the right to flood such areas of land as specified in the permit; and

(e) the right to discharge water or waste in accordance with prescribed conditions and standards.

In all instances, the holder of a water use permit is required to keep records of all activities pertinent to the permit use, and to allow access to the Board, its servants or agents to carry out inspections and measurements. During a drought, the Director of Water Resources may restrict or suspend the exercise of a permit by a notice in the *National Gazette*, in order to ensure water is available for supplying the essential needs of other water users during the period of drought.[409] In relation to consumptive use, annual charges are levied on the basis of volume taken multiplied by the basic charge, and further multiplied by the so-called use factor.[410]

Unfortunately, the Bureau of Water Resources has not maintained accurate records of the total number of water use permits issued to date. Hence, it has only been estimated that more than 800 water use permits have been issued to date.[411] The *Report to the Special Committee on Review of Water Resources Act* found that the permit process is complex and lengthy. Long delays in granting approvals are experienced due to the infrequent (quarterly) meetings of the Board. Hence, the Board itself finds the system largely inappropriate and, therefore, the Minister has, in the majority of cases, exempted the Board from complying with the statutory procedures. In practice, water uses that involve major environmental issues are directed to proceed under the *Environmental Planning Act* (Ch 370). This means that an environmental plan must be prepared and submitted, as required under that Act.

The water use permit can be revoked for non-compliance with a prescribed condition,[412] or for non-use.[413] Upon the sale of land over which a water use permit has been granted and remains in force, the permit is transferable to the transferee under s 41 of the *Water Resources Act*. However, the transferee is required to give written notification to the Board within 14 days of becoming the permit holder.[414]

Water investigation permits

A water investigation permit must be obtained to:

- carry out investigations or surveys into water resources; or
- carry out pumping tests or to test drill to collect soil or geological samples; and
- install and inspect, operate and maintain gauges, instruments or appliances.[415]

Such a permit is not necessary if a person is authorised in writing by the Director of Water Resources to carry out investigations into water resources in the area on behalf of the state.[416] A

---

[409] See *Water Resources Act*, Pt IX.

[410] The varying use factors and minimum annual charges are set out at Sch 2 of the Act. As for non-consumptive use, ie the discharge of wastes etc, into watercourses, the fees are stipulated under Sch 3 of the Act.

[411] *Report to the Special Committee on Review of Water Resources Act* (Prepared by New Zealand law firm, Brandon Brookfield, 1988).

[412] See *Water Resources Act*, s 45.

[413] Ibid, s 46.

[414] Failing to do so is an offence punishable with a fine not exceeding K100: *Water Resources Act* (Ch 205), s 41(3).

[415] See *Water Resources Act*, s 50.

[416] Ibid, s 50(a).

water investigation permit "does not confer the right to authorise the doing of any act prejudicing any customary rights to the customary use of water".[417]

To obtain a water investigation permit, a person must apply to the Director of Water Resources in the prescribed form[418] and submit the appropriate fee.[419] The Director may then grant the permit for a non-extendable period of one year, attaching specific and appropriate conditions.[420] The permit may be revoked if the holder of the permit does not comply with such prescribed conditions or fails to comply with any other provisions or the *Water Resources Act*.[421]

A water investigation permit is not assignable without the written consent of the Director.[422] Within two months of the expiration or revocation of the permit, the former permit holder is required to furnish to the Director a report of the investigations of water resources carried out under the permit, giving details of the hydrological, geographical, geological and geophysical information collected.[423]

Control mechanisms in a drought situation

The *Water Resources Act* does not define what may amount to a "drought situation". "Drought" has been defined[424] as an extended and continuous period of very dry weather, or a period in which water supply is insufficient to meet usual domestic, agricultural and industrial demands.

When a drought situation is threatening, the Water Resources Board meets and reports accordingly to the Director of Water Resources. If "the Director considers that there has been or is likely to be" a reduction or alteration in the flow or supply of water in a water source, or an alteration of a watercourse, he or she may, by notice in the *National Gazette*, declare that Pt IX (relating to action in case of drought) shall apply in respect of the period and the water sources, or part of the water source, specified in the notice.

After publishing the notice of the drought or the impending drought in the *National Gazette*, the Director may give notice in writing to the holder of a water use permit in a specified area. The notice may require the holder to operate water works for a reduced period, or it may suspend the operation of the permit.[425] During this period, the holder of the water use permit will only be allowed to use water for the "minimum essential needs" in the following descending order of priorities of purposes:

- domestic purposes;
- watering stock;
- irrigation and industrial purposes; or
- generation of hydro-electric power.[426]

---

417 Ibid, s 50.
418 The prescribed form is Form 3 of Sch 1 of the Act.
419 See Schs 2 and 3 of the Act. However, for current fees, see Department of Environment and Conservation.
420 See *Water Resources Act*, s 49.
421 Ibid, s 53.
422 Ibid, s 51.
423 Ibid, s 54.
424 Jones, Robertson, Forbes and Hollier (eds), *Collins Reference Dictionary of Environmental Science* (Collins, London, 1990), p 130.
425 See *Water Resources Act*, s 52(2).
426 Ibid, s 53(3).

Failure to comply with these conditions is an offence punishable with a fine of up to K500 for every day on which the breach is allowed to continue.[427]

Catchment management areas

In addition to the four major mechanisms to control and manage water resources, the Water Resources Board has adopted catchment management plans (CMP) in an attempt to provide for the best possible use, or combination of uses, of water and land resources to meet all foreseeable short and long term needs within a defined watershed. In this regard, a former Director of Water Resources aptly explained that:

> "The basic objective in the formulation of catchment management plans is to provide the best use, or combination of uses, of water and water-land resources to meet all foreseeable short and long term needs within a defined watershed. In pursuit of this basic conservation objective, planning from management of catchments with competitive uses of water usually takes into consideration economic development objectives, whilst at the same time considering preservation and social issues of concern."[428]

Watersheds can also be studied for specific resource management objectives. Such objectives may include solving a problem caused by water (that is, for flood control or water quality improvement), the locating of a dam site for hydro-power development, or meeting a demand for water supply such as for municipal and industry use.

Under this management approach, the factors that are usually taken into consideration in planning for a CMP are the competitive uses of water within the particular catchment, the overall economic development objectives, and any conservation or social issues of concern within the catchment area. Needless to say, customary water use right of indigenous Papua New Guineans will also have to be given serious consideration in the planning of a CMP.

So far, there have been two major catchment management studies carried out by the Bureau of Water Resources for the Water Resources Board. These are of the Yonki and Upper Wahgi watersheds.

While the *Water Resources Act* does not specifically deal with the CMP management approach, it is argued that this management approach can be adopted and properly implemented by the Water Resources Board as a management tool pursuant to the powers and functions under s 15(1) of the Act. This section stipulates that the functions of the Board include the examination of problems and planning relating to "the allocation and quality of water".

6.5 COMPLIANCE MONITORING AND ENFORCEMENT

Enforcement

The Director of Water Resources is authorised, under s 17 of the *Water Resources Act*, to conduct official investigations, either personally or through employees, agents or other persons. The

---

427 Ibid, s 55(4).

428 Bisa, *Integrated Approach to Water Conservation and Planning in Papua New Guinea* (unpublished Waigani Seminar paper, Bureau of Water Resources, Port Moresby, 1993), p 4.

Director may enter any land to carry out such investigations concerning the taking and management of water resources. The Director may adopt measures for:

(a) water conservation, regulating the flow of water and to prevent the contamination of water;

(b) the protection of the bed and banks of any watercourse, lake or shore, and to remove any obstructions from the bed or banks; or

(c) removing or destroying any unauthorised works affecting the use, flow or control of water.[429]

The Director, or any of his or her agents, are also authorised "to enter on any land within a water control district and carry out such works relating to the use, flow and control of water" in a water control district.[430] Any act or omission causing hindrance or obstruction of the Director, his or her employees or agents during official investigations is an offence.[431]

Furthermore, the Director is empowered[432] to appoint inspectors for the purposes of enforcement of the Act. Inspectors are empowered to enter any land, buildings, water works and/or watercourses at reasonable times,[433] and to examine and make inquiries in respect of:

(a) the state and condition of any buildings and water works;

(b) the flow or control of water;

(c) the contamination of water;

(d) land use; and

(e) any prohibited act referred to in s 24.[434]

Hindrance or obstruction of an inspector in the exercise of his or her duty in accordance with the Act is an offence punishable with a fine of up to K500.[435]

In terms of enforcement, s 58 is an important provision that includes a general enforcement section:

"(1) A person who, being the holder of a permit, contravenes or fails to comply with a condition, to which the permit is subject, is guilty of an offence.

(2) A person who, not being the holder of a permit:

---

429 See *Water Resources Act*, s 17(1)(a).
430 Ibid, s 17(1)(b).
431 Ibid, s 17(2). The offence is punishable with a fine not exceeding K2,000.
432 *Water Resources Act*, s 18.
433 Ibid, s 19(b).
434 The relevant provision of s 24 of the *Water Resources Act* is s 24 (1), which reads:
"Subject to this section, in a water control district a person who:
(a) ring-barks, cuts down or destroy trees; or
(b) constructs, alters, removes, repairs, cleanses or scours a drain, trench or channel; or
(c) constructs, alters, removes an embankment against a water course or lake; or
(d) constructs, alters or removes an embankment in such a way as:
(i) to alter or likely to alter the course; or
(ii) to impede or be likely to impede the flow or movement or surface water; or
(e) sinks or constructs a well or water bore; or
(f) burns off trees, shrubs, plants, grass or foliage, is guilty of an offence.
Penalty: not exceeding K500.00."
435 See *Water Resources Act*, s 20.

(a) dams a river or stream; or

(b) diverts any water; or

(c) discharges water or waste into any water; or

(d) discharges water containing waste onto land or into the ground in circumstances that result in:

(i) the waste; or

(ii) other waste emanating as a result of processes from the waste, entering water; or

(e) being the occupier of land, causes or permits waste, emanating as a result of processes from matter previously placed on or discharged onto the land or into the ground, to enter water; or

(f) takes or uses water; or

(g) knowingly causes or permits any chemical, metallic or organic wastes or any unsightly odours, litter, waste or refuse to enter any water, is guilty of an offence.

(3) A person who acts in contravention of, or fails to comply with, a provision of this Act, or a direction, notice, order or requirement given or made under this Act is guilty of an offence.

Penalty: A fine not exceeding K5000.00 for every day for which the breach is permitted to continue."

If a corporation is convicted of any offence under the Act, and it is established that the offence was committed as a result of the act, omission or negligence of a director, manager, secretary or an agent of the corporation, the person concerned and the corporation can be made personally and severably liable for the offence.[436]

In spite of these provisions and the occurrence of possible breaches of the *Water Resources Act*, no person has been prosecuted, nor have civil proceedings commenced under any of the provisions of the Act to date.

Monitoring

On compliance monitoring visits to water use permit holders, a former Director of Water Resources observed that:

> "It is important to conduct regular compliance monitoring inspections of water users licensed to either take water or discharge wastes into natural watercourses. Compliance monitoring visits are conducted to ensure the permit holders comply with the terms and conditions of the permit, and the regulations and standards of the government. There are over 800 water users licensed throughout the country under the *Water Resources Act.* Due to severe manpower and financial constraints, it has been very difficult for the Bureau of Water Resources to visit every permit holder's water abstraction or waste

436 Ibid, s 60.

disposal location. Therefore, visits to forestry, mining and petroleum, agricultural and municipal waste disposal sites are conducted quarterly."[437]

For the purposes of meaningful public participation in the water resource management process, s 56 of the *Water Resources Act* is significant. It extends standing (locus standi) to any person, either personally or on behalf of a group or class of persons, to institute proceedings, either criminal or civil, for breaches of any of the provisions of the Act. Section 56(1) stipulates:[438]

> "Subject to Subsection (2) a person may, on his behalf or on behalf of a group or class of persons representing that group or class or the public as a whole, take proceedings:
>
> (a) where an alleged offence against this Act has occurred or is likely to occur; or
>
> (b) where there is an alleged failure to perform an act or duty under this Act that is not discretionary, in court against:
>
> (c) the state; or
>
> (d) a government body; or
>
> (e) another person,
>
> or all or any of them jointly."

6.6 COMPENSATION

Section 16 of the *Water Resources Act* imposes liability on the holder of a permit (a water use permit or a water investigation permit) to pay compensation to landowners (customary, leasehold or freehold) or other occupiers of land in respect of the permit holder's entry on, or occupation of, the land. Compensation is to be paid for:

(a) the deprivation of the use and enjoyment of the surface of the land or any part of it, or of rights to water customarily associated with the land. However, if there has been a reservation in favour of the state by the landowner of his or her rights to the use and enjoyment of the land in issue, then compensation may not be payable;

(b) damage to the surface of the land, any part of the land, any improvement on the land, or to any flora and fauna caused by the carrying on of operations under the permit;

(c) rights of any easements; and

(d) any damage consequential on the holder's use or occupation of the land, or use or control of water or a water source on or in the land.

Landowners or other occupiers of private land adjoining, or in the vicinity of, land occupied by the permit holder are also entitled to compensation for any loss or damage sustained as a result of any operations carried on by or on behalf of the permit holder.[439] The procedure for ascertaining and obtaining the compensation payment is set out under s 16(4)-(14). Generally, the parties themselves can agree on the amount of compensation and the manner and time of payment. If there is disagreement, then either party can apply to the Minister responsible for a decision on the

---

[437] Bisa, op cit n 39, p 5.

[438] It does this without restricting any other rights that a person or class of persons may have under any other law.

[439] This also includes any loss or damage sustained as a result of any operations carried on by reason of a right of way acquired by the permit holder.

amount of compensation and the manner and time of payment. Any person who is aggrieved by the Minister's decision can apply to the National Court by way of appeal. Where the compensation is not paid as agreed or as determined by the Minister, the aggrieved person can also apply to the Water Resources Board seeking cancellation of the holder's permit.[440]

The *Water Resources Act* does not provide for compensation for all landowners who are deprived of the use and enjoyment of their land when it has been declared a water control district, as discussed above. By not providing for just compensation, this part of the Act appears to be inconsistent with s 53 of the *Constitution*, which protects every citizen from the unjust deprivation of their right to their land and the use of it. To the extent of that inconsistency, the constitutional provision prevails. Despite the lack of compensatory provisions, compensation must be paid to those landowners (customary, freehold or leasehold) who are affected by the declaration of a water control district under s 23 of the Act where such landowners are deprived of the use and enjoyment of their land.

The courts have not had the opportunity to interpret the operation and application of s 16 of the Act on this issue of compensation, despite the fact that more than 800 water use permits and/or water investigation permits have been granted to date.[441]

In *Pen Rumints v The State and Western Highlands Provincial Government*,[442] the plaintiff proceeded under s 16 of the *Water Resource Act* for compensation, and not for private nuisance at common law. The plaintiff argued that the state (or the officers of the Department of the Western Highlands Provincial Government) or the owners of Rui Plantation required a permit[443] to undertake water works that would consequently alter or increase the flow of the river. The plaintiff further argued that, under s 16(1), (2) and (3) of the Act, the defendant was liable to pay compensation to the owners or occupiers of other land within the vicinity for any damage or loss caused by them.

The plaintiff was a customary owner of land at the junction of the Poli and Gumanch rivers, where he had been farming for many years with coffee, banana trees and subsistence agriculture. The defendants, by their officers, and Rui Plantation workers performed drainage work upstream on the Poli River. This increased the flow of the Poli River and washed down the sand and soil, which was settled on the plaintiff's land near the junction of the Poli and Gumanch rivers. The increased flow of the Poli River also increased the flow of the Gumanch River, and that caused severe erosion to the plaintiff's land. After a while, much of the plaintiff's land became flooded, waterlogged and eroded, resulting in the loss of coffee and banana trees and the use of much of the land. The relevant district officers and agricultural field officers conducted statutory investigations into the plaintiff's claims, and confirmed the claims. They recommended to the Western Highlands Provincial Government that the plaintiff be compensated. The provincial government did not accept the recommendation. The plaintiff then filed proceedings unsuccessfully in the National Court, claiming damages on the basis of private nuisance at common law.

In dismissing the plaintiff's case, his Honour Woods J said (at 97):

---

440 Under s 16(13) of the Act, a person who fails to pay the compensation within the time determined by the Minister is liable to face criminal prosecution with a fine of up to K1,000.

441 Settlement on compensation may have been negotiated, agreed and payments duly made.

442 *Pen Rumints v The State and Western Highlands Provincial Government* [1993] PNGLR 94 at 97.

443 Water use permit: see *Water Resources Act*, Pts V and VII.

> "The law has always recognized that in the case of water coming onto the lower land from land higher up consideration must be given to what is the normal expectation. A flood of water from higher up if it is not created by the positive intervention of people living higher up cannot lead to any liability."[444]

After making reference to the relevant cases on private nuisance at the common law, his Honour continued:

> "The water was natural, it was always on or coming onto the land by the work of nature, the State was merely assisting its flow by digging better drains and ensuring the free flow of the river. This is where the water naturally accumulating is allowed to flow freely, in its natural state it would eventually flow down the rivers. There is nothing artificial or unnatural about the draining of a swamp or repairing the banks of a river to ensure a safer flow. People in the Highlands are always digging drains or barrats to drain their garden land. This drainage work cannot be an exception and actionable. Any damage done may just be one of the vicissitudes of life which people face who have land on the banks of a river."[445]

His Honour's judgment did not refer to the existing legislative enactments on water resource law[446] and did not, therefore, develop an appropriate underlying law along those lines. His Honour observed that unless there is no "positive intervention" by people living upstream to cause flooding and erosion, then there could be no liability in this case.[447] With respect, his Honour's observations that "there is nothing artificial or unnatural about the draining of swamps or repairing the banks of a river" may be doubted in law. Parts V, VI and VII of the *Water Resources Act*, Ch 205 require water use permits to be obtained if a person wishes to discharge water into any watercourse or if such person wishes to divert a normal flow of the water sources.

6.7 EFFECT OF LEGISLATION ON RIPARIAN RIGHTS AND CUSTOMARY WATER RIGHTS

The *Water Resources Act* provides a legal and administrative system relating to the use and distribution of water resources. It also provides the machinery to adjust conflicts between water users. Realising that water is not capable of ownership at common law:

> "The *Water Resources Act* does not refer to ownership of water, but, instead, provides for the vesting in the State of the right to the use, flow and control of water. The important point to note, then, is that the *Water Resources Act* does not, in any way, affect the 'ownership' of water, but is aimed at regulating the use of water."[448]

It is important to consider the effect of the *Water Resources Act* (Ch 205) on riparian rights and customary water rights.

---

444 *Pen Rumints v The State and Western Highlands Provincial Government* [1993] PNGLR 94.
445 Ibid at 98-99.
446 Namely, *Water Resources Act*, s 16, but the case was argued in nuisance.
447 It is respectfully submitted that the facts of the case clearly show that there was "positive intervention" by the actions of the officers of the defendants, which caused the flooding and erosion of the plaintiff's land and, therefore, the defendant should have been held liable and compensation paid.
448 Ward and Fordyce (eds), *Review of Papua New Guinea Water Resources Legislation* (unpublished discussion paper, June 1989).

Riparian rights

When s 5(1) of the *Water Resources Act* vests the right to the use, flow and control of water on the state and regulates the right of riparian holders under s 22 of the Act, it merely regulates such rights, but does not in any way extinguish riparian rights. Under s 22 of the Act, riparian rights are now restricted to taking water for domestic purposes, watering of stock for oneself or any family members or employees resident on the land, fire fighting, and access for oneself, family members or employees resident on riparian land to part of the bank of a watercourse. However, under s 22(2) of the Act, the Director of Water Resources may place restrictions on the quantity of water a riparian tenement holder may use.

Effectively, riparian rights have not been extinguished by the Act. It follows that "even where licences have been issued ... the common law right will survive to enjoin an upstream diverter from taking water in excess of his licence ... In such a case, a riparian will also have a right to claim damages, based on his riparian right, for any injury caused by the excessive diversion".[449] As late as February 1995, the New South Wales Supreme Court, in *Van Son v Forestry Commission of New South Wales*,[450] awarded damages for pollution of a riparian owner's water supply by silt. In a commentary on the decision, Lipman noted:

> "Cohen J concluded on a claim for damages that the effect of the *Water Act* 1912 (NSW) was that riparian owners retained their residual common law right to 'use and take water for domestic purposes without sensible alteration in its character or quality'. Cohen J also found for the plaintiff in private nuisance arising out of an unreasonable interference and enjoyment of land."[451]

It is submitted that this judgment is consistent with the effects of the statutory underpinning of the common law riparian rights under s 22 of the *Water Resources Act*.[452]

Customary water rights

Section 5(2) of the *Water Resources Act* provides:

> "This Act does not affect customary rights to the use of water by the citizens resident in the area in which customary rights are exercised."

This means that customary rights are recognised and specifically preserved under this provision. The effect of a tacit recognition is to legitimise any notion of ownership of water and/or watercourses that may exist in the customary legal order. Since customary water rights are specifically preserved, it necessarily follows that customary water rights can co-exist with any water use rights that may be conferred by the statutory licensing process.

In the event of conflict or interference with the exercise of a customary water use right, compensation is payable to the customary right holder under s 16(2)(a) of the *Water Resources Act*.[453]

6.8 WATER SUPPLY AND SEWERAGE SERVICE

The regime for articulated water supply and sewerage services is covered under the *National Water Supply and Sewerage Act* 1986.[454] That Act essentially establishes the Water Board as a

---

449 Clark and Renard, "The Riparian Doctrine and Australian Legislation" (1970) 7 MULR 475 at 498-506.
450 *Van Son v Forestry Commission of New South Wales* (unreported, NSW Sup Ct, Equity Div, Cohen J, 3 February 1995).
451 Lipman, "Riparian Rights Reconsidered: Van Son v Forestry Commission of New South Wales" (1995) 12 EPLJ 215.
452 For a detailed analysis of this topic, see Kalinoe, op cit n 2.
453 It should be noted that similarly under s 154 of the *Mining Act* 1992 and s 81 of the *Petroleum Act* (Ch 198) compensation is payable to customary right holders.
454 This legislation also repeals and replaces the *National Water Supply and Sewerage Act* (Ch 393) and the *Water Supply (Papua) Act* (Ch 328) in the

corporation,[455] and charges it to provide co-ordinated water supply and sewerage services throughout the country.[456] The Water Board has, inter alia, the following objectives:

(a) to provide and promote water supply and sanitation services by:

(i) making water supply and sewerage services available on a commercial basis to many people in the urban areas; and

(ii) promoting water supply and sanitation with community participation on self-help bases in the rural areas;[457] and

(b) to keep abreast of, and contribute to, developments in the field of water supply and sanitation management, and to improve and extend water supply and sanitation services in the light of such developments, bearing in mind the needs, goals and aspirations of the people, governments and business enterprises.[458]

In keeping with these objectives, some of the functions of the Water Board, as provided under s 5 of the *National Water Supply and Sewerage Act* 1986, are:

"(a) to provide water supply and sanitation services to meet the reasonable needs of the urban population, Governments and business enterprises; and

(b) to promote water supply and sanitation in rural areas and urban fringe areas through community participation on self-help bases and where necessary with the help of loans, grants or aid; and

(c) to maintain its assets in good order; and

(d) to exercise such control as the Water Board may determine over persons and organizations providing water supply and sanitation services, or services relating to water supply and sanitation; and

(e) to set standards as the Water Board may determine for materials and equipment used in water supply and sanitation; and

(f) to advise the National Executive Council on all matters relating to water supply and sanitation; and

(g) to engage in research related to water supply and sanitation activities."

Under s 27 of the *National Water Supply and Sewerage Act* 1986, the Water Board recommends to the relevant Minister[459] for a particular area to be declared a water supply district[460] or a sewerage district.[461] Upon declaration by the Minister in the *National Gazette*,[462] the Water

---

Revised Laws of PNG.

455 *National Water Supply and Sewerage Act* 1986 (No 68 of 1986), s 4.

456 Ibid, preamble.

457 Ibid, s 6(c).

458 Ibid, s 6(f).

459 At the time of writing the relevant Minister was the Minister for Works.

460 Under s 3 of the *National Water Supply and Sewerage Act* 1986, a "water supply district" is merely defined as "an area declared under Section 27 to be a water supply district". This clearly refers to a given geographic location as specified in the instrument of declaration.

461 Under s 3 of the *National Water Supply and Sewerage Act* 1986, a "sewerage district" is defined as "an area declared under Section 27 to be a sewerage district". Again, this refers to a geographic location as specified in the declaration.

462 *National Water Supply and Sewerage Act* 1986, s 28.

Board acquires the exclusive right to operate and maintain water supply and sewerage systems in that area. Since the Act came into operation,[463] and by invocation of this process, the Water Board has been responsible for all water supply and sewerage services in the country,[464] except the National Capital District (NCD). Until mid-1996, the National Capital District Commission (NCDC), being the responsible urban city council, was empowered under the *National Capital District Commission Act* to operate and maintain water supply and sewerage services for a fee in the NCD.[465] Since then, the water supply and sewerage functions have been taken over by a state-owned company, called Eda Ranu, incorporated under the *Companies Act*. Eda Ranu now provides all water and sewerage services in the NCD.

The Water Board is also responsible for formulating policy and setting standards for, and establishing and maintaining a system of, licensing and regulation of plumbers through the country.[466] Even in areas where the Water Board does not operate water supply and sewerage systems, it is the responsible authority to license and set licensing fees for the operation of such systems by another person or authority.[467] Section 26(4) of the *National Water Supply and Sewerage Act* 1986 provides:

> "A person who, without the prior approval of the Water Board, constructs, operates or manages any public water supply and sewerage system, is guilty of an offence.
>
> Penalty: A fine not exceeding K10,000."

In relation to water quality standards to be observed and enforced for the purposes of the Act, the water quality standards set under the *Public Health Act* (Ch No 226)[468] and the *Water Resources Act*[469] are adopted.

Riparian and customary rights to extract water for domestic use

The interaction between the water use rights provisions of the *Water Resources Act* and the *National Water Supply and Sewerage Act* 1986 is not clear. In relation to riparian rights and customary rights to take water for domestic purposes or for stock watering purposes in a water supply district declared under the *National Water Supply and Sewerage Act*, the following opinion is offered.

First, under ss 21 and 22 of the *Water Resources Act*, a riparian right holder is allowed to take water without charge from a watercourse for domestic or stock watering purpose by that person or members of his or her family resident on the land, and for his or her employees so resident.[470] To do so, the riparian right holder is allowed to "place a permanent installation for taking water in, or on the land adjacent to, the water course".[471] Viewed liberally, this may, in some instances, depending on the number of family members and employees resident on the riparian land, amount to a small to medium-sized water supply scheme. Could this be in breach of s 26(4) of the

---

463 All provisions of the Act, except s 39(b), came into effect in January 1987. Section 39(b) came into effect on 1 July 1987.
464 To date, this has been mainly in the urban areas.
465 There has been tension between the two organisations as to who should control the water supply and sewerage services in the NCD.
466 *National Water Supply and Sewerage Act* 1986, s 26(1).
467 Ibid, s 26(2). Note that under s 26(3), "[a]ny tariff set in respect of a water supply or sewerage system not operated by the Water Board shall be submitted to the Water Board and shall have no effect until approved by the Water Board, except that any such tariff in effect immediately before the coming into operation of this Act shall be deemed to have been approved by the Water Board until further advise by the Water Board."
468 *Public Health Act* (Ch 226). See s 56 of the Regulations, which provide minimum water quality standards. These are discussed later in this chapter.
469 Quality standards for water are provided under Sch 4 of the *Water Resources Act*. These are discussed later in this chapter under the subject of pollution.
470 *Water Resources Act* (Ch 25) Revised Laws of PNG, s 22(1)(a).
471 *Water Resources Act*, s 22(4).

National Water Supply and Sewerage Act, rendering such activity illegal? Depending on the scale and whether or not the riparian owner charges fees, the issue is arguable. If it is on a small scale and fees are not levied, the riparian right holder is most likely acting within rights accorded under other legislation or common law for a specified purpose. On the other hand, where the riparian right holder supplies water at a fee to other members of the public within his or her vicinity, it may well be in breach of s 26(4) of the *National Water Supply and Sewerage Act*.

Secondly, by operation of s 5(2) of the *Water Resources Act*, "customary rights to the use of water by the citizens resident in the area in which those customary rights[472] are exercised" are not affected in any way by the regulatory regime of the Act. That means that customary right holders are at liberty to use water as they see fit in accordance with their custom. The question then is posed: could customary right holders organise themselves and set up articulated water supplies and provide such service to the other members of their community who are not necessarily members of their clan or village? Provided such an activity can be established to be "authorized by custom",[473] the question is answered in the positive. Undoubtedly, however, customary right holders are at liberty to obtain water through pipe installations for their domestic, agricultural and other associated usages, even if this requires large organised communities, because, although the extraction of water through mechanised installations may improve the technique and technology of delivery, it serves the same customary usage and purpose.

Application of the Water Resources Act to the Water Board

The Water Board is a corporation created by the *National Water Supply and Sewerage Act* 1986 for the exploitation of water by "co-ordinating planning, design, construction, management of, and charging for, water supply and sewerage services through the country": s 1. Just as the other corporations are subject to the various regulatory regimes of their resource sectors,[474] the Water Board is subject to the water resource management and regulatory regime under the *Water Resources Act*. This means that the Water Board is required to obtain the necessary water use permits and observe all the other regulatory provisions pertinent to the exploitation and utilisation of water under the *Water Resources Act*.[475]

---

[472] In s 2 of the *Water Resources Act* (Ch 205), customary rights are referred to as "customary rights to the use of water" and defined as "rights to the use of water: (a) that are authorised by custom; and (b) that are being availed of at the time in question or, in the normal course of land management, would be availed of in a customary manner within a reasonable period after that time".

[473] Ibid.

[474] For example, the Mineral Resources Development Company (MRDC), a government-owned company engaged in the mining and petroleum industries, is subject to the *Mining Act* 1992 and the *Petroleum Act* (Ch 198) Revised Laws of PNG.

[475] Unless exemption is granted under s 4(1) of the *Water Resources Act* (Ch 205): "The Minister may, on the recommendation of the Board, exempt: (a) a person or class of persons; or (b) an area; or (c) a water use, from any provisions of this Act."

Public Health Act and the Water Board

The following by-laws made under s 141 of the *Public Health Act* (Ch 226) are relevant to the activities of the Water Board:

(a) the *Public Health (Sanitation and General) Regulation* provides the general regime for the provision and manner of discharge of sewerage and other refuse;

(b) the *Public Health (Septic Tanks) Regulation* sets out the standards and regulations for septic tanks;

(c) the *Public Health (Sewerage) Regulation* sets out the sewerage treatment standards and regulations; and

(d) the *Public Health (Underground Water Tanks) Regulation* sets out the guidelines and standards for the installation of underground water tanks.

These by-laws are of equal application to any person or entity engaged in the construction, provision or maintenance of septic tanks, sewerage treatment disposal systems and underground water tanks.

6.9 POLLUTION CONTROL AND WATER QUALITY STANDARDS

Effluent discharge

The principal statutory provision that deals with unauthorised discharge of effluents into water and, hence, causing water pollution is s 58(2) of the *Water Resources Act* (Ch 205). That provision reads as follows:

> "A person who, not being the holder of a permit:
>
> ...
>
> (c) discharges water or waste into any water; or
>
> (d) discharges water containing waste on to land or into the ground in circumstances that result in:
>
> (i) the waste; or
>
> (ii) other waste emanating as a result of processes from the waste,
>
> entering water; or
>
> ...
>
> (g) knowingly causes or permits any chemical, metallic or organic wastes or any unsightly or odorous litter or waste or refuse to enter any water,
>
> is guilty of an offence."

The offence attracts a penalty of a fine not exceeding K5,000 for every day for which the pollution is unabated.[476]

---

[476] See also *Water Resources Act*, ss 59 and 60.

Rivers are important as a water source for agriculture, power generation and industry. They are also used to flush out effluent and waste. Wisdon has noted:

> "The enjoyment of river water exists either in its removal for public supply, industry, agriculture, etc, or its use within the channel for fishing, navigation, recreation and so forth. A further benefit of a river is its potential as a dispository for effluents and waste water, provided that neither water pollution nor flooding is occasioned."[477]

Regulations made under the *Public Health Act* (Ch 226) also provide for the prevention of the pollution of natural watercourses and the maintenance of the purity of water supply. The most relevant regulation is the *Public Health (Sanitation and General) Regulation.* Under reg 55, "water supply" is expansively defined to include "a river, spring, stream, water course, creek, swamp, waterhole, lake, pond, tank, dam or reservoir" Regulation 58 provides:

> "A person who deposits or permits to be deposited in any place any offensive matter or thing by which a water supply is liable to be polluted is guilty of an offence.
>
> Penalty: a fine not exceeding K1,000.00."[478]

Apart from these statutory provisions, under common law, pollution of water that interferes with property rights attaching to rivers and watercourses may give rise to a civil action for damages and/or injunction. A civil action in such an instance may generally be based on private nuisance and/or negligence. The authoritative judgment by Lord M'Naghten in *John Young & Co v Bankier Distiller Co* is often cited:

> "Every riparian proprietor is thus entitled to the water of his stream, in its natural flow, without sensible alteration in its character or quality."[479]

These common law principles apply in PNG as part of the underlying law.[480]

The effluents that may be lawfully discharged into a watercourse by obtaining a water use permit under the *Water Resources Act* fall under three categories:

(a) sewage;

(b) industrial wastes of the nature of agricultural and horticultural wastes, meat processing and packaging industry wastes etc; and

(c) industrial wastes of agricultural and horticultural origins associated with coffee, oil palm, cocoa, sugar and food processing.

The applicable fees charged under the Act for discharge of wastes are set out in Sch 3, which is set out as Table 1 at the end of this chapter.

When an application is made for a water use permit to discharge waste or water into a watercourse,[481] the applicant is required, among other things, to give details of the watercourse to

---

[477] Wisdon, *Aspects of Water Law* (Barry Rose (Publishers) Ltd, Chichester, West Sussex, 1981), p 56.

[478] For effective punishment and deterrence, it would be advisable to prosecute offenders under s 58(2) of the *Water Resources Act* (Ch 205).

[479] *John Young & Co v Bankier Distiller Co* [1893] AC 691 (HL).

[480] See *Constitution*, Sch 2.

[481] See *Water Resources Act*, s 28(1) and Form 2, "Application for water use permit to discharge water or wastes".

which the discharge is to be made, the volume of water to be discharged and the nature and characteristics of the waste. In particular, the applicant must specify biochemical oxygen demand and variation, pH and variation range, temperature and variation range, appearance, colour, smell and variations, and chemical nature, including chemicals present and likely to be present, etc.

Water quality

In relation to water quality standards, reg 7(2) of the *Water Resources Regulations*, (Ch 205) provides:

> "Any discharges to, or use of, water must not cause a lowering of water quality below the prescribed standards, subject to the allowance for mixing of wastes with the receiving water."

Regulation 7(6) and (7) provides:

> "(6) The water quality standards specify, unless stated otherwise, maximum permissible levels or limits of various substances and parameters unless the natural level is greater.
>
> (7) A discharge into, or use of, water must not increase the level of any substance or parameter above that prescribed or above the maximum level to be found naturally.
>
> Penalty: A fine not exceeding K5,000.00.
>
> Default penalty: A fine not exceeding K2,000.00."

Water quality standards are stipulated under Sch 4. These are set out at the end of this chapter in Tables 2 and 3.

In the event that reliable scientific data indicates that work quality standards are not appropriate for particular specified waters or for the use of those waters, the standards may be modified by the Water Resources Board to meet the requirements pertaining specifically to those waters and their uses.[482] It should be noted that the water quality standards as set out in Table 2 may be changed when scientific advances necessitate their modification.[483]

6.10 CONCLUSION

Water resource management generally refers to the task of regulating water uses amongst competing and varied demands of users, mainly through the permit licensing process. This process has evolved by necessity through increasing competition for resources and the need to allocate them and maintain a record of what resources are being used, by whom, and for what purposes, so that best management practices and approaches can be adopted and developed.

The *Water Resources Act* essentially provides for the regulation and control of the taking, discharge and damming of water in PNG for purposes other than those associated with domestic, fire fighting and customary uses. It does not, however, provide for the management and

[482] *Water Resources Regulations* (Ch 205), s 7(4).
[483] Ibid, s 7(5).

conservation of rivers and/or lakes as entities, soil conservation and erosion control of such watercourses, acceptable levels of in-stream flow, or other utilisations of water resources, such as for fishery purposes.

TABLE 1: FEES FOR DISCHARGE OF WASTES

1 Sewage

Basic charge = K0.05/m^3/year.

FORMULA:

Annual charge (K/year) = 0.05 x volume (K/m^3) x treatment factor (m^3/year).

Type of Sewage Treatment	Treatment Factor
No treatment – this includes sewage that is screened and macerated	1.0
Primary treatment (screened and settled) providing the retention time in sedimentation tank is at least 45 minutes	0.6
Secondary treatment (trickling filters, activated sludge, oxidation ponds or lagoons), providing sewage loadings do not exceed manufacturers recommendations	0.3
Tertiary treatment (all forms of advanced sewage treatment)	0.01

2 Industrial wastes

Basic charge K0.34/kg biochemical oxygen demand (5 day)/year.

These include:

(a) agricultural and horticultural wastes; and

(b) meat processing and packaging industry wastes; and

(c) wastes of a similar kind, consisting predominantly of organic wastes,

that contain substantial numbers of bacteria and viruses pathogenic to humans.

3 Industrial wastes

Basic charge K0.25/kg biochemical oxygen demand (5 day)/year.

These include:

(a) agricultural and horticultural wastes associated with:

  (i) coffee; and

  (ii) oil palm; and

  (iii) cocoa; and

  (iv) sugar

  industries; and

(b) food processing wastes consisting predominantly of organic wastes that are free of bacteria and viruses pathogenic to humans.

SOURCE: *Water Resources Act* (Ch 205), Sch 3.

TABLE 2: QUALITY STANDARDS FOR WATER

Parameters	Fresh water (g/m^3)	Sea water (g/m^3)
Arsenic	0.05	0.05
Barium	1.0	1.0
Boron	1.0	2.0
Cadmium	0.01	0.001
Chlorine (total residual)	0.005 at pH6	0.005
Chromium (as hexavalent form)	0.05	0.01
Chlorine (total residual)	0.005 at pH6	0.005
Chromium (as hexavalent form)	0.05	0.01
Colour	No alteration to natural colouration	
Cobalt	Limit of detectability	
Copper	1.0	0.03

Cyanide (as HCN)	0.05	0.01
Faecal coliform bacteria	(See Note under Table 3)	
Fats	None	None
Fluoride	1.5	1.5
Grease	None	None
Insoluble residues	No insoluble residues or sludge formation to occur	
Iron (in solution)	1.0	1.0
Lead	0.05	0.004
Manganese (in solution)	0.5	2.0
Mercury	0.0002	0.0002
Nickel	1.0	1.0
Nitrate (as No_3 -/+ No_2)	45.0	45.0
Odour	No alteration to natural odour	
Oil	None	None
Oxygen	Not less than 6.0	Not less than 5.0
Pesticides	None	None
pH	No alteration to natural pH	
Phenols	0.002	0.002
Potassium	5.0	450
Radioactivity	None	None
Selenium	0.01	0.01
Silver	0.05	0.05
Sulphate (as SO_4-)	400.0	-
Sulphide (HS)	0.002	0.002
Tars	None	None
Taste	No alteration to natural taste	
Temperature	No alteration greater than 2°C	
Tin	0.5	0.5
Toxicants, miscellaneous	None	None
Turbidity	No alteration greater than 25 NTU	
Zinc	5.0	5.0

TABLE 3: MAXIMUM PERMITTED CONCENTRATIONS OF AMMONIA-NITROGEN

Temperature °C	**pH value** 7.0	8.0	9.0
5	16.1	1.6	0.2
10	**11.0**	1.1	0.1
15	7.5	0.8	0.09
20	5.2	0.5	0.07
25	3.6	0.4	0.06
30	2.6	0.3	0.05
35	1.6	0.2	0.04

Note: Faecal coliform bacteria standards

Based on no fewer than five samples taken over not more than a 30-day period, the median value of the faecal coliform bacteria content of the waters must not exceed 200 per 100 mi.

CHAPTER 7

PROJECT FINANCING IN PAPUA NEW GUINEA

John Sagir Kawi and Wilfred W Golman***

7.1 INTRODUCTION

Negotiating and securing financing packages for major projects can be difficult. Papua New Guinea (PNG), like other developing countries, can encounter difficulties in realising suitable financing packages to satisfy its distinctive requirements. The following are typical for most developing countries:

- limited capital funds, and a lack of skilled labour and modern technology;
- inadequate social and economic infrastructure;
- foreign capital and other economic assistance sourced offshore; and
- financers' judgments about the viability of the project, the worth of the investment, the safe and efficient use of their funds, and repayment of their funds.

These difficulties are linked directly to the business environment in that country. The borrowing host country will be expected to be politically and economically stable, to have a proper regulatory framework and to have appropriate industrial and labour policies in place. If the host country's business environment is unstable, any potential foreign investor will be reluctant to lend. However, if investors fund projects, they assume high risks and, in doing so, expect higher returns to compensate for those risks. In many cases, investors share these risks by involving others in the project. Consequently, structuring a finance package usually involves many parties and instruments. *Project financing* is often used in funding major projects.

Project financing occurs in the context of very high capital cost projects undertaken in three sectors:

- extractive industries (for example, oil, natural gas and mining);
- chemical and process plants (oil refineries, steel mills, cements, fertiliser and power plants); and
- transportation (oil and gas pipelines, such as the gas pipeline from Kutubu to Kikori then to North Queensland).

This chapter considers project financing in general, and some of the major projects in PNG funded through project financing in particular.

* Solicitor General for PNG.
** Lecturer in Law, Department of Law, UPNG.

7.2 NATURE OF PROJECT FINANCING

Project financing has become increasingly popular. Commercial banks and financial institutions are being asked to consider more applications for this type of financing. There is no precise definition, but it is sometimes loosely referred to as project lending, or project loans. However, a few general comments may be made.

First, the term *project financing* commonly describes the various methods that banks and institutional lenders use to finance the construction of new projects, on a basis whereby payout is anticipated from the revenue stream generated by the project. Project financing often involves a loan to a new entity formed specifically to own a project.[484] The requirement under this method is that the funds utilised in a project must be repaid wholly out of revenues realised from the particular project. There are some projects where parent companies of the sponsors of projects assist in financing, while no funding from outside is required.[485] Under such an arrangement, a repayment is devised according to the terms agreed to by parent companies and their subsidiaries that are sponsors of projects. *Infra-company financing* is a term appropriate in describing such financing arrangements. It is often made between a parent and its subsidiaries, or between various member of a corporate family that extends across national and international boundaries.[486]

Secondly, since most major projects take several years to complete, project financing generally involves raising funds over a period of years in stages as the project progresses. This *phase financing* enables the types of finance to be tailored to meet the needs of each stage of the project and, if the finance plan is sufficiently flexible, to tap the world's capital markets at the most appropriate times.

Thirdly, project financing is generally *off balance sheet* for the major sponsors of the project. *Off balance sheet* financing is financing that does not show as a direct liability on the balance sheet of the sponsors of a project.

Fourthly, project financing tends to be complicated and to involve extensive legal documentation designed to ensure that the cash flow from the project will be sufficient to repay the debt raised for the project, or that the debt will be serviced by some credit-worthy party even if the cash flow is inadequate or is interrupted.

Fifthly, in order for companies to extend finance, such projects require security. Legal instruments are designed to ensure such protection. These legal instruments include *mining development contracts*, *petroleum development contracts*, *joint ventures* and *state agreements*. These legal instruments perform a number of functions:

> "... they allow the investors to negotiate with the ... Government specific terms of the investment. Such terms include the sharing of revenue from the project, the taxation regime, employment and training of nationals, provision of social and economic infrastructure, and laying down environmental programs and standards."[487]

---

[484] Grover, "Castle, Project Finance Guidelines for the Commercial Banker" in *Journal of Commercial Bank Lending* (April 1975) at 14.

[485] Ibid.

[486] See also Sargent, *International Trade Law and Practice; Public and Private Funding in International Trade* (London, 1983), p 14.

[487] Nonggorr, "Foreign Investment in the Mining and Petroleum Sectors of Papua New Guinea: Benefit Sharing and Customary Land Issues" in Eustan Quah et al (eds), *Law and Economic Development: Cases and Materials from South East Asia* (1993), p 343.

More importantly, the legal instruments must provide an effective form of resource security or a degree of security to the project developer and its investment. The term *resource security* is used here to cover not only the "developer's ability to rely upon an existing contractual right to proceed with the development, but any alternatives which the developer may have to seek to recover its loss, where it is unable to rely upon a contractual right".[488] These alternatives include a possible right to compensation or restitution, since "the offer of appropriate compensation is an important element in providing investment security for industry".[489]

Security of foreign investment depends upon the legal framework and the manner in which these instruments are used. Other legal instruments that can provide security are:[490]

- adoption of rules of international law;
- reference to international arbitration for dispute settlement;
- creation of particular corporate structures;
- reliance upon rights of property;
- finality of the decision-making process;
- contractual limitations upon the exercise of power;
- formulation of management plans;
- formulation of codes of practice;
- creation of rigorous administrative systems; and
- limited power to vary or revoke particular administrative decisions.

It must be noted that none of these mechanisms provide absolute security. Within a legal system, the law governing these forms of security can be changed, even if the law itself restricts the manner of change. Whatever system of security is created by the law, the law itself is liable to be changed.[491]

7.3 TYPES OF FINANCE

In complex project financing it is common to use different types of financing to fund different stages of the project. For example, *equity funds* may be used to finance feasibility studies and preliminary design and engineering, *short-term revolving credits* often finance major equipment, and *development bank funds* may be used for longer term financing. In short, most project finance involves a blend of several different types of funding. One of the major challenges in any project financing is to combine these different types into a package that provides the lowest cost for the project.

Equity or debt finance

The basic distinction is, of course, between *equity* and *debt* funds. Equity is frequently referred to as the *ownership interest* in a project, as it generally determines how ultimate control over a

---

488 Rigney, "The Resource Development Contract – How Is It?" in Gardner (ed), *The Challenge of Resource Security: Law and Policy* (1993), pp 89-90.
489 Ibid.
490 Fisher, "The Meaning and Significance of Resource Security" in Gardner (ed), op cit n 5, pp 16-17.
491 Ibid.

project is divided. Equity is also the risk element of any finance package, since the providers of equity funds have no assurance that they will ever be able to recoup their invested funds. In this regard, it should be noted that equity contributions to financing can be in kind as well as cash. Because they want to minimise the amount of cash or risk, corporations involved in international projects often try to make their equity contributions in the form of equipment, technology, patents or know-how.

Debt financing is based on a *contract* (that is, a loan agreement), which spells out the terms and conditions under which funds are advanced. The providers of debt funds generally receive interest periodically, and are entitled to receive repayment of the funds they advance in accordance with a schedule for repayment.

Types of finance

Another way of classifying types of finance is by the method or structure of the financing. Methods commonly used include contract-based financing, production payment financing, advance payment financing, compensatory financing arrangements, and leveraged lease financing. These methods are summarised briefly.

Contract-based financing

In contract-based project financing, lenders advance funds to the project on the basis of a contractual commitment by clearly credit-worthy parties to use the project facilities. These contractual commitments generally involve agreement to purchase output from the project.

Production payment financing

Production payment financing is a specialised method of financing that has been commonly used in petroleum-related projects. There are a number of types of production payment financing, but its essence is that the actual physical product produced (for example, petroleum or a mineral) is assigned to, or for the benefit of, the lender, and debt service is provided out of the proceeds from the sale of production.

Advance payment financing

In this type of financing, a company makes advance payments to subsidise exploration and development, with the loan repaid out of production if the venture is successful. Of course, if the venture is unsuccessful, the company making the advance payment assumes the risk of non-payment.

Compensatory financing arrangements

Compensatory financing is a type of finance that is growing in importance in financing east-west trade and investment. In essence, this contractual obligation is designed to generate the hard currency to repay loans made to finance the project.

Leveraged lease financing

Leveraged lease financing is a method of project financing in which the ultimate user of a project facility leases the facility during the period of its useful life, rather than owning the facility in its own name. Lease financing is often used to finance power plants or industrial facilities in the United States.

7.4 PROJECT FINANCING IN PNG: FINANCING NATURAL RESOURCE PROJECTS

Mining and petroleum developments require large capital inputs. Given the huge capital costs and the risks involved in mineral and petroleum developments, a project developer may not want to be the sole developer. All resource development projects in PNG have been undertaken by a group of companies combining their capital and expertise together to carry out the task.

Through project financing, a number of major projects in mining and petroleum have been developed in PNG. These are discussed below.

Bougainville copper mine

The first substantial foreign investment that took place in PNG through project financing was the financing and development of the Panguna copper project on the island of Bougainville in the mid-1960s. The mine mobilised the largest investment in any Australian territory at that time, and proved to be the first of many PNG resource projects. It required huge loans from overseas banks. This project cost more than A$423 million, two thirds of which was borrowed internationally, and the balance was in equity, including a 20 percent equity participation by the host government. The total borrowing was US$334 million. However, this was broken down and financed as follows:[492]

1. Bank of America syndicate – US$110 million.
2. Commonwealth Trading Bank syndicate – US$67.4 million.
3. Japanese cash and equipment loans – US$60 million.
4. US Export-Import Bank equipment loan – US$56.8 million.
5. Equipment loans from Australian suppliers – A$25 million.
6. Commonwealth Savings Bank Housing loan – A$12.5 million.

At full production the mine yielded 90,000 tons of copper per day. The main driving force for the success of the mine was CRA (Conzinc Rio Tinto of Australia, a subsidiary of Rio Tinto Zinc of England) with Bougainville Copper Limited (BCL) as its project company, all within the framework of the Bougainville Copper Agreement of 1967 (the agreement).[493] This agreement was given legal force when the House of Assembly of PNG passed the *Mining (Bougainville Copper Agreement) Act* 1967. It was this legal instrument that governed the operations of the mine, as well as providing the general investment regime, including taxation component, payment of royalties, environmental management, employment and training of nationals, and provision of infrastructure. The mine was operated by BCL on behalf of CRA,[494] and, until its forced closure by militant landowners in 1989, it was the major source of foreign exchange earnings for PNG. While the mine has been important to the development of PNG in terms of investment security, the investment regime created by the 1976 agreement gave rise to serious problems culminating in the mine's closure in 1989.

---

492 Wilshire, "Financing the Project" in Stephenson (ed), *The Establishment of a Copper Mine, Foundation* (2000) *Australian Journal of Architecture and Engineering* at 161.

493 Denoon, *Getting Under the Skin: The Bougainville Copper Agreement and the Creation of the Panguna Mine* (2000), p 3.

494 Bougainville Copper Ltd (BCL) was a project company incorporated in PNG by CRA to manage and operate the mine. The shareholders in BCL were CRA (53.6%), PNG Government (20%) and members of the public (26.4%).

The problems encountered on Bougainville are twofold.[495] The first problem, and possibly the biggest problem affecting the security of any kinds of foreign investments in PNG today, was accessing land required for any resource developments. In Bougainville, land was required on a grand scale to develop the copper mine, and all land was traditional land owned by the indigenous people, who simply refused to sell or surrender their lands. This forced the colonial administration to acquire the lands by compulsory acquisition, and they then flew in riot police to clear the way for further surveying and for the mining operations to begin.[496] While land required for the project was owned by traditional landowners, and its ownership and usages were regulated by traditional rules of custom, the huge investment was made under foreign laws. As noted above, the investment regime was created by the *Mining (Bougainville Copper Agreement) Act* 1967 and, where relevant, the *Mining Act* 1928-1966 (now the *Mining Act* 1992). This statute vests ownership of all minerals in the state, even where they occur on customary lands, a concept that was hardly accepted on Bougainville[497] and all over PNG. The legislation governing acquisition of land for the development of Bougainville copper was the *Land Ordinance* 1962 (now the *Land Act* 1996).

Again, this legislation embodies western values and concepts of land ownership, which are contrary to the customary rules on land prevailing in PNG today.[498] The confrontation between the government and the company on one hand, and the government and the local landowners on the other, is well encapsulated by statements of three Bougainvilleans who bitterly opposed the compulsory acquisition of their lands for mining activities. Their sentiments were expressed in this manner:

> "Land is our physical life – food and sustenance. Land is our social life, it is marriage, it is status, it is politics, in fact, it is our only world. When you [the administration] take our land, you cut away the very heart of our existence. We have little or no experience of social survival detached from land. For us to be landless is a nightmare which no dollar in the pocket or dollar in the bank will allay, we are a threatened people."[499]

This statement demonstrates how valuable land is to indigenous people. Such possessive and emotional attachment to land makes it very difficult to acquire land for any development. Land-related issues in PNG are real concerns that should be treated with care in investment planning decisions, for they would no doubt affect the security of the project and investment if not treated with caution.

The second major problem encountered on Bougainville also arose out of the investment regime created under the 1967 agreement. This time, it related to how the investment benefits were distributed. First, the state agreement establishing the mine, the *Mining (Bougainville Copper Agreement) Act* 1967, was entered into between the Australian colonial administration in PNG and Bougainville Copper Limited. There was no provision in the agreement or the ratifying legislation providing for participation by local landowners, as well as the provincial government of Bougainville. This omission was to be the cause for much grievance and debate, which aggravated the already existing tensions. The result was that the terms of the agreement proved to

---

495 Nonggorr, op cit n 4.
496 Ibid. See also Denoon, op cit n 10, for a detailed account of landowner opposition and refusal to sell their lands.
497 Denoon, ibid, p 1.
498 Nonggorr, op cit n 4. See also Ch 3 of this book.
499 Dove and Togolo, "Mining Bitterness" in Sack (ed), *Problems of Choice: Lands in Papua New Guinea's Future* (1974), pp 181-182.

be more favourable to the company than to the government. In particular, critics argued that the provisions dealing with taxation and payment of royalties treated the host government shabbily.[500]

Clause 7 of the agreement set out the tax regime in detail. Some of the key features were:

- a three-year tax holiday was to commence when commercial production began;
- capital expenditures, including plant and equipment and other expenses for purposes relating to the construction of the mine, were deductible from returns for income tax purposes for as many years as may be necessary;
- BCL was entitled to a 20 percent exemption on its taxable income after the three years and after the depreciation deductions;
- any taxable income (after the tax holiday and the depreciation deductions) was to be taxed at the then existing company rate of 25 percent. After 15 years this rate was to rise to a maximum of 50 percent, and no further until the 26th year, when it would rise by an annual 1 percent to a maximum of 66 percent; and
- BCL was expressly exempted from paying other taxes, including any tax on interests accruing from moneys borrowed, export tax, import tax for mine equipment and other rates and duties.[501]

As to the royalty, BCL was to pay the national government a royalty of a quarter of the market value of the minerals produced.

The other important terms of the agreement that were to have a significant bearing on future resource agreements and developments were:

- **State equity participation:** The administration was limited by the state agreement to take 20 percent equity in the project.
- **Environmental management:** Under cl 15(a), the company was required to dispose of mine waste, including tailings, in "a manner which is reasonably safe and results in as little damage or disturbance having regard always to the need for the company to carry out its said operations efficiently and economically".
- **Compensation for loss of land and other rights:** Under cl 15(d), it was stated:

  "Notwithstanding that the same [mine waste] may have been disposed of in an area in a manner approved, the company shall make compensation for any loss suffered by any indigenous or other inhabitant of the said Bougainville Island or other islands adjacent thereto resulting from any damage done (whether to land, anything on land, water or otherwise) or any interference with any right to use land or water in the course of or tailings produced as a result of its operation under this Agreement."

Furthermore, under cl 15(e), "[t]he company shall not be liable for any loss, damage, disturbance or interference caused by the disposal by the company of any of the said overburden or tailings".

These provisions on environmental management, compensation and royalty payments were to serve as the catalyst for the secessionists' uprising and the civil war later. Overall, it has been said

---

500 Momis, "Bougainville Copper: The case for Re-negotiation" in Zorn and Bayne (eds), *Foreign Investment, International and National Development* (1975), pp 121-122.

501 See the Bougainville Copper Agreement 1967, cl 9.

that the 1967 agreement catered largely for the interests of the investor and the administration. The investor was given favourable terms as an incentive to develop the mineral deposit. Since this was the first major investment ever to be undertaken in the territory, the terms were designed so that other overseas investors could also be attracted to invest in PNG. Concerns about political risks because of the likelihood of PNG becoming independent, the risks of expropriation (which had occurred in other third world countries), and the refusal of the Australian Government to guarantee the security of investment, led CRA to press for and win favourable fiscal provisions.[502]

The administration, on the other hand, was to benefit from its equity holding, the payment of taxes and royalties, and the employment and training of local people. Again, the terms of the agreement on these matters were in favour of CRA. One of the main reasons why the administration did not seek maximum benefits from the mine, by the imposition of higher taxes and other developmental obligations, was that Australia was coming under constant criticism from the United Nations for not preparing PNG well enough for political independence.

Ok Tedi copper and gold project

The second mining project to be governed by a state agreement was the Ok Tedi copper and gold mine in the remote western province. While the mine commenced operations in 1984, legislation providing for the investment and the mine operations, namely the *Mining (Ok Tedi Agreement) Act*, Ch 363, was passed in 1976 to give the force of law to the agreement entered into between the government of PNG and BHP of Australia. As the mine development has progressed, this agreement has been the subject of several amendments through supplemental agreements, all of which have been ratified and given the force of law.

The project financing of Ok Tedi involved many financial institutions and a number of government institutions. Numerous agreements relating to guarantees, assignments and recourse financing were made between the project developers and the various financial institutions.[503] The main features of these financial arrangements are outlined to illustrate how the issue of risks was allocated as a form of project and investment security. The principal shareholders were three large companies from three countries that were important to PNG – BHP of Australia, Amoco of the United States, and Kupfer (short for Kupfer Explorations Gesellschaft), a consortium of two German companies and a German government agency. As the principal developers along with the government of PNG, these companies negotiated various loans from commercial lenders and export credit lenders after giving in return various guarantees, some of which bind the PNG government.[504] The commercial lenders were:[505]

- Citicorp Bank of Australia;
- overseas private investment from the United States; and
- Kreditanstalt fur Wiederaufbau from West Germany.

[502] O'Faircheallaigh, *Mining and Development: Foreign-Financed Mines in Australia, Ireland, Papua New Guinea and Zambia* (1984), p 228.
[503] McGill, "Project Financing Applied to the Ok Tedi Mine – A Government Perspective" in *Natural Resources Forum* (1983), p 115.
[504] Nonggorr, "Economic Development Contracts and Investment Security in Papua New Guinea" (1992) AMPLA Yearbook 686 at 714.
[505] Ibid.

The export credit lenders who supplied the machinery and the equipment for the project were:

- Export Credit Guarantee Department from the United Kingdom;
- Export Development Corporation from Canada; and
- Oesterreichische Kontrollbank Aktiengesellskhaft from Austria.

There were two Papua New Guinean companies involved in these financial arrangements. The first was the Mt Fubilafi Development Co, and the second was the Star Mountains Holding Co Pty Ltd. The provincial government and the local people of the project area owned both.[506] Ok Tedi Mining Limited (OTML) was then incorporated by the major shareholders as a specially built company to manage and operate the mine on behalf of the shareholders.[507]

The second key feature of this financing scheme was that the PNG government approved and gave certain important undertakings, since the project lenders had refused to lend without such approvals and undertakings.[508] Furthermore, the state obtained a loan from Germany to pay for a part of its equity participation in the construction of the major road for the project. This brought the German government directly into the project. The German government then contributed to the loan advance from Kreditanstalt fur Wiederaufbau, under an arrangement with Kupfer, the German consortium, in order to assist its own corporations in securing long-term supplies of raw materials.[509] Thirdly, the various lending institutions tied into the loan agreements completion times for the various stages of the project development, and set project production levels. A default would carry penalties, including reduction of the loan repayment periods or an increase in interest rates.[510] Although the state resisted and refused to be party to completion guarantees, which carried political risks, the complex nature of these financing schemes bound the state to some of these guarantees, which were given on behalf of the project.[511]

This shows that if PNG acts in a way that seriously affects the project, the consequences may be financially and politically disastrous. PNG would be put under heavy pressure, or even counter action by involved foreign governments and agencies, as well as the international financial institutions and local companies which are also involved. Hence, security of the investment is a great concern to the investor. Consequently, the investor will adopt any measures, including obtaining undertakings from the host government, to protect its investment.[512]

Porgera, Misima, Lihir and Tolokuma gold mines

These projects were also project financed using foreign capital provided by many overseas lenders, with the state taking up equity in all projects. One common feature about all of these mines is that they are located in some of the least-developed and very remote areas of the country, where there little or no social and economic infrastructure was in place until major resource developments occurred. Porgera, Misima and Tolokuma, like Bougainville and Ok Tedi, are located in remote and very rugged mountains, while Lihir and Misima mines are located on small and remote coastal islands. There are many risks associated with developments of resources in

506 Ibid.

507 Ok Tedi Mining Ltd is a project company incorporated in PNG. It has three shareholders: BHP (52%) PNG Government (30%) and Inmet Mining Corp of Canada (18%). The initial German shareholders sold off their shares to Inmet Mining and withdrew from the project after they discovered the destruction caused to the environment and its likely consequences.

508 McGill, op cit n 20, p 115.

509 Ibid, p 120.

510 Nonggorr, op cit n 21.

511 Ibid.

512 Ibid.

such remote areas, the most important being accessing traditional land for the development of these projects.

The other notable feature of these projects relates to the legal framework governing the investment. The Bougainville and Ok Tedi projects are governed by their respective state agreements. All other projects are governed by either ordinary mining or petroleum development contracts, as the case may be. A mining or development contract or petroleum agreement may not necessarily give the project developers as great a sense of investment security as would a state agreement.

There are two other notable departures from Bougainville and Ok Tedi. The first is that project developers are now placed under a contractual obligation to encourage and assist local people to undertake and participate in associated and spin-off business activities.

The second important departure has been the direct involvement of both the landowners and the provincial governments in the investment decision-making process and in the sharing of benefits. In 1988, in light of the unfolding landowner crisis on Bougainville, the government adopted a new policy, under which all major investments are to be discussed in a *development forum*. This is a forum where, prior to the commencement of a project, representatives of the state, the project developers, the provincial government/s, and the landowners all meet to discuss and iron out all areas of potential dispute concerning the project. The objective of the forum is to get all concerned parties together to discuss the project openly, so that misunderstandings and conflict can be avoided. For landowners, this is an avenue for participation in the investment decision-making process. The development forum process is now a mandatory procedure, following its incorporation into the *Mining Act* 1992 and the *Oil and Gas Act* 1998.

Following the development forum discussions, a series of contracts are signed. For instance, in the case of Porgera and Misima, the national government entered into separate contracts with the landowners, the provincial government and then the project developers. The agreements with the landowners provide that the government may sell 50 percent of its equity, that is, 50 percent of its 30 percent equity in the case of Porgera, and 50 percent of its 20 percent equity in the case of Misima. The government further undertook to ensure that 23 percent of royalties are paid to the landowners. On their part, the landowners have agreed to co-operate with the government and the investor companies to ensure that the project and investment are not disrupted in any way.[513] The agreements between the government and project developers have no relationship to the landowners. Despite this, the project developers, the landowners and the provincial government maintain a very close working relationship.

Kutubu petroleum project

This was the first petroleum project that was financed using project financing. Located in the very remote and rugged Southern Highlands Province, the project is operated by a joint venture of six entities, with Chevron Niugini as the project manager.[514] The usual arrangements made in the negotiation and making of contracts with landowners and the provincial governments in Porgera and Misima were invoked in the Kutubu project. The only departure was that the state had to

---

513 Ibid.

514 The state holds 22.5% equity in the project. Other shareholders are: Chevron Niugini Pty Ltd, a subsidiary of Chevron Corp USA (19.375%); British Petroleum Development Pty Ltd owned by British Petroleum (19.375%); Ampol Exploration of Australia (16.46%); BHP (9.69%); and Oil Search Ltd, a public company incorporated in PNG (7.76%).

enter into four separate contracts, because there were two provincial governments of two separate provinces and two landowner groups involved in the project. The first provincial government and landowner group is from the Southern Highlands Province where the oil fields are located. The second is the Gulf Provincial Government and the Kikori landowners, located where the 260 km pipeline will carry the oil into the Gulf of Papua for shipment.

Arrangements similar to those in Porgera and Misima on infrastructure development, royalty sharing, employment and training, equity options and assistance to local communities on business development and participation were made with the two provincial governments and landowner groups. These contractual terms are important in terms of risk mitigation arising from accessing traditional lands for development. It is now accepted that these new policy changes and developments on landowner and provincial government participation in negotiations have been, and will continue to be, applied in all mining and petroleum projects.

7.5 THE LEGAL FRAMEWORK

Mining development contracts and standard petroleum agreements

In the mining sector in PNG, the statutory requirement is now for a detailed *mining development contract* to be entered into between the state and the project developer/s at the time when the special mining lease for any mineral development is granted.

The requirement for a *mining development contract* arises from s 18 of the *Mining Act* 1992,[515] while that for oil and gas developments arises under ss 183[516] and 184[517] of the *Oil and Gas Act* 1998 for petroleum and gas respectively.

The mining development or the petroleum or gas development is then undertaken in accordance with the respective agreements. A standard agreement, known as the *standard petroleum agreement*, has now been drawn up. This consolidates the terms of both petroleum and gas into one agreement. Detailed mining contracts were negotiated and entered into with the state and the joint venturers developing the Porgera, Misima, Lihir and Tolokuma mines, while similar petroleum and gas agreements were entered into in respect of the Kutubu petroleum and Hides gas projects.

Before entry into the respective mining development contract or the standard petroleum agreement, there is a statutory requirement for an approved proposal for a mining lease or a petroleum development licence and how it should be considered and approved by the Minister. One issue that may arise under such contracting systems relates to the degree of security offered to an investment under a mining development contract or a standard petroleum agreement. While

---

[515] Section 18 of the *Mining Act* 1992 states: "Where the Minister considers, on reasonable grounds, that the size or distribution of a mineral deposit, the method of mining or treating it, the infrastructure required for it or financial or economic considerations make a mining development contract necessary, the Minister may require that the mining of that deposit takes place under a special mining lease and under the terms of a mining development contract."

[516] Section 83 of the *Oil and Gas Act* 1998 states: "Petroleum Agreement: The Minister may, on behalf of the State, execute a petroleum agreement with a licensee, providing for:

(a) the definition of the extent of a particular petroleum project and petroleum operations for that petroleum project for the purposes of this Act and any other law; and
(b) the application of the provisions of this Act to that petroleum project; and
(c) where permitted by other Acts, the application of those other Acts to that petroleum project; and
(d) the transfer and assignment of State Equity interests in the petroleum project to MRDC [Mineral Resources Development Co] and any other matters agreed to by the parties thereto and such a petroleum agreement will have effect to the extent permitted by law."

[517] The section states that the Minister may, on behalf of the state, execute a gas agreement with a licence.

the capacity of the state to enter into a contract is unquestionable, questions may arise as to how secure a party's rights will be under the contract.

A resource developer entering into a mining development contract or a petroleum agreement with the state must be in a position to evaluate the degree of security offered by that contract or agreement. Furthermore, before committing financial and other resources to the project, the developer must be able to rely upon some pre-existing set of rights and obligations.[518] Hence, it has been argued that prior to the expenditure of funds, a resource developer should be able to ensure that a valid contract exists. Given the special immunities and privileges that a sovereign state enjoys, a developer may experience difficulties in proving the existence of a valid contract.[519] Of the difficulties that may be encountered, three significant ones are discussed below.

The doctrine of executive necessity

There has been judicial recognition that a term can be implied into a government contract that it must be read subject to the future exercise of executive power in public interests. The power of the state to use its executive power in the interests of the public is part of the doctrine of executive necessity.[520] This doctrine was first given judicial recognition in the case of *Commissioner for Crown Lands v Page*.[521] In that case, Lord Devlin stated that the:

> "covenant or promise must by necessary implication be read to exclude those measures affecting the nation as a whole which the crown takes for the public good".[522]

For instance, under s 28(2) of the *Mining Act* 1992, the Minister may refuse to extend the term of an exploration licence if "he considers it in the interests of the State to do so". Hence, where a resource development contract is breached by the state in exercising its statutory powers in the public interests, a project developer may be left without a remedy due to the state's "power to override contractual obligations".[523] However, the application of this doctrine to the *Mining Act* 1992 and the *Oil and Gas Act* 1998 is highly questionable, because mining and petroleum agreements made under both statutes now allow the Minister to exercise discretion which can be fettered under such contracts.

Undertakings about the exercise of statutory discretion

In developing countries, it is quite common for the state and statutory bodies that exercise statutory discretion to contract to do, or not to do, things that normally would, in other countries like Australia or New Zealand, be regarded as unusual because the undertaking involves obligations to exercise discretion in a certain way.[524]

Clause 13.2 of the standard petroleum agreement, which deals with currency, is an example of how the state can contract to be bound by the exercise of a future discretion. This clause provides

---

518 Rigney, "The Resource Development Contract – How Is It?" in Gardner (ed), *The Challenge of Resource Security: Law and Policy* (1993).
519 Ibid.
520 Ibid.
521 *Commissioner for Crown Lands v Page* [1960] 2 QB 274.
522 Ibid at 292.
523 Rigney, op cit n 35.
524 Hair, "Operating Mining Project in Papua New Guinea: A Case Study" (1995) AMPLA Yearbook 152 at 161-162.

that certain loans and other transactions that require the approval of the Central Bank under the *Central Banking Act* (Ch 138) "shall be approved by the Bank". Similarly, cl 4.1 of the mining development contract for Porgera (which is now a standard term in all mining development contracts) provides that the special mining lease and certain other ancillary tenements, the grant of which involves the exercise of a statutory discretion, "will be granted".

In Australia and other common law countries, as noted above, any promise or undertaking which fetters the future exercise of executive power or statutory discretion may be held to be invalid in the public interest.

Contracting with landowners

As noted earlier, following the development forum, a series of contracts are signed. The mining development contract or the standard petroleum agreement is primarily an agreement between the state and the project developers. The developers are not parties to the agreements between the national government, the provincial government and the landowners. Notwithstanding this, obligations are imposed on the landowners and the provincial government, who undertake to ensure that the project is not disrupted in any way.[525] Such obligations have now become standardised, and apply to all such agreements.

The single biggest problem in contracting with landowners relates to the enforcement of contracts.[526] In nearly all cases, the agreement is entered into with landowners who are mostly illiterate. Although there may be a few educated persons in the area who may explain what these agreements are all about, the signing of the agreement is done by clan or tribal leaders who are illiterate elderly men who do not even speak English, let alone other official Papua New Guinean languages, Pidgin or Motu.[527] Usually the signature is indicated by a thumb imprint or the making of the "X" on the paper using a pen, which cannot even be grasped properly.

In western societies, the making of a contract shows a commitment to be bound by its terms. Such commitments are usually backed up not only by legal enforcement, but also involve other personal commitments, which, if not performed, reflect badly on the integrity and standing of the person who made the contract. To an illiterate Papua New Guinean landowner, these concepts are all foreign and mean very little, including the act of holding a pen and putting signature to the paper.[528]

The other serious problem is to actually enforce the contractual obligations against the landowners. The obligation not to disrupt the project in any way has no mechanism in place to affect landowners in the event of a breach. Consequently, the landowners will not feel inhibited by such obligations. Hence, to claim damages for breach of contract where, for example, a blockade results in an operation losing millions of dollars, it is unreasonable to expect that the landowners will pay damages for the losses.[529]

---

525 An example of such standard landowner undertakings is to be found in Pt C of the agreement between the national government and the Southern Highlands landowners in respect of the Kutubu Petroleum Project. Such terms have now been standardised.

526 Nonggorr, "Resolving Conflicts in Customary Law and Western Law in Natural Resource Developments in Papua New Guinea" (1993) 16 UNSWLJ (2) 433 at 449.

527 Ibid at 449-450.

528 Ibid at 450.

529 Ibid.

State agreements

The other legal device that has been used in the resources development was the statutory ratification of a *state agreement.* The state agreement was first pioneered on the Bougainville copper agreement of 1967, namely, the *Mining (Bougainville Copper Agreement) Act* 1967. The only other resource project that is governed by a state agreement is the Ok Tedi mine.

Essentially, a state agreement takes the form of a contract between the government and the private companies engaged in a resource project, ratified by Parliament,[530] and comprises two elements – the agreement between the state and the investor, and the legislation that gives it legal force. The contract usually deals with five different matters. These are:[531]

- resource title;
- infrastructure development;
- local and provincial government;
- environment protection; and
- government revenue.

According to Leigh Warnick, there are several reasons why legislative ratification provides a greater degree of security to the developer.[532] These are:

1. It places beyond doubt the power of the state to make the agreement and the authority of the person signing on its behalf.
2. It gives effect to any necessary modification of existing law.
3. It cures any failures to comply with mandatory procedures.
4. It enhances the security of the agreement against inconsistent action by the government in its executive capacity.

Three major advantages arise from legislative ratification. First, the government agreement provides a means of co-ordination of the numerous regulatory controls applicable to a major resource project. Secondly, it allows the parties to create a unique legal regime for each major resource project, thereby avoiding deficiencies of the ordinary legal system. For instance, if environmental controls applied in the general law are inappropriate for any reason, they can be modified and replaced by specific controls set out in the state agreement. Thirdly, it may overcome constitutional limitations imposed upon the states, a feature which is very important in Australia.

---

[530] Crommelin, "A New Era of Concessions? The Government Agreement in Australia" (1996) AMPLA Yearbook 693 at 694. See also Barnett, "State Agreements" (1996) AMPLA Yearbook 314.
[531] Ibid.
[532] Warnick, "State Agreements" (1988) 62 ALJ 878 at 882.

7.6 PROJECT FINANCING: RISK IDENTIFICATION AND ALLOCATION

In project finance, risk is the chance of an event occurring which would cause actual project circumstances to differ from those initially assumed when forecasting project benefits and costs. A financier will participate in project financing where it expects that the project's sponsor will derive benefits when it participates in the project. These benefits will outweigh any anticipated costs, including financing costs, and are of sufficient magnitude to satisfy the financier's requirement for a security buffer.[533] Such expectations are normally based on a projection of the project benefits and costs.

Indeed, a major advantage of project financing is the process of risk analysis and allocation. This process shapes not only the overall structure of the financing, but also identifies the issues that require special consideration by the financier. Project financing, like other forms of financing, involves the financier in a detailed analysis of the risks associated with the project. However, the difference between project financing and other forms of financing tends to be that in project financing the financier is trying to create, as far as possible, "a close circuit of the risks".[534] This means, all the risks that have a bearing upon the project must be identified, analysed and allocated between parties best able to manage them, and a detailed legal mechanism must be structured to manage the risks. Indeed, it has been said that:

> "The detailed identification, analysis, allocation, and management of risks associated with any project financing is itself so fundamental that it should be regarded as one of the defining features by which project financing is differentiated from other kinds of finanacing."[535]

There are a number of reasons for identifying and allocating risks to a party best able to manage.[536] First, the project is a new business, the attributes of which are primarily defined and created by the contracts that provide for its creation and funding. In this regard, there is no pre-determined set of risks that the parties to the project accept, allocate and mitigate. Hence, it is up to the parties to decide how they intend to deal with the risks.

Secondly, the term of the project funding is also important. If the term is longer, then there is a real likelihood that the risks will crystallise, and so it becomes very likely that the actual circumstances will differ from those which were assumed when the initial projection of the project benefits and costs were made. In such a situation, risk assessment and allocation becomes very important.

Thirdly, risk assessment and allocation assumes more importance and becomes complicated when a sovereign state is a participant in the project. The involvement of the state in many projects means that more attention will be given to risk identification and allocation than would be given in a purely private sector project. This is especially true for PNG, which is an equity participant in all resource projects. In a private sector project, the starting point for risk identification and

---

533 Furnell, "Risk Identification and Risk Allocation in Project Finance Transactions" (unpublished paper presented to students in the "Project Finance" course, University of Melbourne, 8-22 May 2000), p 1.

534 Naughton, "Project Financing" in Mallesons Stephen Jacques Solicitors (ed), *Australian Finance Law* (4th ed, 1999), p 244.

535 Ibid.

536 Furnell, op cit n 50.

allocation is purely financial. The involvement of the state, however, may involve many reference points, "given that its project benefits and costs are unlikely to be characterised in purely financial terms".[537] This is so, given that the state's primary focus is on the provision of goods and services to its people. Hence, this complicates the risk allocation.

The project financing of Ok Tedi, and how risks were assessed and allocated between the project developers and the state, as discussed above, provides a good illustration of the importance and complexities of risk assessment where the state is a participant in a project.

While it is difficult to generalise about the risks applicable to project financing, certain risks, such as political risks and operational risks, are universal, while different types of projects have their own special kinds of risks. For instance, a major risk that requires consideration in an oil and gas pipeline is the competition law risk, which is not found in other financings.[538]

Even if a risk is universal, meaningful analysis and management of this risk will depend on the particular industry. Finally, the individual circumstances of a particular project, its financiers and participants will also affect the nature and extent of the project risks.[539]

With these qualifications in mind, it is now proposed to discuss some of the risks that are normally considered by financiers and project developers in PNG when analysing a mineral or petroleum project, and the legal issues that may flow from that analysis. There are many risks that have a bearing upon the project. However, of these, the only three discussed here are political risks, environmental risks and customary title risks.

Political risks

The basic requirement in the assessment of political risk events is that the political environment of the country "must be reasonably friendly and stable".[540] There is no clear definition of "political risk", rather, various categories of risks are considered in assessing this risk. The different kinds of risks embraced by the term are not necessarily interconnected, nor do they stem from a common source. At its most extreme, political risk extends to the loss of control by a sovereign government over its people so that, as a result of civil war or insurrection, the project is forced to close completely.[541] The forced and continued closure of CRA's Bougainville copper mine as a result of the secessionist war, partly precipitated by the mine, is a good example of this. In less extreme cases, the government remains in control but economic difficulties and political unrest can cause political and economic dislocation. In the short term, this affects the orderly carrying on of business, but in the longer term it affects the confidence of bankers in the stability of the country.[542]

Nonetheless, a workable definition of "political risk" would be as follows:

> "Political risk is the risk that:
>
> (i) war or civil disturbance involving a host country will prevent or interfere with; or

---

537 Ibid.
538 O'Rourke, "Pipelines: Structuring New Projects" (1995) AMPLA Yearbook 279 at 285.
539 Naughton, op cit n 52.
540 Nevitt, *Project Financing* (4th ed, 1993).
541 Naughton, op cit n 52, p 249.
542 Ibid.

(ii) the government of a host country or an entity controlled by that government will, in a discriminatory manner, prevent or interfere with (or seek so to do, by lawful means or otherwise and either directly or indirectly); or

(iii) immunity, insolvency or illegitimacy of the government of a host country will prevent or interfere with, the exercise of the right of a foreign investor with,

respect to its assets or investments in that host country."[61]

It is apparent from this definition that political risks may take a number of forms, including four principal categories which are often described in contracts of guarantee or insurance policies issued by institutions covering political risks. These four categories are[62] expropriation, exchange control restrictions, war or civil unrest, and repudiation of contract.

1. **Expropriation:** A direct action of a government which may affect a project is when a government expropriates or nationalises a project. This is often referred to as "sovereign risk", where the state uses its legal power in its jurisdiction to take over or compulsorily acquire private property. Fear of expropriation and nationalisation of the private investment by the host government is, therefore, a prominent political risk event.

2. **Exchange control restrictions:** This risk is a restriction imposed by the host government, through its central bank, on the conversion of local currency into foreign currency or its transfer out of the country. Convertibility and transferability go together, in that a foreign investor will want to exchange local currency in the host country for foreign currency held offshore.[63]

   Similarly to other developing countries, PNG has a system of exchange control administered by the Central Bank under the *Central Banking (Foreign Exchange and Gold) Regulation.* This regulation was enacted under the *Central Banking Act*, Ch 138. The regulations control dealings in foreign currency and outflows of funds. Under the regulations, such transactions are permitted only with the authority of the Central Bank or an authorised dealer, which are usually the commercial banks. Under the mining development contracts, mining companies are offered additional assurances that they will be given authority to maintain foreign currency accounts, retain foreign currency in them for specified purposes and, in some cases, to repatriate capital. In this way, currency risks, which mining companies bear in bringing foreign currency into PNG, are controlled.

3. **War and civil disturbance:** Thee principal risks here are the damage, destruction or loss of tangible property resulting from war or civil disturbance. Civil disturbances include riots, insurrections, revolutions, rebellions, sabotages and other similar politically motivated hostile acts in the host country. A further risk is that the foreign investor might lose the use of facilities or be unable to operate a project due to the civil disturbance or war.[64] The Bougainville secessionist war by landowners demonstrates this. The host government has a huge task to use all available resources to curb such uprisings, so that the investors feel secure in financing major projects.

4. **Contract repudiation, re-negotiation and unilateral changes:** Contracts with the host governments run the risk of being repudiated or frustrated by those governments in

61 Williamson, "Commentary on Coping with Political Risks" (1991) AMPLA Yearbook 536.
62 Ibid.
63 Frecker, "Coping with Political Risk" (1991) AMPLA Yearbook 508.
64 Ibid.

circumstances where the foreign investor is left with no enforceable remedy in domestic courts or tribunals, either because of sovereign immunity or through other factors such as restrictions on fettering the future exercise of powers by authorities.[543] One solution is for the contract to be given statutory ratification in the host country so that it has the force of law, as is the case with the Bougainville and Ok Tedi projects. Although this would give some protection, it is not a complete security.

Some of these risks are highlighted by other problems relating to, or arising out of, the investment regimes and changes to the terms of the mineral or petroleum agreements, including the forced re-negotiation of the Bougainville copper agreement and the forced re-negotiation of the additional equity for the state in the project.

This shows that project agreements (state agreements, mining development agreements and petroleum agreements) with the investor and the host governments have not been entirely successful in providing stability to the agreed terms of the investment. Rowland Brown summarised the situation when he said:

> "Contracts and concessions, even carefully drafted by expensive lawyers, seemed a poor defence against demands for change."[544]

Hence, the risks of repudiation, re-negotiation and unilateral changes of the terms of the investments are significant considerations in the assessment of political risk.

Environmental risks

The 1980s, culminating in the 1992 Rio Earth Conference, showed a growing awareness of environmental issues and more focused attention on the interactions between the natural environment and economic development. While many countries have translated environmental concerns into overall developmental policies, the main strategy has been for minimising damage to the environment. In this regard, governments have adopted and passed legislation dealing with specific environmental standards for the construction and operation of commercial facilities.

Mining and petroleum projects are no exception to these environmental standards. These standards are imposed not only on new projects, but also on existing ones. Indeed, application of stringent environmental standards to existing projects has caused much concern and, in some cases, tremendous financial loss. PNG's Bougainville and Ok Tedi mines are living testimonies to the environmental issues and problems that arise from a mining project. Risks arising from the environment reflect the impact sensitivity that a project may have on the environment. If not handled correctly, environmental risks have the potential to immediately halt a project.[545]

There are many concerns about the environmental impact of a project.[546] First, many developing countries have a legal requirement to assess the environmental impact of resource projects and to ensure that standards are met during the construction and operation of a project. Secondly, returns from an investment, and even the investment itself, can be ruined if a particular project does not comply with, or adhere to, environmental standards. Thirdly, social responsibilities involve local,

---

543 Williamson, op cit n 61 at 548.

544 Brown, "The Relationship between the State and the Multinational Corporation in the Exploitation of Resources" (1984) 33 ICLQ 2218.

545 Fry, "Native Title: Joint Venture Solutions" (1996) AMPLA Yearbook 108 at 115. See also Naughton, op cit n 52, p 248.

546 Razavi, *Financing Energy Projects in Emerging Economies* (1996), p 209 suggests they fall into three categories.

regional or even global environments. These are broader concerns that may be raised by governments, governmental agencies, bilateral and multilateral development agencies, including financial institutions like the IMF and the World Bank, and various environmental groups (as well as local and neighbouring communities that may be affected).

As a result of these concerns, financiers have insisted that project sponsors address relevant environmental impacts sufficiently, because environmental problems can result in serious financial loss. Furthermore, financiers are increasingly committed to the prevention of environmental damage resulting from projects, and set strict guidelines for reviewing environmental impacts of such projects.[547]

A host country is required to establish a policy and administrative structure defining the overall objectives of environmental obligations. In this regard, the government has to establish environmental standards for proper assessment, monitoring and remedying of any environmental deterioration. Following that, the government has to decide what regulatory system to adopt, including drafting laws and regulations which set standards. The environmental standards can either be part of the law or part of the project agreement. Such standards should be practical, realistic and applied consistently throughout the life of a project. Finally, the government has to adopt an administrative approach for environmental supervision.[548] Such an approach can be sectoral, integral or self-regulatory.[549]

PNG is no exception to such environmental management approaches. Like other developing countries, it has a diverse natural environment within which resource developments take place. Long before the world began to talk seriously about integrating developmental objectives and sustainable environmental use, culminating in the 1992 Rio Earth Conference, PNG adopted comprehensive statements on the protection and sustainable use of its natural resources in the preamble to its *Constitution*, in the form of the National Goals and Directive Principles of 1975.[550]

These broad commitments to conservation and sustainable use of the environment were followed by the enactment of specific legislation relating to environmental management. These Acts are:

547 Ibid, p 211.

548 Omalu and Zamora, "Key Issues in Mining Policy. A Brief Comparative Survey on the Reform of Mining Law" (1999) 17(1) JENRL 13 at 35.

549 Ibid. According to Omalu and Zamora (at 35): "... the sectoral approach refers to a situation where each economic sector has an environmental office of its own. In the integral approach, environmental management is entirely in the hands of a central Environmental Ministry [and a Department]. The better approach to adopt would depend on the peculiar circumstances of each country. Ordinarily, the integral approach would be preferred but in countries with an active mining industry but undeveloped environmental management bodies, the sectoral approach would prove to be a more practical approach to adopt as a start."

550 The National Goals and Directive Principles No 4 of the *Constitution* states: "We declare our fourth goal to be for Papua New Guinea's natural resources and environment to be conserved and used for the collective benefit of us all, and be replenished for the benefit of future generations. We accordingly call for: wise use to be made of our natural resources and the environment in and on the land or seabed, in the sea under the land, and in the air, in the interests of our development and in the trust for future generations; and the conservation and replenishment, for the benefit of ourselves and prosperity, of the environment and its sacred, scenic, and historical qualities; and all necessary steps to be taken to give adequate protection to our valued birds, animals, fish, insects, plants and trees."

On a discussion of the constitutional protection and the environment, see Taylor, "Putting Ok Tedi in Perspective" in Banks and Ballard (eds), *The Ok Tedi Settlement: Issues, Outcomes and Implications* (LRC, Port Moresby, 1997), p 12.

- the *Environmental Planning Act*;
- the *Environmental Contaminants Acts*;
- the *Conservation Areas Act*;
- the *Dumping of Waste at Seas Act*; and
- the *Water Resources Act*.

These Acts provide the general legal regime by which PNG intends to enforce its environmental policies. In addition, the *Mining Act* 1992 and the *Oil and Gas Act* 1998 impose conservation requirements specific to resource developers involved in mining and petroleum activities. With the enactment of the *Environment Act* 2000, which repealed the *Environmental Planning Act*, the *Environmental Contaminants Act* and the *Water Resources Act*, all new projects have to comply with the requirements of the new law.

In addition, PNG has ratified a number of international conventions which contain environmental management regimes, including the United Nations Convention on the Law of the Sea, and the Convention for the Protection of the Natural Resources and Environment of the South Pacific Region, and the accompanying Protocols on Dumping at sea and Pollution Emergencies and the Kyoto Protocol on Climate Change.

Although PNG has taken positive steps in ensuring general protection of its environment, it needs to make a specific effort to enforce measures against those who ignore their obligations under either the environmental laws or the project agreements. Because of the lax attitude of the government, the landowners along the Fly River have suffered the most massive environmental destruction in the history of this country. In its daily mining operations, Ok Tedi dumps over 80,000 tonnes of tailings directly into the Ok Tedi River – a tributary of the Fly river. This has caused widespread deforestation, extensive killing of fish, disruption of local food production and several other social and environmental problems.[551] Construction of a tailings dam was a requirement under the *Environmental Planning Act*. However, the failure by the implementing agency to ensure that such a dam was constructed, has caused irreplaceable damage to the surrounding environment, and the landowners' livelihoods have been severely affected.

Customary title risks: land issues as risks affecting resource development

In PNG, project developers engaged in resource development, or developers engaged in any social or economic infrastructure development, including the state, have encountered problems. These problems connect with land. Almost all land in PNG is customarily owned by the people. The traditional laws and customs govern land use and norms of ownership. Resource developments, on the other hand, are undertaken by developers in accordance with laws that PNG inherited largely from Australia and England. These laws relate to land ownership, land acquisition, payment of compensation and environmental protection and management. The mining and petroleum statutes, and other legal instruments such as state agreements, joint venture agreements, mining development agreements and petroleum agreements, are all foreign and often conflict with traditional concepts of land use, access to land and ownership norms and values. Such conflicts can give rise to misunderstandings and suspicions, and lead to physical confrontations and disruption of the project.[552]

---

551 Kalinoe, "Water Resource Management in PNG Law, Policy and Practice" (1994) Mel LJ 23.
552 Nonggorr, op cit n 43 at 435.

The main areas of conflict relate to land ownership and land rights. There are four basic land problems that can affect the development and operation of a project.[553] First, the outright acquisition of land from customary owners is inconsistent with their concepts of land ownership. Secondly, the separation of mineral ownership from the land is unacceptable to the indigenous people. By custom, land includes not only the physical soil, but also what grows on, and what is below the surface of, the physical soil. Thirdly, the payment of a purchase price for outright acquisition of land creates problems. Fourthly, the legal instruments used, such as agreements, in transactions with traditional landowners, under which interested parties share rights and duties, do not really solve the problems.

Land tenure: traditional concept of land

The main difference between western concepts of land ownership and a Papua New Guinean (Melanesian) concept of land lies in what constitutes land and the norms relating to its ownership. By western standards, land is individualised and is regarded as an economic factor of production by which it can be alienated. For the Melanesian, land fulfils a very complex social, economic, cultural, religious, psychological and, therefore, legal, role, which makes it difficult to analyse in straightforward economic terms as simply a factor of production.[554] There is, therefore, a special attachment between the indigenous person and the land. As a result of these complex obligations, customary owners of the land (often described as landowners) maintain a very emotional and possessive attitude towards their lands. This makes it very difficult to acquire traditional land for resource development projects. Hence, the risk here is primarily accessing and acquiring traditional land held under the complex land tenure system for economic development.

Ownership of land

Customary land tenure systems prevail over nearly all of PNG. While recognising the complexity of land in PNG, economic analysis is important in one respect. Of PNG's total land area of 47,615,700 ha, 46,310,419 ha (or 97.25 percent) is customary or unalienated land, and remains directly under the control of its traditional owners pursuant to their customary laws and traditions.[555] What is distinctive about this communal ownership is the inability of a group to alienate interests in its lands in most circumstances, except to the government. This is where problems arise when land is required for economic development. Traditionally, the main characteristics of these systems are that absolute ownership of the land is vested in the clan, who are the corporate institutions that control land use and allocation. Within the group, individuals and their families are allocated land use rights for gardening and other uses.[556] The remaining three percent of PNG's land is alienated, and its ownership is vested in the state.[557] These alienated lands have been acquired from its customary owners, either voluntarily or through compulsory acquisition by the government, in order to carry out essential development projects.

Accessing land for resource developments

Given the complex land tenure systems, the fundamental problem encountered by resource developers is accessing and acquiring customary land. Section 132 of the *Land Act* 1996 prohibits the transfer of land or interests in customary land, except in accordance with custom. A further exception is made to this rule when the state transacts with customary owners for development to take place. All mining and petroleum developments occur on traditional land. Given the

---

553 Ibid.

554 Trebilcock and Knetsh, "Land Policy and Economic Development in Papua New Guinea" (1981) Mel LJ 102.

555 James, *Land Law and Policy in Papua New Guinea* (LRC, Port Moresby, 1985), p 64.

556 Eaton, "Customary Land Disputes: Should Lawyers Be Kept Out?" (1983) 11 Mel LJ 47.

557 James, op cit n 77, p 169.

difficulties encountered in accessing customary lands under s 132, the state has always acquired customary land through the compulsory acquisition process, and then leased to the project developers to carry out the proposed developments.[558] There are many problems associated with such practices.[559]

First, compulsory acquisition of another's land is prohibited by custom. Forced or outright acquisition of land is regarded as an act of stealing, and is sufficient reason for tribal war. Secondly, under customary tenure, land cannot be transferred except in very limited circumstances sanctioned by custom itself. Thirdly, by custom, land is held by the clan in trust for the living, the dead and the unborn. Consequently, the living members lack authority to transfer or sell land. Fourthly, the compensation moneys paid for the acquisition of lands by the state are usually made in a lump sum. This cannot totally compensate for the loss of land, as people are not used to being permanently divested of their lands. Furthermore, the living members use up all the compensation moneys paid, with nothing held for the future generations who, years later, make compensation demands on the basis of some reversionary interests in the same lands.

There are also problems with the values of the land itself.[560] When customary land is acquired, its value, for compensation purposes, is measured by western-based market value principles of land. There are problems with the application of this market value concept to customary land. First, customary land is never a marketable commodity. Secondly, landowners are not always willing to part with land, as demonstrated by the Bougainville conflict. Thirdly, there are other non-market values of land, such as the sentimental and spiritual or religious values, which are not taken into account when computing the market value of the land.

With all these complex social, economic, cultural and religious responsibilities inherent in traditional lands, there is a very complex relationship between the foreign investor and the landowners, as well as the government. Tensions and conflicts have arisen in such relationships, often manifested by violence and criminality, with landowners always demanding more monetary compensation from the project developers as a means to justify their actions. Indeed, unreasonable landowner demands for compensation challenge the national government's inability as a resource owner and regulator to effectively regulate such demands, is often a cause for concern for investors. As a regulator, the state has failed on many occasions to effectively deal with landowner demands, hence, increasing risks associated with traditional landholding.

---

[558] For a detailed discussion on the exercise of the state's power to acquire customary lands through compulsory acquisition, see Muroa, "Constitutional Constraints on the Power of Eminent Domain" (1995) 23 Mel LJ 95.

[559] Nonggorr, op cit n 43 at 435.

[560] For a discussion of these problems in the context of acquiring customary land for mineral or petroleum developments, see Kawi, "Protecting and Recognizing Indigenous Land Rights. Legal Framework, Land Management, and Compensation Issues Arising from Acquisition of Traditional Land for Resource Development: Some Comparisons between Australian Aborigines and Papua New Guinea" (unpublished LLM research paper, University of Melbourne, August 2000).

Accessing resources

While land on which resource developments occur is owned by, and its usage is regulated by, the customs and traditions of indigenous people, the mineral and petroleum reserves found under the surface of these lands are owned by the state. Section 5 of the *Mining Act* 1992 and s 6 of the *Oil and Gas Act* 1998 vest ownership of minerals and petroleum reserves in the state. The basis of the state's ownership of minerals and petroleum under traditional land stems from the position at common law.

At common law, minerals formed part of the land in which they were located. This position is summarised in the maxim, *cujus est solum, ejus est usque at coelum et usque ad inferos*, which is more a presumption that a landowner is entitled to all that lies above and below the surface of his land. The exceptions were the royal metals comprising gold and silver, which were owned by the crown by virtue of its royal prerogative.[561] These exceptions were applied to PNG in the colonial era, and then extended to cover all other minerals and petroleum and helium reserves. The position has remained unchanged.

This system has given rise to conflicts and disagreements, because surface and subsurface rights over the same land are being governed and exercised independently, a regime that landowners simply cannot accept. For one thing, legal principles vesting these resources in other persons are seen as an attempt to deprive traditional landowners of their lands.

7.7 MITIGATING RISKS

Mitigating political risks

In an effort to attract foreign investment, a host country often gives legal guarantees or assurances against the various types of political risks and, in some cases, to lessen the adverse consequences of such risks. Such guarantees can be in the form of legislation or other legal instruments, such as a resource development contract governing a project. The resources legal system in PNG has such guarantees in place.

Legislation

The primary legislation that seeks to promote foreign investment in the country is the *Investment Promotion Act* 1992. The Act prescribes detailed guarantees under s 37. It prohibits expropriation or nationalisation of the property of a foreign investor, except where:

- it is in accordance with a law;
- it is made for a public purpose which is defined by law; and
- compensation is paid as defined by law.

[561] Crommelin, "Australian Mineral Law as a Resource Management Regime" (1981) *Australian Journal of Forensic Sciences* 2.

These guarantees mirror those set out under s 53 of the *Constitution*, which protects the citizens only from the consequences of unjust deprivation of their property rights and interests.

The foreign investor is also given a right to remit debt service and earnings overseas, and to repatriate capital, but subject "to the availability of foreign exchange and to any laws relating to taxation". Furthermore, the foreign investor is permitted to remit overseas any compensation received for expropriated property. Also, the foreign investor is given an assurance that suitably qualified non-citizens may be employed if there are no suitably qualified nationals.

Section 38 of the *Investment Promotion Act* 1992 adopts all the guarantees set out under Art 15 of the Multilateral Investment Guarantee Agency (MIGA) Convention as if these were enacted under the Act. Under s 39, the Act implements the terms of the MIGA Convention relating to disputes over the terms of an investment between a host government and the foreign investor.

There is, therefore, sufficient protection given to a foreign investor under this legislation.

Investment protection agreements

These are bilateral agreements of treaty status between states, which aim to promote the flow of investment between two countries by providing the investor with a range of guarantees and assurances.[562] This form of investment security has also been termed *political leverage*.[563] A good example of this is the 1991 Agreement For the Protection of Investment between Australia and PNG. Three of the principal categories of political risk that are covered are expropriation, currency exchange restrictions and war or civil disturbance. The agreement also prohibits other discriminatory actions, limits legislative interference, contract repudiation and nullification and forced re-negotiation and sale of the investment, as well as compensation for any losses as a result of the host government's actions.[564]

Mining development contracts and petroleum agreements

In some ways, the difference in the contractual arrangements between a mining development contract and a petroleum agreement reflects the different risk profiles of the two sectors. The most specific means by which the mining development contract and the petroleum agreement help to overcome political risk, relates to currency exchange.

Under the *Central Banking (Foreign Exchange and Gold) Regulation*, the general rule is that all proceeds of exports from PNG must be remitted back to the country and converted to the local currency. However, mining development contracts and petroleum agreements now contain standard clauses by which the state commits itself to give, and to ensure that the Central Bank gives, special treatment to the contracting companies to convert and transfer currency overseas and to retain the currency in an overseas account. From an investor's perspective, there is no greater assurance against the risk of currency exchange restrictions:

---

562 Frecker, op cit n 62 at 515.

563 Nonggorr, "Investment Security in Papua New Guinea" (1992) AMPLA Yearbook 687 at 706.

564 See Arts 7 and 8 of the agreement. For a detailed discussion of this agreement, see Nonggorr, op cit n 84 at 706-712; and Frecker, op cit n 62 at 515-517.

> "than the right to retain a portion of the proceeds of the sale of product in foreign currency in an account in the company's name outside the country".[565]

This portion of moneys will be effectively outside the reach of any restrictions that the host country may impose. A further measure of protection, which has now been inserted into some Papua New Guinean agreements, particularly joint venture agreements, is a clause which seeks to obtain the benefit of the Agreement for the Protection of Investment between Australia and PNG, on the basis of non-discrimination. This clause mirrors the "most favoured nation" clause.[566]

Governing law and stabilisation clauses

Parties to a resource development contract are free to agree on the law that will govern their contract. This is because the contract will be construed in accordance with the governing law. Any changes to the terms of the contract, and any contractual liabilities arising as a result of the host country making unilateral changes to the terms of the contract, will be determined by the applicable law. Hence, the choice of applicable law is very important.[567]

All of PNG's mining contracts and petroleum agreements provide for the law of PNG to be the governing law. However, to lessen the risk of abrogation of contractual rights under its laws, respective contracts or agreements provide that the rules of international law will apply where relevant.[568]

In addition, to overcome the risk of changes to domestic law, some state contracts contain stabilisation clauses. There are many forms of stabilisation clauses,[569] but the one that is commonly included in contracts is the one which states that if local laws are changed to the detriment of the foreign investor (for example, changes to the tax laws), the state will compensate the foreign investor for the loss incurred.[570]

The investment guarantees under s 37 of the *Investment Promotion Act* 1992 are examples of stability clauses that have been provided under respective contracts, but which have now been "codified" and extended to all other investments of foreign investors.

Any form of stabilisation clause raises the issue of whether it can be overcome by the state exercising its sovereign powers. In PNG, the common law doctrine of executive necessity may render any contract provisions fettering the exercise of executive power unenforceable, although the application of that doctrine to mining contracts and petroleum agreements is questionable as a result of the wide discretion given to the Minister to fetter the exercise of discretion.

---

565 Frecker, ibid at 523.

566 This clause is in the following terms: "The State shall treat the investment and activities of each of the Joint Venturers in Papua New Guinea pursuant to this Contract on a basis no less favourable than that accorded to investment activities associated with investments of other foreign owned or controlled companies in Papua New Guinea under any bilateral investment protection treaty between the State and any other country, and accordingly, if under any such treaty other companies receive the benefit of any undertakings by the State relating to:
(a) expropriation and nationalisation and compensation therefore; or
(b) the transfer of currency and remittances of currency out of Papua New Guinea
which are more favourable than those contained in this Contract, the Joint Venturers will be treated as though those undertakings extended to them."

567 Nonggorr, op cit n 85 at 690.

568 For instance, cl 23 of the Misima Mining Development Contract and cl 25 of the Porgera Mining Development Contract read: "this agreement shall be governed by and construed in accordance with the laws of the Independent State of Papua New Guinea, which the Parties acknowledge and agree include, so far as they are relevant, the rules of international law".

569 Stabilisation clauses can be clauses that attempt to freeze the applicable law by providing that it is the law of the state in force at the date of the contract. Alternatively, they may be clauses for adjustment in the event of changes in the domestic law or provision under which the state guarantees that it will not enact laws that unfavourably alter the rights or obligations of the foreign investor.

570 For a detailed discussion of this issue; see Nonggorr, op cit n 85 at 690-697.

Arbitration and dispute resolution

With any contract, a critical issue is whether or not it can be enforced. Contracts governing the development of resources are no exceptions. Foreign investors want an international forum to pursue and settle their claims. Since there is no international judicial system, international arbitration is the answer. International arbitration can be set up on an ad hoc basis in accordance with the arbitration clause[571] in the relevant contract, or by the use of appropriate international forums.

In PNG, the mining contracts or petroleum agreements provide for dispute resolution by international arbitration through the International Centre for Settlement of Investment Disputes (ICSID), which deals with most arbitration involving investment disputes. PNG has ratified the ICSID Convention, which is implemented domestically by the *Investment Dispute Settlement Act* (Ch 346).

Under Art 54 of the ICSID Convention, each contracting party will recognise an award made under the convention, and enforce that award domestically as if it were a final judgment of a domestic court. The *Investment Dispute Settlement Act* provides specifically for the registration of convention awards, which then have the same force as a judgment of the National Court and can be enforced domestically. Hence, the contractual obligations of PNG can be legally enforced domestically as well as internationally. This should provide sufficient avenue for redress in the event of a breach of the terms of a resource contract.

Political risk insurance

Project finance is all about risk sharing. Hence, while political risk remains the traditional responsibility of the host government, project sponsors can also take steps to mitigate such risk in order to make the project risk acceptable to the banks. A specific way for project sponsors to do this is by taking out political risk covers through institutions such as the Export Finance and Insurance Corporation (EFIC) of Australia[572] or through MIGA. EFIC has indeed issued political risk covers for projects in PNG. As of 30 June 1990, EFIC's political insurance cover for PNG alone was A$88.2 million, and by 1995 it had categorised the political risk in PNG in the "D" category, which is the highest risk category.

Mitigation techniques undertaken by a project sponsor should, however, not be a concern for the host government or an excuse for the host government to shy away from its risk mitigation responsibilities. Host governments should continue to strive to establish legislative and contractual mechanisms, as well as policy directives, to offer investors and would-be lenders a sense of investment confidence and security.

---

[571] An example of this is the arbitration between the Government of PNG and developers of the Misima mine, which began in 1998 in Sydney. A clause in the Misima Mine Development Contract provided for "fly in fly out" arrangements for all expatriate employees of the mine to Cairns, Australia, every month. When a new government assumed office after the 1997 general elections, this clause was abrogated, leading to the dispute. An arbitrator was then appointed under the arbitration clause of that contract without the need to arbitrate under the ICSID facilities. See also *Kuwait v Aminoil* (1982) 66 ILR 518; *Texaco v Libya* (1978) 53 ILR 389; *Liamco v Libya* (1977) 62 ILR 140.

[572] EFIC is established under the *Export Finance and Insurance Corporations Act* 1981 (Cth).

Mitigation of land risks

A common technique of dealing with risk is to pass it on to the other party best able to manage the risk, whenever this can be done efficiently. The private sector does this when it is cost competitive to do so, rather than retain the risk. Such practice has been termed "rational risk allocation".[573]

Risks arising from, or associated with, acquiring or simply accessing customary land are very serious and pose real threats to the security of any foreign investments and resource projects. Furthermore, the host government's ability to regulate these risks has often been of concern to foreign investors, as well as financial and capital lenders. As a result, it is argued that, in dealing with this risk profile, it is not simply a question of project developers passing on the risk to the host government to address. Rather, it is submitted that this risk profile must be addressed by all parties involved in the project, that is, the national and provincial governments, the project developers and the local community, particularly the landowners. In this way, this risk profile can be shared by all parties, rather than leaving it to only one party.

There are a number of ways in which both the central and provincial governments and the project developers have addressed and overcome the adverse consequences of this risk profile.

7.8 LAND OWNER PARTICIPATION IN RESOURCE PROJECTS

Traditionally, much of the investment in developing countries has taken place with the key players being the central government and the project developer. This is particularly so in the mining sector. Such an approach has been termed by the World Bank as the *enclave model*.[574] The enclave model is characterised by negotiations and agreements with the central government, taxes and royalties paid to the central government and all other services focused on the mine. There is no involvement of local communities, let alone the provincial governments and the landowners. Instead, the mine and its activities are dominated by the mining company, thereby generating a culture of dependency on the part of the local people.[575]

From a risk management perspective, this model may help in mitigating other traditional mine-associated risks, such as completion risk, project risk, etc, but it does nothing to overcome or mitigate risk associated with traditional landholding. The non-involvement and consultation of both the provincial governments and the landowners in the negotiation, development, and then participation, in the investment decision-making process and the investment itself, has been a grave cause for concern. After all, it is the peoples' land that contains the minerals. This happened in the Bougainville and Ok Tedi projects, where the mining companies dominated all of the investment terms and services prescribed by the respective regimes. In Bougainville, a consequence of this mine-dominated approach meant that the mine operators, BCL and CRA, were not adequately aware of the developments among the landowners, nor their changing leadership patterns, in order to counter the moves and involve the national and provincial governments at an early enough stage to prevent the drastic consequences of the landowner revolt.

---

573 Arndt and Maguire, *Private Provision of Public Infrastructure: Risk Identification and Allocation Project: Survey Report* (University of Melbourne, 1999), p 44.

574 Strongman, "Mining and the Community from Enclave to Sustainable Development" (Paper presented at the Mining and the Community Conference for Asian and Pacific Nations, Madang, 26-29 July 1998), pp 2-3. See also Ch 8 of this book.

575 Ibid.

In calling for new behaviours in the mining sector, a new approach, which the World Bank now advocates, takes into account environmental considerations as well as consultation with, and participation of, the local communities in the resource project. The World Bank termed this the *new sustainable model.*[576] In this approach, the key players are the central and provincial governments, the project developers and, more importantly, the local community.

Some of the key features of this model are:

- Negotiation and agreements are not limited to the central government and the mining company, but also involve the local communities and the provincial and local-level governments.
- Taxes and royalties are shared between the central government, provincial governments and local-level governments, and the local communities.
- Compensation includes social and economic infrastructure services to build the community-based assets.
- Training includes support for building skills and institutional capacities for the mine and the community.
- Mine services are available to the community.

Spin-off business opportunities may be available to enable local community participation in business activities, and most employment positions are filled by local communities rather than by outsiders.

In PNG, a policy change in 1988, under the shadow of the developing landowner crisis in Bougainville, saw the government adopting a new approach that mirrors this new sustainable model. As discussed earlier, this new sustainable approach is now encapsulated in the development forum process.[577]

As noted, this was a major departure from the Bougainville and Ok Tedi Agreements. The development forum is a mandatory statutory procedure, which aims at the inclusion of local and regional interests into the mine development process. It is a consultation process involving the central, provincial and local-level governments, the project developers and the landowners, culminating in the signing of three-way agreements.

These agreements are complex and detailed and spell out the various responsibilities of the parties to the mine development, including the development of social and economic infrastructure. The agreements also spell out the terms of the distribution of government income from the mine, the split of royalties between the provincial government and landowners, and the terms under which landowners and the provincial government would be offered equity in the project.

The Porgera mine was the first in PNG where landowners and the provincial government were offered up to five percent equity in the project. It has since set a precedent for similar arrangements for new developments and, retrospectively, to existing mines, although in Misima

---

[576] Ibid.

[577] For a discussion on this development forum process, see Nonggorr, op cit n 85 at 446-450. See also Ch 8 of this book.

landowners refused the equity offer, instead opting for the mine to provide social and economic infrastructure to the local community to build up the community asset base.

It is only after the conclusion of the development forum that the main mining development contract or the petroleum agreement is signed. From a risk management perspective, the development forum is an acceptable compromise between the competing interests of the central government and the project developers. The involvement of landowners and the provincial governments, first in the investment decision-making process, and then as equity participants in the project, as well as sharing in the project benefits, gives them a sense of having ownership interests in recognition of their traditional land rights.

Equity participation by the state

State participation in a resource project is motivated by many factors. Some of these factors include transfer of technology, prevention of transfer pricing, generation of national skills and employment, national mineral resource management or other broad political considerations. There is a trend in the international mining industry towards reliance on the various forms of joint venture arrangements.[578] These arrangements could be between public and private sector companies, or built upon state minority holdings in otherwise privately owned companies, as is the case in PNG, where the Mineral Resources Development Company (MRDC) Ltd acquires a participating interest on behalf of the state. As noted earlier, under existing government policy, the state has a right to acquire up to 30 percent equity in mining projects and up to 22.5 percent in petroleum projects.[579] The state acquires its interests at the time when the development approval is given, by purchasing the interests from the project developers at sunken costs.

From a risk management perspective, state participation should be assessed on the basis of two issues.[580] First, would state participation reduce the political risks to the investor? In other words, does participation increase the expectation of political stability? Secondly, how does participation affect the investor's assessment of technical and commercial risks inherent in a project? Does participation decrease the risk of absolute loss, or reduce the scale of investment?

From a project developer's perspective, equity participation is said to provide some political comfort, in that the host government is unlikely to take expropriatory action or place undue restrictions on the operations or profitability of a project in which it has substantial interests.[581]

From the state's perspective, it may be that participation gives it access to information and a degree of control over the project which, under normal circumstances, it would not otherwise have.[582]

On the other hand, it has been argued that equity participation by the government is not well regarded in the mining industry because equity ownership presupposes a common business purpose. This is certainly not so in the mining sector, where the social, economic and national objectives of the government are usually not the same as those of the investing company.[583]

---

[578] Omalu and Zamora, op cit n 70 at 17-18.
[579] *Mining Act* 1992, s 16A; *Mining Regulations*, s 1(1); *Oil and Gas Act* 1998, s 165.
[580] Omalu and Zamora, op cit n 70.
[581] "Anatomy of a Mining Project in Papua New Guinea: A Case Study" (1995) AMPLA Yearbook 132.
[582] Ibid.
[583] Omalu and Zamora, op cit n 70.

Furthermore, joint venturing between non-homogenous partners, such as a foreign mining company and a government, tends to complicate the decision-making process, and increases:

> "by way of the compromises typically implicit in joint venture processes, the costs of operation significantly. There is accordingly, less profit and less taxes to be had from joint ventures with the government".[584]

In PNG particularly, it is argued that because capital for any other social and economic infrastructure is scarce, available financial resources of the state could be better utilised if injected into providing and meeting the primary needs of its citizens, rather than putting up capital on risky mining ventures.

A greater problem for the state as an equity participant is the potential conflict of interests between the state's role as an equity participant and its role as a regulator of the project. This is particularly so in the application of laws relating to environmental regulation and management.

The environmental problems along the Ok Tedi River, resulting from the failure of the mine to build a tailings dam and the dumping of wastes into the Fly and Ok Tedi rivers, demonstrate this conflict. In Ok Tedi, the initial 1976 agreement prohibited the dumping of wastes into the river systems. After the collapse of a tailings dam in 1983, the state enacted the supplemental agreements of 1984 and 1986, which suspended the requirement for a tailings dam to be built, and allowed the mine to dump wastes into the river systems. Subsequently, rather than insisting that the company take other steps to mitigate environmental damages, when the landowners sued BHP and OTML in the Supreme Court of Victoria claiming compensatory damages for environmental destruction, the state responded in favour of the project developers by enacting two statutes which abolished the rights of landowners to sue BHP and OTML for compensation. Moreover, the legislation made it a criminal offence for landowners or any other person to pursue compensation proceedings in a foreign court in respect of a mining or petroleum project in PNG.

Given these problems, the modern emphasis is to see a separation of the commercial sphere, being exclusively the domain of the private sector, and the government sphere, characterised by an arm's length, regulatory, licensing and supervisory function. Mixing these two may produce inefficient results for everybody, and does not help to distinguish what each type of organisation does best. Hence, business is for companies, public purpose regulations are for the government or its agencies, and neither is good at the other's tasks.[585]

Equity participation by landowners in resource projects

A valid reason for the state's equity participation in resource projects in PNG is the increased desire of landowners to also share in equity participation. The state does this by parcelling part of its equity interests to the landowners. As pointed out earlier, one set of agreements that are signed between the national government and provincial government and landowners after the development forum relates to equity participation by the landowners and the sharing of royalties.

The policy is for the national government to give landowners options to acquire part of the equity held by the government in the resource project. In Porgera, for instance, landowners acquired five

584 Ibid.
585 Ibid.

percent from the state's 30 percent share. In Kutubu, landowners of the two provinces hosting this project opted to acquire seven percent and five percent respectively from the state's 22.5 percent equity holding. As a risk management regime, it is submitted that such an approach in equity participation brings to landowners a sense of fulfilment, a sense of ownership and a sense of belonging and of being involved in the project. Prominent Bougainvillean landowner, Mr Paul Nerau made this point when he said:

> "The extension of this ownership by way of equity participation or ownership in resource companies brings to Papua New Guineans a sense of fulfilment and a feeling of being involved. They are then satisfied that they are part of the decision making process."[586]

Provision of social and economic infrastructure

A common feature of resource development in the mining and petroleum sectors is that the developments are located in very remote and rugged mountain terrain of the country. In these areas, social and economic activities are either minimal or simply non-existent. Mining and petroleum are the only industries able to provide basic social and economic services, which neither the national nor provincial governments can provide.

Owing to the lack of developments, there is now a standard clause in all mining development contracts and petroleum agreements for the project developers to provide, in addition to the mine infrastructure, other social and economic facilities to the local areas. In many remote areas where resource developments are taking place, such social and economic infrastructure[587] includes the building of mining towns and associated services, airstrips and airports, wharves and other transport facilities, roads and bridges, schools and other educational services, postal and telecommunication services, water supply and reticulation systems, aid-posts, clinics and hospitals, and law and order facilities, including the construction of police stations. Project developers also provide assistance in other services, such as advice on small businesses development, employment and training of nationals, and ensuring that spin-off businesses are available to local people.

Recognising the importance of private sector contribution to the development of social and economic infrastructure in resource development areas, the government introduced the Infrastructure Tax Credit Scheme into the *Income Tax Act* as an incentive to encourage more private sector investment in this area. Under this scheme, project developers are required to incur expenditure of up to 0.75 percent of their assessable income on infrastructure development. Such expenditure is then treated by the state as income tax paid by the developer. For instance, the inception of this scheme made it financially attractive for Placer Pacific Ltd, the project manager for Porgera mine, to be the de facto service provider in the Enga Province where the mine is located.

---

586 Nerau, "Landowner Participation in Spin-off Benefits in the Resource Industry" (Paper presented at a seminar on PNG resource projects, Port Moresby, February 1993).

587 The definition of social and economic infrastructure here is taken from the Parliament of New South Wales, Public Accounts Committee, *Infrastructure Management and Financing in New South Wales, Vol I: From Concept to Contract – Management of Infrastructure Projects* (Reports No 73, 1993), p 4. This committee defines "infrastructure" as the: "Infrastructure [that] comprises the physical assets required to satisfy the public's need for access to major economic and social facilities and services. It may be divided into two broad types:

> Economic infrastructure, comprising roads, railways, ports, airports, dams and reservoirs, water headworks, water treatment and reticulation facilities, telecommunications and postal facilities, power generation facilities.
>
> Social infrastructure, comprising schools and other educational facilities, hospitals, clinics and other facilities, housing, recreational facilities, law and order facilities.

The principal characteristics of such infrastructure facilities are: they have high initial capital costs, they are time consuming to build, they have long lives, they exist to support other economic and social activities, not merely as an end in themselves."

This trend of resource developers providing services to the local community is certainly in line with the *new sustainable model* advocated by the World Bank. By being service providers to the local people, apart from carrying out their traditional mining activities, project developers also contribute to the mitigation of any risks that may arise or be associated with traditional landholding, rather than leaving this responsibility to the government and landowners to sort out.

7.9 MITIGATING ENVIRONMENTAL RISKS: INTEGRATING ENVIRONMENTAL CONSIDERATIONS INTO RESOURCE DEVELOPMENTS

Resource developments, particularly those involving mineral resources, impact upon the natural and human environments. The single biggest trend forced by mining and other natural resource development "is the re-orientation of international and national laws and regulatory framework to comply with the new paradigm of sustainable development".[588] The concept of sustainability reflects a compromise between the dual aspirations of promoting economic growth and development and, at the same time, protecting environmental quality.[589] The United Nations' World Commission on Environment and Development (the Brundtland Commission) proposed a solution that sought to maximise both aspirations by merging them into a new concept called *sustainable development.*[590]

Sustainable development practices in resource projects

One way of mitigating environmental impact is to integrate the new concept of sustainable development into mining and petroleum development codes and management practices, in an effort to promote economic growth and, at the same time, to protect the quality of the environment around it. For all types of developments, including mining, sustainability requires:[591]

- the preservation of options for generations;
- promotion of social and community stability; and
- maintenance and restoration of environmental quality.

For mining specifically, sustainability requires:

- alleviation of poverty;
- meeting basic human needs;
- environmental impact assessment;
- pollution abatement;
- minimisation of environmental impact;
- conservation of resources;
- adequate worker health and safety standards;

---

588 Pring, Otto and Naito, "Trends in International Environmental Law Affecting the Mineral Industry" (1999) 17(1) JENRL 39 at 45.

589 Ibid.

590 "Sustainable development" is defined by the World Commission on Environment and Development (WECD), *Our Common Future* (1987) as "development that meets the needs of the present without comprising the ability of future generations to meet their own needs"

591 Pring, Otto and Naito, op cit n 110 at 46.

- community betterment; and
- protection and restoration of the environment.

The application of the principle of sustainable development to the mining sector may be difficult to achieve, given that mining deals with non-renewable, and therefore non-sustainable, resources.

Notwithstanding this inherent difficulty, sustainability is applied to mining, insofar as its above requirements "encourage the rational use of non-renewable resources and the preservation of a country's social, cultural, economic and environmental resources".[592]

This new approach in law requires new behaviours[593] in mining and resource development activities, since the goal is to "maximise ecological, cultural and economic concerns simultaneously", making them work together and mutually reinforce each other. To meet the requirements of sustainability-based laws, it has been said that international and national government officials and mining industry leaders should not concentrate solely on maximising current short-term economic achievements, but should also maximise protection of the environment, quality of life issues and the well-being of future generations.[594]

Environmental impact assessment

Another way of mitigating environmental impact is to carry out an environmental assessment of the project area before the project commences. One of the requirements of the *Environmental Planning Act* and the *Mining Act* 1992 is the need to carry out an environmental plan for each project. This plan is submitted, in addition to the feasibility studies, as part of the assessment process. The government only approves the project after it is satisfied with the environmental plan. During the life of the project, developers are required to submit quarterly reports on their operations and their impact on the environment.[595]

The problem here has been the lack of sufficient skilled labour on the part of the government agencies, particularly personnel from the Department of Environment and Conservation and the Department of Mining and Petroleum, to monitor and carry out their own independent environmental assessments of the projects. In addition, these government regulatory authorities lack financial resources to carry out detailed environmental impact studies. Such lack of resources creates an additional constraint in the form of an imbalance in accessing information between the developers and regulators. Government monitoring agencies simply rely on the project developers to submit the reports, and when this is done, these regulatory agencies do not evaluate them based on their own sampling and analysis.[596] The state's equity participation in the various projects does nothing to improve this situation.

[592] Ackermann, "Is Mining Compatible with Sustainable Development? A World Bank Perspective" (1998) 6(2) *International Council on Metals and the Environment (ICME) Newsletter* 1.

[593] Strongman, op cit n 96.

[594] Pring, Otto and Naito, op cit n 110 at 46.

[595] Asafu-Adjaye, Mawuli and Kameata, "Integrating Environmental Considerations into Economic Decision-Making Process: The Minerals Sectors in Papua New Guinea" (Report prepared for the Economic and Social Commission for Asia and the Pacific, 1997), p 29.

[596] Ibid.

Social impact assessment and social monitoring

In addition to the requirement for an environmental plan, social impact assessment and social monitoring of development projects is also a requirement under the *Environmental Planning Act.* The Department of Environment and Conservation and the Treasury Department are responsible for carrying out systematic social impact assessment and social monitoring programs in all development projects. However, these institutions have failed to implement these responsibilities, again owing to lack of skilled labour and adequate financial resources.

The failure of the state in carrying out this social aspect of environmental impact mitigation is highlighted by the start of the Bougainville crisis. In Bougainville, a study carried out by a consultancy firm revealed that there had been no social monitoring program during the years following the 1974 renegotiation of the agreement.

This continued failure by the state as an owner and regulator of the resources does not accord well with the objectives of sustainable development. Although PNG has good legislation in place to achieve environmental objectives, the legislation by itself is not sufficient to achieve these objectives unless it is backed by adequate human and financial resources and institutional support.[597]

7.10 CONCLUSION

Resource development in PNG, particularly in the mining and petroleum sectors, is undertaken primarily by foreign investors and financed by cross-border financing. Foreign capital is risk averse, and therefore legal instruments are drawn up to overcome disadvantages, including measures to overcome risks, so that foreign capital can be secured. Each country has a risk profile that requires proper assessment and management. In PNG, three risk profiles that are often the subject of much concern to foreign investors are political risks, native title or risks arising from accessing or acquiring traditional lands for resource developments, and environmental risks and how local people respond to the environmental impacts.

An examination of the regulatory framework reveals that PNG has a sufficient regulatory regime in place to overcome these risks or the adverse consequences of these risks. There are also adequate mechanisms and policies in place to mitigate many of these risks factors. For instance, investors in the mining and petroleum sectors enjoy additional concessions not ordinarily available to other sectors of the economy. The positive impact of these concessions is an added attraction to foreign investment. In terms of resource security, the mechanisms in place should assure investors that their investments are safe and secure.

However, it is the management of these risks, especially on the part of the state, that is often called into question and becomes a concern to investors. The continuous changes of government and political party allegiances do nothing to improve political stability and the political risks profile. Similarly, the state's inability to regulate risks arising from accessing and acquiring traditional land required for resource development, particularly regulating unreasonable demands from landowners, is a matter of concern. An area of great concern relates to the ability of the state

[597] Ibid.

to participate as an equity participant in a project, and at the same time regulate and enforce its laws on environmental management and control as a resource owner and regulator. In this regard, the state's ability to integrate the requirements of sustainable development practices, particularly in the mining and petroleum sectors, is questionable.

CHAPTER 8

STATUTORY RECOGNITION OF CUSTOMARY RESOURCE OWNERS' COMPENSATORY RIGHTS AND INTERESTS

*George Tapya Yapao**

8.1 INTRODUCTION

This chapter examines the nature and the extent of compensation to the people of Papua New Guinea (PNG) for their natural resources. It considers a selected number of resource-related statutes, including the *Constitution*, and the extent to which those statutes have recognised customary landowners' compensatory rights and interests.

8.2 RESOURCE HOLDER COMPENSATION IN PNG: GENERAL

This chapter considers compensation payment to resource holders for extraction, depletion, destruction or use of their natural resources. Compensation payments are not directed primarily at the resource developers for the loss or damage they have caused to the resources. Rather, the main aim of compensation payments is to indemnify the resource holder for the loss or damage to their resources. The introduction of money in the traditional PNG market economy, and the increase of customary alliances, is promoting the growth of the "compensation industry", which has resulted in increasing demands for very large sums of money by landowners.

Some of these claims by resource holders are genuine, while others are not.[598] In some cases, where the landholders are informed by inside sources that the paying authority, particularly the developers, will be putting up infrastructure for the project's development and paying compensation to resource owners, they will make many gardens and put up buildings where none had been before.[599]

Some of these claims are well substantiated by detailed valuation reports provided at cost by registered valuers, while many are not. In few instances, people place their own values on

---

* Lecturer in Law, Law School, UPNG.

598 In many parts of the highlands it has become a practice that, where roads are in the process of being constructed, people living along the roads quickly plant grown-up crops, such as coffee and bananas, on the site of the proposed roads, with the view to demanding compensation from the constructors and the government agents involved in these roadworks and, in many cases, slowing down development, and, in very extreme cases, completely preventing development.

599 See Jackson, *Cheques and Balances: Compensation and Mining in Papua New Guinea* (Australian National University, Law Reform Commission of Papua New Guinea Monograph 6, 1996), p 115.

resources, as opposed to values fixed by the Valuer-General's Office.[600] Most, if not all, the values placed by the Valuer-General's Office are now outdated, as they have not been updated[601] in the light of changes over the years.

The fact that the prices of all other commodities and goods have increased should be an important argument for increasing the values of natural resources. The values fixed by the Valuer-General's Office have not been reviewed for a long time. Some of the figures do not represent the true market value in comparison with the values of such natural resources elsewhere. This means that the compensating authorities, usually corporate entities and government instrumentalities, continue to use these outdated values to assess and compensate the resource holders. This obviously amounts to unfair and unjust compensation payments. Unless various factors are taken into account in making the assessment of just and fair compensation to the concerned landholding clans, the purpose and objective of the law of fair and just compensation for customary land will not be achieved. Let us now consider the relevant legislation that allows compensation to be paid to customary resource owners including landholders.

Natural resources under legislation

Successive governments in PNG have enacted legislation to regulate the exploitation of natural resources. Most of these statutes provide for compensation payment for the depletion of these resources. To some limited extent these laws give effect to the fourth goal of the National Goals and Directive Principles.[602] They include the *Constitution*,[603] the *Land Act* 1996,[604] the *Mining Act* 1992,[605] the *Oil and Gas Act* 1998,[606] the *Water Resources Act* (Ch 309),[607] the *Environmental Contaminants Act* (Ch 73)[608] and the *Lands Acquisition (Development Purposes) Act* (Ch 9).[609]

Most, if not all, natural resources in PNG are extracted from unalienated or non-governmental land. It is the author's proposition that the natural resources belong to landholders of unalienated land and under common law. The maxim *cujus est solum ejus est usque ad coelum et ad inferos*[610] applies to them. This maxim has some relevance in the PNG land tenure system in that whoever owns the land owns anything that belongs to that land.[611]

When any customary land is purchased, expropriated or compulsorily acquired, or if anything is done at all to take away such rights and interests attached to that land and other resources, the injured persons must be fairly and justly compensated.

---

600 Under the *Valuation Act* (Ch 327), the Valuer-General places value on various natural plants and other resources, which becomes the basis of assessment for compensation payments to resource holders.

601 The *Valuation Act* came into operation in 1984. Since then, the values placed on resources have not been reviewed regularly, while values placed on all other commodities have increased by more than 50%.

602 The fourth goal of the *National Goals and Directive Principles* relating to natural resources and environment is set out in the preamble to the *Constitution*. Although the *National Goals and Directive Principles* are not justiciable, they are intended for use as guides and yardsticks in pursuing and achieving national aims and objectives.

603 *Constitution*, s 53.

604 *Land Act*, Pt IV, ss 19-47.

605 *Mining Act*, ss 154-160.

606 *Oil and Gas Act* 1998, s 118.

607 *Water Resources Act*, ss 16 and 57.

608 *Environmental Contaminants Act*, s 61.

609 *Land Acquisition (Development Purposes) Act*, Pt III, ss 16-34.

610 The maxim means "he who possesses the land also possesses that which is below and above it". See also Muroa's views on this maxim in Ch 3 of this book. The maxim is clearly in line with the strongly held views of the customary landholders that they own the land and everything that is above and beneath it: *Land Dispute Settlement Act* (Ch 45), s 2.

611 Muroa argues that the maxim does not have relevance in PNG. The writer is, however, of the view that whatever the activity is that the other person is involved in, the use of the owner's land by that person is at the pleasure of the owner. The owner can stop the user any time he or she wants to use the land himself or herself. Thus, the maxim does have some relevance in PNG.

Recognition of resource holder rights and interests under the Constitution

The *Constitution* and the *Organic Laws* (the *Constitution*) are the supreme laws in PNG. All other laws that are inconsistent with the *Constitution* are, to the extent of that inconsistency, invalid and ineffective.[612]

The fourth goal of the National Goals and Directive Principles in the preamble of the *Constitution* stipulates:

> "We declare our Fourth Goal to be for Papua New Guinea's natural resources and environment to be conserved and used for the collective benefit of us all, and be replenished for the benefit of future generations."

Section 53 of the *Constitution* deals with compensation payment for acquisition or expropriation of natural resources, particularly land. It states:

> "(1) Subject to Section 54 (special provision in relation to certain lands), and except as permitted by this section, possession may not be compulsorily acquired, except in accordance with an Organic Law or an Act of the Parliament, and unless the property is required for:
>
> (i) a public purpose; or
>
> (ii) a reason that is reasonably justified in a democratic society that has a proper regard for the rights and dignity of mankind,
>
> that is so declared and so described, for the purposes of this section, in an Organic Law or an Act of Parliament."[613]

During the colonial era, the state acquired land by compulsory acquisition under various Acts.[614] Compensation payments were made at nominal prices that were often criticised.[615] Compulsory acquisition was continued after independence under the *Land Act* (Ch 185), and currently under the *Land Act* 1996. Under the current Act, the state can acquire customary land that has mineral or other natural resource deposits.[616] The state, in return, arranges compensation to the landholders from whom the land is expropriated for that purpose.

---

612 See *Constitution*, s 11.

613 Section 53 of the *Constitution* is designed to protect property owners, including those who own customary tenure.

614 See *Land Ordinance* 1906, s 35; *Land Ordinance* 1911-1914, s 60; *Land Ordinance* 1922-1941, s 71; *Imperial Ordinance* 1903, s 1; *Lands Acquisition Ordinance* 1914, ss 13 and 26; *Land Acquisition (Town Planning) Ordinance* 1949, ss 4 and 5; *Land Acquisition Ordinance* 1952, s 14; *Lands Ordinance* 1962, s 17. The *Land Ordinance* amalgamated all the laws relating to land, including some new provisions. Some form of compensation for acquisition of those lands was allowed by the colonial administration, and later at an improved level. See Montgomery, *Land Settlement Branch Manual* (Department of Lands, Surveys and Environment, Port Moresby, 1978), pp 113-120. See also Muroa in Ch 3 of this book.

615 See Dove, Miriumg and Togolo, "Mining Bitterness" in Sack (ed), *Problems of Choice: Lands in Papua New Guinea's Future* (1974), pp 181-183 for an analysis of the circumstances surrounding the acquisition of land for mining in Bougainville. Compensation to landowners for acquisition of their land was grossly unfair in the light of the huge profit Bougainville Copper Mining Ltd was going to make, and this caused resentment among landowners whose land was compulsorily acquired.

616 The *Land Act* 1996 consolidated and amended legislation relating to land in PNG. Part II (ss 6-18) deals with compulsory acquisition of customary land by the state, while Pt IV (ss 19-47) deals with compensation to landowners whose land is compulsorily acquired.

Section 53(2) of the *Constitution* provides that:

> "... just compensation must be made on just terms by the expropriating authority, giving full weight to the National Goals and Directive Principles having regard to the national interest and to the expression of that interest by the Parliament, as well as to the person affected."[617]

The rationale of compulsory acquisition is that the land is deemed to be "acquired for public purpose"[618] or that the land is required for "a reason that is reasonably justifiable in a democratic society that has a proper regard for the rights and dignity of mankind".[619]

Apart from compensation payment to private landowners pursuant to s 53(2) of the *Constitution*, the *Constitution* also makes it mandatory for the state to show that the land is used bona fide for the purpose for which it was acquired.[620] That is why the two conditions under s 53(1)(a)(i) and (ii) of the *Constitution* are required to be set out in the form of an Organic Law or an Act of Parliament, so that the interested public, particularly the private landowners from whom the land was acquired, will know that the government was genuine and had no hidden motive in acquiring their land.[621]

It is important to note that an individual person's constitutional rights to his or her property or land under s 53 of the *Constitution* is not an absolute or unlimited right. Like all fundamental rights and freedoms under the *Constitution*, except the right to freedom from inhumane treatment, the rights or interests of a person to his or her property are qualified. The qualifications, as stated above, are that, first, the property must be acquired for public purpose, and secondly, that the property must be acquired for a reason that is reasonably justifiable in a democratic society that has a proper regard for the rights and dignity of humankind.[622] The acquisition of customary land either for a "public purpose" or "acquired for a reason that is justified in a democratic society having proper regard for the rights and dignity of mankind", under s 53(2) of the *Constitution*, makes it mandatory for compensation to be paid to those landholders dispossessed of their land. This provision does not just call for payment of compensation. It further states that compensation payments must be "just compensation on just terms".

The terms "just compensation" and "just terms" are not defined by the *Constitution*, the *Land Act* nor any of the other resource-related legislation.[623] These terms were, however, considered in the case of *Frame v The Minister for Lands, Surveys and Environments.*[624] This case related to compulsory acquisition of land belonging to the appellant, Mr Frame, under the provisions of the

---

617 See *Constitution*, s 53(2).

618 In general terms, "public purpose" means the goal of society to its citizens. Specifically, the doctrine examining governmental action and measuring the ultimate benefit to the public, as with the acquisition of customary land to build a general hospital. See s 1 of the *Land Act* 1996, which comprehensively defines "public purpose". See also Muroa, "Constitutional Constraints on Power of Eminent Domain" (1995) 23 MLJ 97.

619 Ibid at 98.

620 See *Constitution*, s 53(1)(a)(ii).

621 See Muroa, op cit n 21.

622 See *Constitution*, s 53.

623 The *Constitution*, the *Land Act* 1996 and other resource-related legislation, such as the *Water Resources Act* 1982, the *Mining Act* 1992, the *Oil and Gas Act* 1998 and the *Environmental Contaminants Act*, do not define the terms "just compensation" or "just terms".

624 *Frame v Minister for Lands, Surveys and Environment* [1979] PNGLR 626. See also discussion of the case by Muroa, op cit n 21 at 108-112.

Land Acquisition Act 1974.[625] The appellant appealed under s 23 of the Act,[626] alleging that the amount determined by the Minister under s 22 of the Act[627] was inadequate. The National Court, most importantly, considered s 53(2) of the *Constitution*,[628] and declared that "just terms" in that section involved full and adequate compensation for the compulsory taking.

Approximately three percent of all land in PNG came under foreign control during the colonial period and was later transferred to, and vested in, the independent state of PNG. The remaining 97 percent remains as customary landholding. The three percent comprises much of the most cultivable, agriculturally rich and productive of the country's land. This situation has generated a lot of resentment against the authorities by the local landholders.[629] Many landholders whose lands were expropriated by the colonial administration believe they were inadequately compensated for their lands. They dispute the payments made to resource holders, on the basis that the payments made by expropriating authorities were inadequate, unconscionable[630] and not based on the true market value of the land at the relevant times.[631] The indigenous landholders argue that the colonial administration took advantage of their ignorance.

Some[632] claim that the expropriating authorities made fraudulent misrepresentations. Others[633] support the colonial administration, and claim that at the material times when the administration purchased land and resources from indigenous landholders, the landholders gave consent. The payments adopted and compensatory payments made were accepted by the landholders as full and final payments. However, in one case,[634] a fertile customary area of about 7.8 ha was sold by the elders of two clans and purchased by the colonial administration for the establishment of their office under the *Land Ordinance* 1962.[635] The elders received, on behalf of their respective clans, only $23 as full and final payment in exchange for that portion of land, and $8.80 for improvements on that land.

Even if one agrees that the above transaction is valid, since the two landholder-chiefs signed the transfer documents on behalf of their respective clans, can it be safely concluded that the agreement binds the members of those two clans?

The National Court considered s 19 of the *Land Acquisition Act* 1974,[636] particularly s 19(3), and held that the determination of the average net profit[637] is to be treated as a valuation exercise (or as a step in such an exercise), and that, considering the whole circumstances of the case, the

625 *Land Acquisition Act* 1974.

626 Ibid, s 23.

627 Ibid, s 22.

628 See *Constitution*, s 53(2).

629 Landholders have held demonstrations against the administration, in fear of losing their lands and their livelihood. See Dove, Miriumg and Togolo, op cit n 18, p 188. See also Muroa, op cit n 21 at 97.

630 Land in "Yeis", belonging to Ibi Pangali, a local leader of the Pyapin tribe, was also given by his father to the colonial administration when asked.

631 Iki Koka of Maini clan claims to have given up his land to missions and now disputes that he was not fairly compensated for his land.

632 Andake Nanenge of Pyapin clan, and a few others whose clans also sold land to the colonial administration who later leased the same to the Lutheran Mission, stated that they wanted to reclaim their land unless compensation was paid in full.

633 Many people who wanted the services rendered by the mission, in terms of the high school established by the Lutheran Mission, including the Yapao family and the Maini clan, did not want anything at all to do with compensation payments. They wanted the services, and in most cases were opposed to landowners claiming compensation.

634 The above example arises from a factual case involving the Maini and the Pyapin clans from Wapenamanda in the Enga Province. They purportedly sold the land known as "Yeis" to the colonial administration on 5 June 1969. The administration then established the first high school (St Paul's Lutheran High School) in the province on that land.

635 See *Land Ordinance Act* 1962, s 85.

636 Section 19 of the *Land Acquisition Act* 1974 sets out the principles for determining the amount of compensation to be paid by the government to the dispossessed owner for acquisition of land.

637 The National Court held that in order to determine the average annual net profit and the value of improvements, full regard should be given to the accepted principles of valuation practice and the current value of the subject land and any chattels which are the properties of the dispossessed owner.

amount of compensation awarded for acquisition of the land was unjust. The court directed that the compensation be increased.[638]

Muroa[639] has argued that, theoretically, the government has inherent power to acquire any land, even without payment of compensation, but practically it will be difficult, if not impossible, to compulsorily acquire customary land without payment of any form of compensation to the dispossessed owner. It should also be noted that, under s 53(3)[640] of the *Constitution*, the compensation need not be in the form of money only. Umeh also supports this view:

> "... equivalent of the property taken but not necessarily in money ... the amount of compensation must be just, equivalent and the principle and the manner of determining compensation must be such as to ensure that it is just and reasonable".[641]

8.3 RECOGNITION OF RIGHTS AND INTERESTS UNDER THE LAND ACT 1996

The *Land Act* 1996[642] deals with land, and defines customary land as:

> "land that is owned or possessed by an automatic citizen or community of automatic citizens by virtue of rights of a proprietary or possessory kind that belong to that citizen or community and arise from and are regulated by custom".[643]

In deciding the measure or quantum of compensation[644] for land acquired by compulsory process under the *Land Act*, various important factors need to be considered. Section 23 of the *Land Act*[645] requires three factors to be considered in assessing compensation:

- the value of the land at the date of acquisition;
- the damage (if any) caused by the severance of the land from other land in which the claimant had an interest at the date of acquisition; and
- the enhancement or depreciation in value of the interest of the claimant, at the date of acquisition, in other land adjoining or severed from the acquired land by reason of the carrying out of, or the proposal to carry out, the public purpose for which the land was acquired.[646]

These factors are not exhaustive. The following factors also need to be considered by the resource developer:

- the National Goals and Directive Principles;
- the expression of the national interests, and interests expressed by Parliament; and

---

638 See *Frame v Minister for Lands, Surveys and the Environment* [1980] PNGLR 433.
639 See Muroa, op cit n 21.
640 *Constitution*, s 53(3). This provision allows compensation to be paid in cash and in kind.
641 Umeh, *Compulsory Acquisition of Land and Compensation in Nigeria* (London, 1973), p 42.
642 The *Land Act* (No 45 of 1996) was passed by the National Parliament and certified on 20 December 1996. It was intended to consolidate and amend legislation relating to land and to repeal various other statutes relating to land.
643 *Land Act* 1996, s 2 (Interpretations).
644 Sections 12, 13, 14, 15 and 19-48 of the *Land Act* are provisions relating to compensation payment for both alienated and unalienated land. In particular, Pt III, Div 5 relates to acquisition by compulsory process, while Pt IV, Divs 1-9, particularly ss 19-49, of the Act, relate to compensation for such acquisition.
645 See *Land Act* 1996, s 23.
646 *Land Act* 1996, s 23.

- just and fair compensation to the persons affected, including future generations.

When dealing with customary land, the following factors also need to be considered:

- various interests vested in the land by both current and future generations of the landholding clans;
- traditional value placed on the land by their ancestors; and
- development or improvements on the land.

Direct dealings in land by outsiders with landholders are prohibited by s 73 of the *Land Act*.[647] The state claims the right of eminent domain[648] over all land and water in PNG, and perhaps it is on this basis that the state also claims ownership of all minerals and petroleum in PNG.

The *Lands Acquisition (Development Purposes) Act*,[649] particularly ss 7-34, refers to payment of compensation upon acquisition of land by the state for development purposes. This does not apply to customary land as stated in s 3(1) of this Act, and is therefore not discussed in detail, as this chapter concentrates on compensatory payments to the indigenous people of PNG for acquisition of customary land.

8.4 RECOGNITION OF RIGHTS AND INTERESTS UNDER THE MINING ACT

"Minerals" here mainly refer to minerals defined by the *Mining Act* 1992.[650] Since most of the minerals are found on customary land in PNG, compensation payments are required to extract those minerals. It is important to mention that the ownership of minerals is vested in the state by s 5 of the Act. Section 5 states:

> "All minerals existing on, in or below the surface of any land in Papua New Guinea, including any minerals contained in any water lying on any land in Papua New Guinea, are the property of the State."[651]

The issue of ownership of minerals is controversial and unsettled.[652] Section 2 of the *Land Dispute Settlement Act*[653] states:

> "'land' means customary land and includes:
>
> (a) a reef or bank;
>
> (b) a house or other structure built on land or over water; and
>
> (c) things growing on land or in land over water, earths and minerals on or under land; and

---

647 Section 73 of the *Land Act* 1996 deliberately prohibits the landholders from directly dealing with foreigners.

648 See Muroa, op cit n 21, and Ch 3 of this book.

649 The *Lands Acquisition (Development Purposes) Act* (Ch 192) was incorporated for the purpose of acquisition of land by the state for development purposes.

650 The *Mining Act* (No 20 of 1992) was passed by the National Parliament and certified on 20 December 1992. It was intended to consolidate and amend legislation relating to mining and to repeal various other statutes relating to land.

651 See *Mining Act* 1992, s 5.

652 Attempts have been made to challenge the issue of ownership of minerals in PNG in *Donigi v The State* [1991] PNGLR 376 and *Akipa v Lowa* [1990] PNGLR 502. See also *Lowa v Akipa* [1992] PNGLR 60.

653 *Land Dispute Settlement Act*, Ch 45, s 2.

(d) an interest in land".

These definitions are in opposition to, and must be read with, the *Mining Act*, which is a more recent enactment than the *Land Dispute Settlement Act* of the 1980s. The controversial nature of the issue of mineral ownership gave rise to the Bougainville crisis. There is potential for more problems in the light of increased compensation and royalty claims by landowners. For the purpose of this chapter, and to avoid any further discussions, the state is assumed to be the owner of the mineral resources.

Mining development forums

Section 6 of the *Mining Act*[654] calls for the Minister to establish mining development forums[655] before granting any special mining leases.[656] The Minister must invite all interested participants, including the landholders of the land that is the subject of the application for the special mining lease or other tenement to which the applicant's proposals relate. This is an important opportunity for the resource holders to directly participate in negotiations leading to the development of mining projects.

The provision requires the Minister to ensure that the landholders are afforded a fair hearing.[657] The Minister can stop the forum from proceeding if he or she considers that the landholders are not represented by qualified people, or if the resource holders will not be afforded a fair hearing. This recognition by the *Mining Act* in allowing the landholders to participate in the mining development forum confirms a statutory recognition of resource holders' rights and interests to the resources for which the state, by virtue of s 6 of the Act, claims ownership.[658]

Compensation

The *Mining Act*[659] recognises the rights and interests of landholders to compensation in respect of entry or occupation of land that is the subject of the tenement for the purposes of carrying out explorations or mining operations. Historically, the *Mining Ordinance* 1907[660] required, at least in Papua:

> "any person about to mine on 'owned and occupied by natives' to inform the warden, who assessed the probable damage, collected the money and held it for later payment to the owners of the land. The warden was to prevent any mining likely to cause 'substantial damage' until the owners of the land and property gave their consent".[661]

These principles were incorporated into the *Mining Act* 1992, Pt VII (Compensation to landholders). The key section is s 154 (Principles of compensation).[662] Section 154(2) sets out the

---

654 See *Mining Act* 1992, s 6.

655 The Mining Development Forum was first introduced by the Namaliu Government to negotiate the Porgera Mining Agreement in 1989, and has now been included in the *Mining Act* 1992. This inclusion was regarded as one of the breakthroughs in the mining industry, because the landholders were directly involved in mine development negotiations for the first time. See *Mining Act*, s 3, and Ch 7 of this book.

656 A "special mining lease" is a lease granted to major mining projects. Part V, Div 2 and ss 33-37 of the *Mining Act* 1992 provide for special mining leases.

657 See *Mining Act* 1992, s 3(1).

658 The state maintains ownership over resources such as minerals and petroleum. By allowing the resource holders to participate in these resource development forums, the state is obviously respecting and recognising their interests and rights to those resources.

659 See *Mining Act* 1992, Pt VII, Div 8. See also ss 154-160.

660 See *Mining Ordinance* 1907.

661 Ibid.

662 See *Mining Act* 1992, s 154.

circumstances under which landholders can claim compensation.[663] The landholders can complain of:

(a) being deprived of the possession or use of the natural surface of the land;

(b) damage to the natural surface of the land;

(c) severance of land, or any part thereof, from other land held by the landholder;

(d) any loss or restriction of a right of way, easement or other right;

(e) the loss of, or damage to, improvements;

(f) in the case of land under cultivation, loss of earnings;

(g) disruption of agricultural activities on the land; and

(h) social disruption.[664]

Section 154(6) refers to land outside mining leases, and it states:

> "Where any land or improvements, adjoining or in the vicinity of the land the subject of a tenement, is or are injured or depreciated in value by the exploration or mining of the tenement, the landholders of that land are entitled to compensation for all loss and damage sustained."[665]

The Ok Tedi and the Bougainville mining projects are covered respectively by the *Mining (Ok Tedi Agreements) Act* (Ch 363)[666] and the *Mining (Bougainville Copper Agreement) Act.*[667] The *Mining Act* expressly states that it does not apply to the legislation on the Ok Tedi and Bougainville mines.[668] Any aggrieved resource holder here may then file a legal suit claiming damages under the *Constitution*,[669] or under the common law,[670] which validly applies in PNG, as did the Ok Tedi[671] and Porgera[672] resource holders.

For compensation[673] to be paid under the *Mining Act* 1992, the landholder does not need to prove loss or damage suffered.[674] The call for payment of loss or damages even before actual loss or damage is proved shows that thc proposed developer should readily pay compensation when merely reported. In practice, the resource developers have denied liability until damages are actually proved.[675] This means that the *Mining Act* makes it mandatory for compensation to be

---

663 Ibid, s 154(2).

664 Ibid.

665 Ibid, s 154(6).

666 See *Mining (Ok Tedi Agreements) Act*, Ch 363.

667 See *Mining (Bougainville Copper Agreement) Act*, Ch 196.

668 See also Kawi and Golman in Ch 7 of this book. Schedule 2 of the *Mining Act* 1992 states that the Act does not affect the *Mining (Bougainville Copper Agreement) Act*, the *Mining (Bougainville Copper Agreement) Act* and the other eight (Ok Tedi Supplementary Agreement) Acts.

669 The constitutional rights of a citizen to sue for protection from unjust deprivation of property are set out in ss 53 and 57 of the *Constitution*.

670 The English common law has been adopted by virtue of Sch 2.2 of the *Constitution* and shall be applied in PNG provided that its application is suitable to the circumstances of PNG.

671 The resource holders from the Ok Tedi mine instituted legal proceedings against BHP in Melbourne, Australia, claiming damages for dumping toxic chemicals into the river system and increased sedimentation. It was claimed that this affected the vegetation along the river system and animals and people living along the Ok Tedi River. The Ok Tedi case was settled out of court.

672 A similar action was instituted by the people of lower Porgera against the Porgera Joint Venture (PJV), claiming damages for dumping toxic chemicals, increased sedimentation, tailings and loss of access to alluvial gold. In the case of Porgera, the landholders filed proceedings in the National Court and, at the same time, disputed offers made by PJV and referred the matter to the Environment Minister for determination under the *Water Resources Act*. The Minister made a determination in 1996 and ordered payment of compensation to the resource holders.

673 See *Mining Act* 1992, ss 154-160.

674 Under the *Mining Act*, landholders are to be paid compensation for all loss or damage suffered, or foreseen or likely to be suffered, as a result of the activities of tenement holders: see *Mining Act* 1992, s 154(1).

675 In the Ok Tedi and Porgera resource holders' claims for compensation for damages to their respective river systems as a result of dumping of tailings

paid, not only upon proving actual loss or damages suffered, but also for loss or damage that is likely to be caused. In other words, if it can be foreseen that landholders will suffer from the activities of exploration or actual mining or ancillary operations in relation to the project, then they will be entitled to compensation.[676] Section 159 of the *Mining Act*[677] makes the compensation agreement binding on the parties. Offences are created by s 67 of the *Mining Act*, and the general penalties are provided particularly by s 168. Under these provisions, a person or a company failing to pay compensation can be penalised and ordered to pay a court fine of about K10,000, or a default penalty of K1,000. These provisions are yet to be tested, because none of the companies involved in the resource development projects have been penalised under these provisions.[678]

Royalties and equity participation

Section 148 of the *Mining Act* provides that royalties for mine products shall be paid in accordance with the *Mining (Royalties) Act* 1992.[679]

From the royalty payment of 1.25 percent[680] in the other mining projects and two percent[681] in the Lihir mining project, the state, as the owner of the resources, is rightfully entitled to those royalty payments for depletion of its mineral resources. However, the state has instead allowed the resource holders and provincial governments of the host provinces to take substantial portions of the royalties from these royalty payments. Section 148 of the *Mining Act* 1992 provides that royalties for mine products shall be paid in according with the *Mining (Royalties) Act* 1992.[682] Section 173(5) of the Act states that provisions of the repealed Act shall continue to apply as if the repealed Act has not been repealed.[683] The *Mining (Royalties) Act* 1992 has not yet been enacted.

Importantly, the Parliament has given recognition to the landholders by allowing them to participate directly in mining development projects through *equity participation*. For example, in the case of the Porgera mine, the landowners now own five percent of the mine. The method by which they came to acquire this equity is even better. In the Porgera case,[684] the landowners were allowed to pay only for 2.5 percent of the equity interest from their royalty money, and the balance could be paid from their dividends from the first 2.5 percent of the equity interest. Thus, these landholders are collectively some of the richest people in the community in comparison with the ordinary people at their own ranks.

---

and other toxic wastes, the companies involved in the development of resources in those areas, namely BHP and PJV, refused to pay compensation until they were referred to relevant authorities who later directed payment. In the case of Ok Tedi, the landholders took the giant mining company, BHP, to court in Melbourne, Australia, while in the case of Porgera, the resource holders filed proceedings in the jurisdiction and further referred the matter for ministerial determination under the *Water Resources Act*.

676 See *Mining Act* 1992, s 154(1).

677 Ibid, s 159.

678 According to the limited research done for this chapter, there is no record of any resource developer being penalised under any of the penalty provisions. One can therefore assume that either no offences are being committed, or that offences are committed but the state has not caught the offenders. It could also be that the state is aware of the offences being committed but does not want to penalise the offenders, for fear of deterring foreign investors.

679 This proposed *Mining (Royalties) Act* 1992 has not been enacted by Parliament yet, so for the purpose of deciding what royalties are to be paid, we need to look at the provisions (Pt XI – Provisions Relating to Mineral Returns and Royalty) under the old *Mining Act* (Ch 195).

680 The royalty rate applying to all major operations in the mining industry has been 1.25%, except the Lihir gold mine in which the rate was increased to 2%.

681 The royalty rate at the Lihir gold mine was fixed at 2% (an increase from 1.25% by .75%) due to much pressure applied on the national government by the provincial governments of resource provinces and the resource holders, demanding an increase of the royalty rate. See also Yapao, "Additional Profits Tax: A Source of Revenue for Papua New Guinea from Mining Operations" (unpublished Masters thesis, Somare Library, reserve section).

682 The Parliament was supposed to enact the *Mining (Royalties) Act* 1992 setting out the rates and methods of payment of royalties. The proposed Act is still pending enactment by Parliament.

683 The *Mining Act* (Ch 195) applies, even though the *Mining Act* 1992 repealed the former *Mining Act*. It is about nine years since the *Mining Act* 1992 was enacted and passed as law, but the *Mining (Royalties) Act* 1992 has not been considered by Parliament.

684 The Porgera SML landowners have 5% equity interest in the giant Porgera gold mine in the Enga Province.

8.5 RECOGNITION OF RIGHTS AND INTERESTS UNDER THE OIL AND GAS ACT 1998

Section 6 of the *Oil and Gas Act*[685] declares petroleum as the property of the state and states:

> "Subject to this Act, but notwithstanding anything contained in any other law or in any grant, instrument of title or other document, all petroleum and helium at or below the surface of any land is, and shall be deemed at all times to have been, the property of the State."

Section 118 of the Act provides for compensation to be paid by a licensee to the owners and occupiers of, and any persons interested in, any private land in relation to their several interests, in respect of the entry on or occupation of the land by the licensee. Section 118(1) of the *Oil and Gas Act* states:

> "A licensee shall be liable to pay compensation in accordance with this Section to the owners and occupiers of, and any person interested in, any private land in relation to their several interests, in respect of the entry on or occupation of the land by the licensee under this Division."

Section 48[686] of the *Oil and Gas Act* makes it mandatory for the Minister responsible for petroleum to convene a developmental forum, which should, among other things, involve resource owners from the petroleum project area. Equally importantly, s 50[687] of the *Oil and Gas Act* states that any agreement that the state makes with the project area resource owners shall be contained in a developmental agreement. These provisions allow the petroleum project area resource owners not only to receive benefits from the development, but also to actually participate in the negotiations leading to petroleum developmental agreements. These forums are directly comparable to mining development forums.

Another important provision[688] under the *Oil and Gas Act* relates to royalty payments to resource holders. The Act states that the tenement holder shall pay to the state royalties at the rate of two percent of the wellhead value of all petroleum produced from the licence area.[689] The state has agreed to allot a certain percentage of the royalties to the resource owners pursuant to s 168[690] of

---

685 *Oil and Gas Act* 1998, s 6.

686 Section 48 of the *Oil and Gas Act* 1998, like s 5 of the *Mining and Petroleum Act*, is the provision providing for development forums.

687 Section 50 of the *Oil and Gas Act* 1998 provides for oil or gas development agreements.

688 Section 159 of the *Oil and Gas Act* 1998 is the provision relating to royalties. Payment of royalties is another recognition of the customary rights and interests of resource holders.

689 Section 159(1) of the *Oil and Gas Act* 1998 relates to royalty rates at 2%.

690 Section 168 of the *Oil and Gas Act* 1998 relates to royalty benefits of provincial governments and landholders.

the Act. Under s 167(4),[691] the state has also agreed to share equity benefits from petroleum operations with the project area resource owners. The resource owners are to receive at least 20 percent of the royalties accruing to the provincial governments.[692] Landholders may further negotiate for an additional share during the petroleum developmental forum process. For example, the Kutubu landholders receive 40 percent of the royalties from Kutubu petroleum, and the Southern Highlands Provincial Government retains 60 percent.

8.6 RECOGNITION OF RIGHTS AND INTERESTS UNDER THE WATER RESOURCES ACT[693]

The *Water Resources Act* (Ch 205) regulates the management and use of water resources in PNG.

Sections 16 and 57 of that Act make it obligatory for compensation to be paid to owners and occupiers of any private land which is being affected as a result of entry, occupation or activity by the water use permit holder or water investigation permit holder.[694] Section 16(1) states:

> "Subject to this section, the holder of a permit is liable to pay compensation to the owners and occupiers of, and any person interested in, any private land in relation to their several interests, in respect of entry on or occupation of the land by the holder."

Section 16(2) identifies the areas for which compensation will be paid. The procedure for assessing and determining compensation and the final payment of compensation is generally provided by s 16(4)-(14) of the *Water Resources Act*. Section 16(6) provides that where the concerned parties are not able to agree on the amount of compensation to be paid, the aggrieved party may then apply to the Minister to have the amount determined. If parties are still aggrieved by this determination,[695] they may appeal to the National Court only on the question of inadequacy of the compensation.[696] Interestingly, certain provisions relating to compensation under the *Water Resources Act* are seen to be in contravention of s 53 of the *Constitution*, which guarantees rights to landholders and any interested persons to just compensation.[697] Section 16(14) of the *Water Resources Act* provides that if compensation is not paid in accordance with an agreement under s 16(4) or a determination under s 16(6), then the Water Resources Board may, on application by a persons entitled to the compensation, cancel the permit.

The first test case[698] to be referred to the Minister for determination under the *Water Resources Act* disputed a compensation payment by the resource developer, on the basis that the compensation was inordinately low. The dispute involved people living along the Porgera river

---

691 Section 167(4) of the *Oil and Gas Act* 1998 relates to equity payments to the provincial governments and resource holders.

692 See Power, *Landowner Compensation: Policy and Practice* in Toft (ed), *Compensation for Resource Development in Papua New Guinea: Resource Management in Asia Pacific Research* (School of Pacific and Asian Studies, Australian National University, Law Reform Commission of Papua New Guinea) (Monograph 6), Canberra, 1997.

693 See Kalinoe in Ch 6 of this book.

694 "Water use permit" or "water investigation permit" holder refers to the developer who is given a water use permit under the *Water Resources Act* to use water for the purposes for which the permit was granted.

695 The Porgera River Alluvial Miners Association protested the sum of K1,746,292, which the Porgera Joint Venture offered to pay the resource owners, occupiers and any interested person under the *Water Resources Act*. This was supposed to be the full and final payment, but the resource owners, occupiers and interested persons refused to accept that proposed offer and referred the matter to the Environment and Conservation Minister under s 16(6) of the *Water Resources Act*.

696 In the case of *Opis Papo v Paul Mambei and Placer (PNG) Ltd* (OS No 340 1996), the court decided that the appeal to the National Court could only be made on the question of inadequacy of the compensation.

697 See Kalinoe, "Water Resource Management in Papua New Guinea" (1994) 22 MLJ 23 at 35.

698 See *Opis Papo v Paul Mambei and Placer (PNG) Ltd* (OS No 340 1996). Opis Papo is the Chairman of the Porgera River Alluvial Miners Association (PRAMA), an association established to challenge the Porgera Joint Venture (PJV) Company over the outstanding environmental pollution allegedly caused by PJV's dumping of tailings and chemical toxic wastes into the river system. Mr Papo, a geologist graduate with not too much experience in public office, was elected as the member for Progera/Paiala in the National Parliament in the following year, after receiving much publicity from this case.

system. These people alleged that the Porgera Joint Venturers (PJV), operating the Porgera gold mine, were disposing of mine wastes and mine tailings into the Porgera river system, resulting in damage to the environment and all living inhabitants, including people, without any payment of compensation. The lower Porgera landholders' claim for compensation in 1989, when the Porgera mine commenced operation, was not accepted and paid by the PJV under the Act. Placer (PNG) Ltd offered to pay the sum of K1,746,292 to the lower Porgera landholders in 1995 as full and final compensation. The compensation package was to cover sedimentation and loss of right to alluvial gold mining and tailings.[699] The landholders then applied to the Minister for Environment and Conservation under that Act for a determination.[700]

The Minster subsequently made a determination[701] in accordance with the Act, and ordered K15,243,415 compensation to be paid as full and final settlement. The payment of the determination has been made to the resource holders, but many people are still opposed to the method of payment adopted by the PJV, claiming that PJV may have used selection criteria favouring PJV supporters more than the members of the opposition faction.

8.7 RECOGNITION OF RESOURCE OWNERS' RIGHTS AND INTERESTS UNDER THE FORESTRY ACT[702]

National forestry resources are regulated by the *Forestry Act* 1991,[703] which gives explicit recognition to customary forest holders/owners. The Act sets out a procedure for the identification of such persons and groups, using the *Land Groups Incorporations Act* 1974.[704]

The *Forestry Act* was made following recommendations by a commission of inquiry,[705] headed by Justice Barnett,[706] into a number of allegations of widespread impropriety and corruption.

Unlike the legislation regulating mining and petroleum operations, there is no provision directly relating to compensation payments to forest resource owners. The state has, instead, set up the

---

699 Placer (PNG) Ltd offered to pay K282,337 for sedimentation, K967,454 for loss of right to alluvial gold and K496,501 for tailings, which brings the total to K1,746,292. Section 16(4) of the *Water Resources Act* 1982 refers to the fact that a water permit holder may agree with any person entitled to compensation under this section as to the amount of compensation and the time of payment thereof.

700 Opis Papo, the chairman of the PRAMA, made an application on behalf of the people of lower Porgera, pursuant to s 16(6) of the *Water Resources Act*, to the Hon Paul Mambei, who was then the Minister for Environment and Conservation and made the first determination in February 1996.

701 After accepting submissions from all interested parties, the Minister made his determination under s 16(6) and (7) of that Act. The Minister determined that the full and final money to be paid as compensation was K15,243,415. If this sum is compared with the amount of K1,746,292 offered by PJV and rejected by resource owners, there is a difference of K13,497,123. The matter was further referred by PJV for review, since the parties were not satisfied with the amount determined. The next Minister for Environment and Conservation reconfirmed the first determination, and PJV finally agreed to pay.

702 See also Kwa in Ch 4 of this book.

703 The *Forestry Act* (No 30 of 1991), approved and passed by Parliament in 1991 and gazetted in 1992, repealed the old *Forestry Act* (Ch 217), the *Forestry (Private Dealings) Act* (Ch 217) and the *Forest Industries Council Act* (Ch 215).

704 The *Land Groups Incorporations Act* 1974 (Ch 147) was an Act purposely enacted to recognise the corporate nature of customary landowning groups etc. The resource owners are to be identified (or in their absence, the agents accepted by the customs of the group concerned) before compensation is paid.

705 A Forestry Commission of Inquiry was established to investigate allegations of impropriety and corruption in the forestry industry. This inquiry reported: "It would be true to say, some of the companies that are now roaming the countryside with the assurance of robber-barons; bribing politicians and leaders, creating social disharmony and ignoring laws in order to gain access to rip out and export the last remnants of the province's valuable timber." See Holzknecht, "Two Sides of the Coin: The Case of Forestry in Compensation for Resource Development" in *Papua New Guinea Resource Management in Asia Pacific Research* (School of Pacific and Asian Studies, Australian National University, Law Reform Commission of Papua New Guinea Monograph 6). This inquiry further led to the resignation of Sir Ted Diro, who was implicated in the inquiry reports. He later resigned as a Member of Parliament.

706 Justice Toss Barnett, a judge of the National and Supreme Court of PNG, was the Chairman of the Commission of Inquiry that was established to investigate the serious allegations relating to forestry.

National Forest Authority[707] and the National Forest Board[708] to assist in the management, development and protection of the forest resources and the environment generally. The *Forestry Act* 1996[709] provides that one member from two nominees representing forest resource owners shall be appointed by the National Executive Council (NEC) to be on the board. Further, s 46 of the *Forestry Act* recognises the customary resource owners' rights and interests, and reassures that the rights of customary owners of forest resources shall be fully recognised and respected in all transactions affecting the resources.[710] It is important to note that the state, in appreciation of the customary resource owners' rights, has agreed to involve them in all transactions relating to their resources. In addition, it has also agreed to ensure that the monetary and other benefits to the customary resource owners are specified in the written agreement and paid.[711]

Forestry operations in relation to forestry resources on customary land can be permitted under s 55(e) of the *Forestry Act*, provided that a forest management agreement has been entered into between the customary owners and the authority under s 58. Section 58(b) of the *Forestry Act* states that the forest management agreement shall be in writing and shall specify the monetary and other benefits, if any, to be received by the customary owners in consideration for the rights granted.[712] The tenure of these customary landholders must first be verified under s 57. Section 57 of the *Forestry Act* ensures that the title of the customary landowners to the land is identified under the *Land Groups Incorporations Act* (Ch 147) or registered under a law providing for the registration of title of customary land.[713]

Section 56 refers to the acquisition of timber rights etc, by the authority, to manage timber on the land. Importantly, s 56(1) and (3) states that no acquisition shall affect the customary rights of ownership of the land. Section 120 of the *Forestry Act* relates to royalties payable by a permit holder to the resource owners on monthly instalments at the rates approved by the Minister responsible for forestry. If a question arises as to who owns the forest produce, then s 128 of the *Forestry Act* presumes that the forest produce is the property of the Forest Authority. Section 130 of the *Forestry Act* further restates that all forest produce is the property of the Forest Authority, and it may seize, detain or remove such produce until the royalties, levies, dues and charges have been paid. If there is default in payment, within 20 days after seizure, they may be disposed of.

Tony Power[714] summarises the problems that resource holders are facing despite various attempts by the government to protect the resource holders' interests, including the enactment of the *Forestry Act* 1991. He states:

---

707 Section 5 of the *Forestry Act* establishes the National Forestry Authority.

708 Section 9 of the *Forestry Act* establishes the National Forest Board.

709 Parliament saw the need to have one Board member representing the timber resource owners so, in s 3 of the *Forestry (Amendment No 2) Act* 1996, Parliament repealed s 10 of the principal Act and included the timber resource owner representative.

710 Section 46 of the *Forestry Act* states that the customary holders/owners are owners of the forest, and that their ownership rights will be recognised and respected.

711 See *Forestry Act*, s 58.

712 Section 58(b) of the *Forestry Act* makes it mandatory for a forest management agreement to be in writing specifying the amount of monetary and other benefits payable to customary owners. This provision is important to the customary forest resource owners, because it is intended to protect their interests in consideration of their rights to forest resources.

713 The *Land Groups Incorporation Act* (Ch 147) was enacted by the National Parliament to recognise the corporate nature of customary groups and to allow them to hold, manage and deal with land in their customary names, etc. Thus, in referring to that Act under s 57(1) of the *Forestry Act*, the Parliament must have wanted the true customary forest resource owners to be identified, to be registered in accordance with the *Land Groups Incorporation Act*, and to have their title to the land registered in accordance with the *Land Groups Incorporation Act*, to ensure that the benefits were received by the genuine beneficiaries: see *Forestry Act*, s 57.

714 See Power, op cit n 95, p 91.

"The State's fiscal arrangement in taking a large slice by way of export tax is a sensible fiscal measure to make the logging companies pay. The State still loses by way of fraud but has taken measures to reduce this by contracting a surveillance company to quantity survey log exports.

Unfortunately, the heavy export tax is at the expense of the resource owners who are not getting the returns of their trees that, for example, landowners in Australia or Switzerland would get. This tax could possibly be construed as unconstitutional by way of being unjust deprivation. Landowners are the big losers in the logging business. Their forest and their environment is degraded and they do not get anything like a fair return. If there is no sustainable development replacing the forest then clearly the returns are not fair. At the very least the State is failing in its fiduciary responsibilities.

The forest industry landowner business arrangements also suffer from the same weaknesses as those in the mining and petroleum industry. The silent managers and directors of the companies manipulate the system for their own benefit. Some logging companies actually promote inequity by fostering a group of so called leaders, usually as company officials, who corruptly receive benefits in return for blind acceptance of the logging company's policies that are not to the advantage of the resource owners. The Forest Authority, through the Forest Management Planning project, has made a big effort to address these issues but progress is slow and indeed a lot more needs to be done to close the gap between talk and action.

The problem with successive governments and ministers is that private greed stands in the way of good government. Too many so called leaders do not want the Forest Authority to work well.

Certain management improvements have been put into place only to wither on the vine due to budget constraint. How can you have a legitimate budget constraint imposed on a so-called Statutory Authority that is responsible for hundreds of millions of export funds and many millions of revenue? An authority which has assumed fiduciary responsibility for billions worth of kina from resources owned by the rural citizens of the country."[715]

The *Forestry Act* has recognised customary owners' rights and interests to their forestry resources. For example, the *Forestry Act* gives explicit recognition to customary forest holders/owners and sets out a procedure for the identification of such persons and groups for payment of compensation. However, practically it has been difficult. Many players in the industry have not followed best practices. There is a great need to improve this sector of the natural resources industry in PNG.

[715] Ibid, pp 91-92.

8.8 RECOGNITION OF RESOURCE OWNERS' RIGHTS AND INTERESTS UNDER THE ENVIRONMENTAL CONTAMINANTS ACT

The *Environmental Contaminants Act* 1978[716] makes it an offence to contaminate the environment, and provides that anyone who does so is to be penalised and is to pay compensation. The Act provides, under s 61, that compensation is to be paid to owners, occupiers or any person having an interest in the environment. Such compensation is to be paid after conviction.

Section 61(1) of this Act reads as follows:

> "Where a person is convicted of an offence against this Act and as a consequence directly or indirectly of the commission of that offence any other person (including the State) has suffered damage or injury or has incurred expenses, that other person may make application to the court for an award of damages or compensation in respect of that damage or injury or expense, and the court may ...".[717]

8.9 CONCLUSION

Successive governments in PNG have started to recognise customary landholders' rights and interests in their resources. Parliament has introduced various Acts with a view to protecting the interests and rights of resource holders. Such Acts include the *Forestry Act* 1991, the *Mining Act* 1992, the *Land Act* 1996 and the *Oil and Gas Act* 1998.

Successive governments have also come to appreciate that, despite their statutory rights of ownership of resources, they should not tolerate conflict between resource developers and resource holders, most of whom are supported by the provincial and local-level governments. Governments need to change their mode of operations to resolve conflicts justly. The change of direction may be due to the Bougainville revolt that started in 1989. In addition, governments have been influenced by landholders, court challenges against the national government and resource developers, both locally and internationally, at the Ok Tedi and Porgera projects in 1995, 1996 and the early parts of 1997.

As the national government faces administrative problems in controlling and monitoring the activities of the resource developers and their technologically advanced methods of operations, the government should examine the need to update laws to address the current problems faced by the industry.

Importantly, the national government should allow the resource holders and local-level governments to participate in resource developments forums, but the state should retain ownership title over resources such as mining and petroleum. The country's desire for national

---

716 *Environmental Contaminants Act* 1978 (No 55 of 1978).

717 The *Environmental Contaminants Act* was passed by Parliament with the intention of criminally prosecuting the offender, and imposing penalties in the form of monetary compensation to the affected people, in the event of serious damage to the environment and the people and other living creatures living in it. To date, however, no developer has been prosecuted under this Act, and it is assumed that everything is fine.

economic growth or development cannot be achieved by allowing individuals, communal or sectional groups of the community to benefit at the expense of the state of PNG. However, resource holders' rights and interests must be recognised and respected.

Meaningful economic growth and development can only take place when a common entity such as the state retains ownership of vital resources, such as minerals, and pursues economic, social and political developments globally (throughout PNG) without fear or favour. Only then can a resource-rich country like PNG grow and prosper.

Index

[References are to page numbers]

Acquisition of land
- administration, by, 37-39, 41, 42-47
  - abuse of power, 48
  - joint administration, 39
  - New Guinea, in, 38
  - ownerless land, 43-48
  - Papua, in, 37-38
  - waste and vacant land, 43-48
- agreement, by, 39
  - condition precedent, 42-43
- compensation, 153, 169-172
- compulsory process, by, 20, 32, 39-41
  - condition precedent, 42-43
- condition precedent to, 42-43
- government, by, 33-35
  - modes, 39-42
  - restrictions, 49
- joint administration, during, 39
- lease, by, 41-42
- ownerless land, 43-48
- pre-annexation period, during, 35-36
- private individuals, by, 35-36
  - restrictions, 35
- protectorate, before, 35, 36
- unjust, 48
- waste and vacant land, 43-48

Additional profits tax, 11

Alienated land
- definition, 16
- private freeholds, 16, 17
- radical title to, 17
- state land, 16, 17
- unalienated land and, division between, 17

Barnett Inquiry, 58-59, 61, 63, 69, 70, 71, 83

Bougainville copper mine
- *Bougainville Mine Agreement of 1967*, 10, 136, 137-139, 145, 159
- compensation claims, 175
- compulsory acquisition of lands, 137
- foreign investment, 136-139
- mining company domination of investment terms, 158-159
- project financing, 136-139
- renegotiation of agreement, 149
- royalty payments, 138
- suppression of landowners' rights to ownership of minerals, 22
- tax regime, 138

Colonial administration, 2-3
- acquisition of land *see* **Acquisition of land**

Commission of Inquiry into Aspects of Forestry Industry
- effect on forestry sector, 58-59

Commission of Inquiry into Land Matters
- recommendations regarding waste and vacant or ownerless lands, 47-48

Compensation
- compulsory acquisition of land, 153, 169-173
- customary resource holder rights and interests, 167-183
  - *Constitution*, recognition under, 169-172
  - *Environmental Contaminants Act* 1978, recognition under, 182
  - *Forestry Act* 1991, recognition under, 179-182
  - *Land Act* 1996, recognition under, 172-173
  - *Mining Act* 1992, recognition under, 173-177
  - *Oil and Gas Act* 1998, recognition under, 177-178
  - *Water Resources Act*, recognition under, 178-179
- environmental contamination, for, 182
- improvements on land, for, 31, 32
- legislation providing for, 168-169
- mining projects, 174-176
- Ok Tedi mine, environmental damage, 179
- petroleum projects, 177-178
- Porgera mine, environmental damage, 179
- value of natural resources, 168
- water use rights, in relation to, 119-121, 178-179

Compulsory acquisition of land, 20, 32, 39-41
- Bougainville copper mine, 137
- compensation, 153, 169-173
- condition precedent, 42-43
- constitutional provisions, 49

Constitution
- compensation for compulsory acquisition of land, 169-172
- formulation, 3
- natural resources provision, 2
- property rights, 48-49
- sustainable development principles, 5

Customary land, 16-17
- access for resource developments, 153-154
- acquisition *see* **Acquisition of land**
- colonial administration, 3
- definition, 16

minerals and petroleum in, 20-23
project development and, 21-23, 151-154

Economy
contribution of natural resources to, 3-4, 6-13
fisheries, 91-93, 106-107
forestry, 50-52
non-renewable resources, 6-13
foreign investment, 4

Environmental Contaminants Act 1978
compensation under, 182

Environmental management and control
environmental impact assessment, 164-165
legislation, 151
mining and petroleum agreements, 12, 150
project financing, effect on, 149-151
resource development projects, 12, 149-151

Equity participation in resource projects
landowners, by, 159, 161-162, 176-177
state, by, 160-161

Export revenue, 4
fisheries sector, 92
forestry sector, 50, 51
non-renewable resources sector, 8

Fisheries resources, 88-93
access agreements, 99
access restrictions, 95, 97, 98-99
artisanal fisheries, 87, 88, 89, 91, 93, 107
catch limits, 95, 97, 101-104
coastal pelagics, 89
coastal sharks, sawfish and rays, 90
commercial fishing sector, 93
development under *Fisheries Management Act* 1998, 97
crustacea, 89
customary landowners, territorial use rights of, 97, 98-99
customary ownership, 87
declared fisheries zone (DFZ), 88
deepwater shrimp, 90
Department of Fisheries and Marine Resources (DFMR), 94
derivation grants, 95
development and management, 86-107
diminishing, 93
economy, contribution to, 91-93, 106-107
enforcement of legislation, 105-106
estuarine stocks, 89
export revenue, 92
extensive fishing grounds, 86, 88
fines for offences, 105-106
Fisheries Act 1984, 94-95
Fisheries Management Act 1998
development of commercial and industrial sectors, 97
effect on sustainable development, 86, 96
gaps in, 96-97
offences against, 105-106
fisheries management agreements, 99
fisheries officers, powers of, 105
fishery management plan (FMP), 98, 100-101
foreign vessels, restrictions on, 100
freshwater resources, 90-91
gear restrictions, 100
individual transferable quotas (ITQs), 97, 104-105
industrial sector, 93-94
development under *Fisheries Management Act* 1998, 97
legal problems, 94-96
licences, 94, 96, 97, 99
maximum number of licence holders, 102-104
transfer, 105
local fishers, 93
management, approaches to, 97-106
monitoring, 105-106
National Fisheries Authority (NFA), 94, 95, 96, 97, 100, 101, 107
enforcement and monitoring, 105-106
restrictions on, 97
National Tuna Management Plan, 97, 100
observers, 105
offences against *Fisheries Management Act* 1998, 105-106
offshore fishery resources, 90
operators, maximum number of, 102-104
overfishing, 95
overview of fisheries sector, 87-88
policy development, 87-88, 94
problems in the fishing industry, 93-97
production, 91-93
provincial governments and, 107
reef and lagoon fish, 89
regulation of fishing practices, 97, 99-101
revenue, 91-93
scientific assessments, 96
sectoral problems, 93-94
sedentary marine resources, 89, 100
sharks and billfish, 90
stocks, monitoring of, 106
subsistence and artisanal sector, 93, 96
subsistence users, 93
sustainable development, 5, 86
territorial use rights of customary landowners, 97, 98-99
Torres Straits Protected Zone, 100, 103-104
total allowable catches (TACs), 97, 101-104
traditional commercial fisheries, 87, 93
commercial development of, 88
tropical coastal resource bases, 88-89
tuna, 90, 91, 93, 97, 98, 100
catch limits, 101
vessel restrictions, 100, 101, 106

Fixtures on land
ownership
buildings and other structures, 29-30
common law, 23-29
customary law, 29-30
degree of annexation, 27
object of annexation, 27
quic quid plantatur solo, solo credit maxim, 23, 25-26, 30
right to remove, 30-31
tests to determine whether object is a fixture, 26-29
things growing on or in water over land, 30
things growing or cultivated on land, 29

Foreign investment, 165
legislation to promote, 154-155
mitigating political risks to attract, 154-158
protection agreements, 155
stabilisation clauses, 156-157

Forestry law
breach of *Forestry Act* 1974, 69
colonial, 62-69
New Guinea, 64-66
Papua, 62-64
Papua and New Guinea, 66-69
evolution of, 62-73
Forestry Act 1974, 69
Forestry Act 1991, 70-71
customary owners' rights and interests, recognition under, 179-182
problems with, 83
Forestry (Amendment) Act 1993, 71
Forest Authority, 70, 71, 75
registration with, 73
Forestry Guidelines 1993, 71-73
opposition to, 72-73
Forest Management Agreement (FMA), 70, 74-76, 83
Forestry (New Guinea) (Amendment) Ordinance 1971, importance, 66-67
Forestry Ordinance of 1936, importance, 65-66
Forestry (Private Dealings) Act, 69
National Forest Board, 70
Native Timber Authority, 63
Organic Law on Provincial Governments, 80-82, 84
post-independence, 69-71
provincial and local-level governments, 79-82
Provincial Forest Management Committee, 70, 75, 77, 78
reforms, 83
Timber Authority, 70

Forestry resources
afforestation, 72
allocation procedures, reform, 70
Barnett Inquiry, 58-59, 61, 63, 69, 70, 71, 83
colonial administration, 3, 55-58
Commission of Inquiry into Aspects of Forestry Industry, 58-59
customary land
Forest Management Agreement process, 74-76, 180
timber authority process, 77-79, 83
transfer, 52-54
customary owners, 52, 53, 61, 67, 82-83
disposal of timber by, 68
recognition of rights, 179-182
share of revenue for, 72
development, 73-79, 83
foreign companies, 73
Forest Management Agreement process, 74-76
licence process, 79
registered forestry industry participants, 73-74
timber authority process, 77-79, 83
timber permits, 70, 75-76
economy, contribution to, 50-52, 82
exploitation, 83
export revenue, 50, 51
distribution, 72, 73
flora and fauna, 82
Forest Authority, 61-62
licences, 79
Local Forest Areas, declaration, 78
local-level governments and, 79-82
National Forest Policy, 61-62, 75
overview, 50-52
ownership, 52, 53, 61, 67
transfer, 54-55
policy development, 55-62, 83-84
colonial forestry policy, 55-58
Commission of Inquiry into Aspects of Forestry Industry, effect, 58-59
1979 policy, 58
1991 policy, 61-62
Tropical Forest Action Plan, effect, 59-61, 70
World Bank, intervention by, 59-61
provincial governments and, 79-82
reafforestation, 72
revenue system, 72, 73
stumpage, 72, 73
sustainable development, 84
timber authority, 77-79
application for, 78
timber permits, 70, 75-76
Timber Rights Purchase, 54-55, 67, 83
transfer of timber rights from customary owners, 54-55

Gobe oil field, 7, 8, 10

Hides gas field, 7, 8, 10

Hierarchy of laws, 21

Infrastructure
resource developers, financing by, 9-10

Kutubu oil field, 7, 8, 10
project financing, 141-142

Land
access for resource developments, 153-154
acquisition *see* **Acquisition of land**
airspace above surface, ownership of, 17-19
alienated, 16-17
annexation, effect on indigenous rights, 34-35
classification of, 16-17
common law definition, 14-15, 17, 23
compulsory acquisition *see* **Compulsory acquisition of land**
customary land, 16-17, 32-33
access for resource developments, 153-154
transfer, 52-54
customary landowner
denial of rights to minerals and petroleum, effect on project development, 21-23
disposal of land by, 36, 37, 38
customary law definition, 15, 19
definition, 14-16
fixtures on
ownership, 23-30
right to remove, 30-31
forestry resources *see* **Forestry resources**
improvements on, compensation for, 31, 32
incidents of land ownership, 17-31
indigenous rights
Australian colonies, 35
British Papua, in, 35
constitutional protection, 48-49
effect of annexation on, 34-35
German New Guinea, in, 35
protection of, 33-35, 37, 38, 39, 47, 48
lease, acquisition by, 41-42
minerals and petroleum found in, ownership, 19-23, 154
conflict between customary and common law, 20-21
denial of customary landowners' rights, effect on project development, 21-23
non-customary land, 16-17
ownerless declaration, 43-48
Commission of Inquiry into Land Matters recommendation, 47-48
ownership *see also* **Ownership of land**
custom, by, 16
incidents of, 17-31
private freeholds, 17
project financing, issues affecting, 151-154
resource development, issues affecting, 151-154
rights above surface
common law, 17-18
customary law, 18
rights below surface of the earth
common law, 19-20
customary law, 20-23
sacred resource, as, 33
shortage, 48, 49
significance, 14
state land, 16, 17
statutory definition, 15-16
unalienated, 16, 17
waste and vacant declaration, 43-48
Commission of Inquiry into Land Matters recommendation, 47-48

Land Act 1996
compensation under, 172-173

Lease
acquisition of land by, 41-42
lease-leaseback scheme, 42

Lihir gold mine, 7, 8, 10
project financing, 140-141

Mineral resources
colonial administration, 3
ownership, 19-23, 154, 173-174
denial of customary landowners' rights, effect on project development, 21-23

Mineral Resource Stabilisation Fund, 11

Mineral Resources Development Corporation, 11

Mining Act 1992
compensation under, 174-177

Mining and petroleum industries
additional profits tax, 11
agreements, 9, 10, 12-13, 142-146
stability, 149
denial of landowners' rights, effect on project development, 21-23
development of sector, 7
economy, contribution to, 6-13
employment creation, 8-9
environmental impact assessment, 164-165
environmental management and control, 12, 149-151
equity participation in projects
landowners, by, 159, 161-162, 176-177
state, by, 160-161
export revenue, 8
extraction methods, 7
government policies, 10-12
government revenue, 7-8
income tax, 8, 11
infrastructure and social services, 9-10
local communities, consultation with, 159
Mineral Resources Development Corporation, 11
mining development contracts, 142-145

arbitration and dispute resolution, 157
contracting with landowners, 144-145
currency exchange, 155-156
doctrine of executive necessity, 143
stabilisation clauses, 156-157
statutory discretion, undertakings about exercise of, 144
mining development forums, 174
petroleum agreements, 142-145
arbitration and dispute resolution, 157
contracting with landowners, 144-145
currency exchange, 155-156
doctrine of executive necessity, 14
negotiations, 177
stabilisation clauses, 156-157
statutory discretion, undertakings about exercise of, 144
principles for development, 10-11
project development on customary land, 21-23
project financing, 136-146
resource rent tax, 11
risks associated with development, 6-7, 11, 146-158
royalties, 176-177
social and economic infrastructure, provision of, 162-163
state agreements, 145
sustainable development practices, 163-164
tax credit scheme, 9-10
training programs, 7, 9
transfer of technology, 9

Misima gold mine, 7, 8, 10
project financing, 140-141
land owner participation, 159-160

Moran oil field, 7, 8, 10

Mt Tolokuma gold mine, 7

National Fisheries Authority (NFA), 94, 95, 96, 97, 100, 101, 107
enforcement and monitoring, 105-106
restrictions on, 97

National Forest Board, 70

Native Timber Authority, 63

Natural resources
Australia, exploitation by, 2
colonial administration, 2-3
exploitation, 1-3
export values, 4
government policies, 10-12
history, 1-5
importance to development, 1, 3-4, 6-13
overview, 1-5
ownership, 2
policy, 1-5
sustainable development principles, 5

Non-customary land, 16-17

Non-renewable resources sector *see also* **Mining and petroleum industries**
additional profits tax, 11
economy, contribution to, 6-13
employment and manpower development, 8-9
environmental management and control, 12
export revenue, 8
government policies, 10-12
government revenue, 7-8
high-risk sector, 6-7, 11
income tax, 8, 11
infrastructure and social services, 9-10
principles for development, 10-11
resource rent tax, 11

Oil and Gas Act 1998
compensation under, 177-178

Ok Tedi copper mine, 7, 8, 9, 10, 139
compensation claims, 175
environmental damage, 151, 161
German participation in financing of, 140
mining company domination of investment terms, 158-159
Ok Tedi Mining Agreement of 1979, 10, 145, 159
project financing, 139-140

Organic Law on Provincial Governments, 80-82, 84

Ownerless land
Commission of Inquiry into Land Matters recommendation, 47-48
declaration, 43-48
definition, 43-44
undeveloped, return to traditional owners, 47-48

Ownership of land, 15
common law, 31-32
communal, 32
custom, by, 16
customary, 16-17, 32-33
transfer, 52-54
fixtures on land
common law, 23-29
customary law, 29-30
incidents of, 17-31
minerals and petroleum, 19-23
conflict between customary and common law, 20-21
denial of customary landowners' rights, effect on project development, 21-23
nature of, 31-33
project financing, effect on, 151-154
rights above surface of land
common law, 17-18
customary law, 19

rights below surface of the earth
common law, 19-20
customary law, 20 23
usufructuary rights, 32

Papua New Guinea
colonial administration, 2-3
colonial protectorate, proclamation as, 33, 35, 36, 37
history, 1
location, 1
natural resources *see* **Natural resources**

Petroleum *see* **Mining and Petroleum resources**

Porgera mine, 7, 8, 10
compensation for environmental damage, 179
equity participation, 159, 177
Porgera Mine Agreement of 1987, 10, 12-13
project financing, 140-141
tax credit scheme, 9

Project financing, 132-166, *see also* **Resource development**
advance payment financing, 135
Bougainville copper mine, 136-139
compensatory financing arrangements, 135
contract-based financing, 135
customary title risks, 151-154
mitigation, 158
debt finance, 134-135
definition, 133
difficulties in obtaining, 132
enclave model, 158
environmental risks, 149-151
mitigation, 163-165
equity finance, 134-135
foreign investment, 165
legislation to promote, 154-155
mitigating political risks to attract, 154-158
protection agreements, 155
stabilisation clauses, 156-157
Kutubu petroleum project, 141-142
land issues, 151-154
accessing land for resource developments, 153-154
mitigation of land risks, 158
ownership, 152-153
traditional concept of land, 152
land owner participation in resource projects, 158-163
legal framework, 142-145
legal instruments, 133-134
leveraged lease financing, 135
Lihir gold mine, 140-141
mining and petroleum developments, 136-146
Misima gold mine, 140-141
mitigating risks, 154-158
environmental, 163-165
land, 147-149
political, 147-149
nature of, 133-134
new sustainable model, 159, 163
off balance sheet financing, 133
Ok Tedi copper and gold project, 139-140
overview, 132
phase financing, 133
political risks, 147-149
contract repudiation, re-negotiation and unilateral changes, 149
exchange control restrictions, 148
expropriation, 148
insurance, 157
mitigation, 154-157
war and civil disturbance, 148
Porgera gold mine, 140-141
production payment financing, 135
resource security, 134
risk identification and allocation, 146-154, 165
customary title risks, 151-154
environmental risks, 149-151
political risks, 147-149
risk mitigation, 154-158, 165-166
social and economic infrastructure, provision of, 162-163
state agreements, 145
Tolokuma gold mine, 140-141
types of finance, 134-135

Property rights
constitutional protection, 48-49

Provincial Forest Management Committee, 70, 75, 77, 78

Ramu cobolt and nickel mine, 7

Resource developers
infrastructure and social services, financing of, 9-10, 162-163
principles for development, 10-11

Resource development *see also* **Project financing**
environmental management and control, 149-151
land owner participation, 158-163
mining development contracts, 142-145
arbitration and dispute resolution, 157
contracting with landowners, 144-145
currency exchange, 155-156
doctrine of executive necessity, 143
stabilisation clauses, 156-157
statutory discretion, undertakings about exercise of, 144
petroleum agreements, 142-145
arbitration and dispute resolution, 157
contracting with landowners, 144-145
currency exchange, 155-156
doctrine of executive necessity, 14
stabilisation clauses, 156-157
statutory discretion, undertakings about exercise of, 144

social impact assessment and social monitoring, 165
sustainable development practices, 163-164

Resource rent tax, 11

Risk *see* **Project financing**

Royalty payments
Bougainville copper mine, 138
mine products, 176-177

Social impact assessment, 165

Social services
resource developers, financing by, 9-10, 162-163

Sustainable development
mining and petroleum codes and practices, 163-164
principles, 5

Tax credit scheme
mining and petroleum agreements, in, 9-10

Tenant
right to remove fixtures, 30-31

Timber authority, 77-79
application for, 78

Timber permits, 70, 75-76

Timber Rights Purchase, 54-55, 67, 83

Tolokuma gold mine
project financing, 140-141

Torres Straits Protected Zone, 100, 103-104

Tropical Forest Action Plan (QFAP), 70
effect on forestry sector, 59-61

Tuna *see* **Fisheries resources**

Unalienated land
alienated land and, division between, 17
definition, 16
ownership, 17

Waste and vacant lands
Commission of Inquiry into Land Matters recommendation, 47-48
declaration, 43-48
challenge to, 45-46
definition, 43-44
undeveloped, return to traditional owners, 47-48

Water law, 108-131
National Water Supply and Sewerage Act 1986, 122-125
Public Health Act, application to Water Board, 126
Water Resources Act, 108, 111-116, 128
compensation under, 178-179
compliance monitoring, 118-119
customary rights, effect on, 121, 122
enforcement, 116-118
riparian rights, effect on, 121-122
Water Board, application to, 125

Water resources
administrative arrangement, 110
catchment management areas, 116
compensation, 119-121
control mechanisms in drought situation, 111, 115-116
customary rights, 108
domestic use, to extract water for, 124-125
effect of legislation on, 121, 122
Director of Water Resources, 110, 112, 113, 114, 115
investigations by, 116-117
drought situation, control mechanisms in, 111, 115-116
effluent discharge, 126-127
fees, 129
enforcement of legislation, 116-118
formal permit system, 108
industrial wastes, 127
fees for discharge, 129
landowners, compensation to, 119-121
management, 108-131
monitoring, 118-119
pollution control, 126-131
riparian rights, 109
domestic use, to extract water for, 124-125
effect of legislation on, 121-122
state control over water use rights, 108-109
statutory water use rights, 111-116
Water Board, 123-124
Public Health Act, application to, 126
Water Resources Act, application to, 125
water control district, declaration of, 111-113
compensation to landowners, 119-120
water investigation permits, 111, 114-115
compensation to landowners, 119-121
water quality standards, 128, 130-131
Water Resources Board, functions and powers,110
water supply and sewerage services, 122-126
Water Board, functions of, 123-124
water use permits, 111, 113-114
compensation to landowners, 119-121
water use rights
state control over, 108-109
customary rights, exemption, 108
formal permit system, 108
statutory, 111-116